Inequality across State Lines

In the United States, one in four women will be victims of domestic violence every year. Despite the passage of federal legislation on violence against women beginning in 1994, differences in how domestic violence is addressed persist across states. *Inequality across State Lines* illuminates the epidemic of domestic violence in the United States through the lens of politics, policy adoption, and policy implementation. Combining narrative case studies, surveys, and data analysis, the book discusses the specific factors that explain why US domestic violence politics and policies have failed to keep women safe at all income levels and across racial and ethnic lines. The book argues that the issue of domestic violence and how government responds to it raises fundamental questions of justice, gender and racial equality, and the limited efficacy of a state-by-state and even town-by-town response. This book goes beyond revealing the vast differences in how states respond to domestic violence by offering pathways to reform.

Kaitlin N. Sidorsky is Associate Professor of Political Science at Coastal Carolina University. She is the author of *All Roads Lead to Power: Appointed and Elected Paths to Public Office for US Women* (2019).

Wendy J. Schiller is Professor of Political Science and Director of the Taubman Center for American Politics and Policy at Brown University. Her publications include *Dynamics of American Democracy* (2021), *Electing the Senate: Indirect Democracy before the Seventeenth Amendment* (2015), and *Partners and Rivals: Representation in US Senate Delegations* (2000).

Inequality across State Lines

*How Policymakers Have Failed Domestic Violence
Victims in the United States*

KAITLIN N. SIDORSKY

Coastal Carolina University

WENDY J. SCHILLER

Brown University

CAMBRIDGE
UNIVERSITY PRESS

Shaftesbury Road, Cambridge CB2 8EA, United Kingdom

One Liberty Plaza, 20th Floor, New York, NY 10006, USA

477 Williamstown Road, Port Melbourne, VIC 3207, Australia

314–321, 3rd Floor, Plot 3, Splendor Forum, Jasola District Centre,
New Delhi – 110025, India

103 Penang Road, #05-06/07, Visioncrest Commercial, Singapore 238467

Cambridge University Press is part of Cambridge University Press & Assessment,
a department of the University of Cambridge.

We share the University's mission to contribute to society through the pursuit of
education, learning and research at the highest international levels of excellence.

www.cambridge.org
Information on this title: www.cambridge.org/9781009279116

DOI: 10.1017/9781009279154

First published 2023

*A Cataloging-in-Publication data record for this book is available from the Library of
Congress.*

ISBN 978-1-009-27911-6 Hardback
ISBN 978-1-009-27916-1 Paperback

This book is dedicated to all those who have been victims of domestic violence.

Contents

Figures

Tables

Acknowledgments

It is estimated that over 10 million people will be victims of domestic violence every year in the United States. The majority of these victims will be women, one-quarter of whom will experience physical violence at the hands of an intimate partner. Domestic violence has not quite made the leap from a "private matter" to a "public health emergency" despite the fact that thousands of women are injured or killed across the country as a direct or indirect result of domestic violence. The fields of public health, criminology, and feminist theory study the topic of intimate partner violence and its collateral effects more deeply than the traditional "political" disciplines. We believe there is a fundamental gap in our understanding of the politics of violence against women. Human security is the foundation of a civil society, and violence among domestic households negatively disrupts that security. By failing to successfully address and mitigate domestic violence through coherent and cohesive national policy enforced and implemented consistently across states, women remain disproportionately at risk. In this book, we demonstrate how failed policy creates four levels of inequality for women: relative to men, across state lines, within states, and across racial and ethnic lines.

We argue throughout this book that women who are not assured safety in their own home and private lives will never achieve the equality they deserve. There is a single national policy on violence against women embodied in the Violence Against Women Act, originally enacted in 1994. Accompanying legislation, known as the Lautenberg Amendment, enacted in 1996, put restrictions on firearm possession and ownership among domestic violence misdemeanants. In 2022, Congress passed the Bipartisan Safer Communities Act (BSCA) which extended protections against domestic firearm violence among dating partners. Despite the existence of these federal policies, states have both different definitions and scopes of domestic violence law and different laws on gun ownership and possession. This variation across state lines creates a patchwork fabric of protections for women who are subject to lethal domestic violence with a gun. Using a collaborative approach, we worked with research assistants at our own institutions to compile a comprehensive data set of these state laws, and we were aware that other researchers were doing the same thing. We are grateful to April Zeoli, Associate Professor in the School of Criminal Justice at Michigan State University and her colleagues for sharing their data on state laws in this arena. Lastly, the nonprofit organization Everytown for Gun Safety has created a working database with a range of gun laws that states have adopted since 1990, and we appreciate having access to that database as well. We use those data in Chapter 4 to demonstrate which factors encourage or discourage state adoption of laws at this intersection of policy.

Studying and researching domestic violence is challenging because so many victims do not want to come forward to report crimes against them for fear of disrupting their family lives, losing streams of income in cases where the abuser is the primary earner, and fear of future retribution by the abuser among other factors. Government agencies do not coordinate well in tracking and sharing data on the intersection of criminal activity and public health; it is only recently, for example, that the Centers for Disease Control (CDC) has persuaded the majority of states to coordinate information sharing between their state and local law enforcement agencies and their public health system. Information about how domestic violence cases are adjudicated is also difficult to find, absent in-depth studies of localized court systems, which can make it hard to generalize to systems outside that jurisdiction. Our solution was to create and administer an original survey of district attorneys and public defenders about their overall caseload, the percentage of cases that were related to domestic violence (40 percent on average) and the outcomes of those cases. We report these findings in Chapter 5.

This project has been a bit of an odyssey for us driven by our determination to put domestic violence more squarely on the map in the disciplines of political science and public policy. We came to this project together, originally as a PhD student and a faculty member and now as equal research partners. Kaitlin Sidorsky started her career at Brown University in 2010 as a PhD student who wanted to study gender and politics. She crafted her original dissertation topic on the influence of women at the state level in nonelective office with Wendy Schiller, Susan Moffitt, and James Morone as her advisers. She published that work as the book *All Roads Lead to Power: The Appointed and Elected Paths to Public Office for US Women* (University Press of Kansas, 2019). She is now a tenured Associate Professor of Political Science at Coastal Carolina University. Wendy Schiller spent most of her research career writing about institutional politics in the US Senate, both current and historical. Her pivot came after the publication of her second research book, *Electing the Senate: Indirect Democracy and the Seventeenth Amendment* (Princeton University Press, 2015) and her promotion to Professor of Political Science at Brown University. At that point, Kaitlin was finishing her dissertation and Wendy suggested they work together to consider the impact of state laws and policies on women's equality, which was a natural extension of Kaitlin's work on the impact of women in public office at the state level. If a state was conducive to women serving in nonelected public offices that had roles in implementing and overseeing policy, was that state a place that worked to ensure that women could thrive in general?

The first place to start to answer that question was the area of women's human security. Our first conference paper looked at what happens to rankings of women-friendly states when incidences of sexual violence are included in the women-friendly index; we found that the rankings changed considerably, which was our first indication that a state's climate of violence against women was not being fully included in assessments of women's equality across states. In our subsequent research on the Women's Rape Movement in the 1970s, we recognized that the issue of sexual, physical, and emotional violence against women committed by domestic partners was only relatively recently brought from the private to the public sphere and was inconsistently done at the state level. We set out to assess how inconsistency across states, and as compared with federal policy, creates inequality for women depending upon where they live. The collaboration has been invigorating and inspiring for both authors, who believe that this book is the beginning, not the end, of a long-term commitment to studying the impact of policy on women and families.

We are grateful to the reviewers of two articles that we published as part of this project. One article, on which Chapter 5 is based, was published in the *Journal of Women, Politics & Policy* (2020); we thank coeditors Heidi Hartmann, Becki Scola, and Melody Valdini for their support. The other article, on which Chapter 4 is based, was published in *State Politics & Policy Quarterly* (2022); we thank coeditors Connor

Dowling, Tracy Osborne, and Jonathan Winburn for their support. For their permission to reprint portions of our articles in this book, we also thank both Taylor Francis and Cambridge University Press, the publishers of the *Journal of Women, Politics & Policy* and *State Politics & Policy Quarterly*, respectively.

We have presented sections of the book manuscript in conference form, and we are grateful to panel participants at the Midwest Political Science Meetings and the American Political Science Meetings for their comments and advice. We also appreciate the input of our colleagues at these conferences, including Scott Ainsworth, Sarah Binder, Sanford Gordon, Jennifer Lawless, Frances Lee, Suzanne Mettler, and Masako Okura. We would like to thank the seminar participants at Brown University, the University of Virginia, and the University of Illinois as well as Kelly Branham Smith for their comments on Chapter 4 of this book's manuscript. We would also like to thank the Women's and Gender Studies writing group at Coastal Carolina University, specifically Ina Seethaler for her endless support as well as Jennifer Mokos and Jaime McCauley for their comments on Chapter 5. Each of our institutions provided financial support for our research, and in particular, Wendy would like to thank the Humanities Research Fund and the Dean of the Faculty's office at Brown University for continuous support.

We would like to the thank the many research assistants whose work was crucial to the completion of this project. At Brown University, we thank research assistants Caleb Apple, Abigail Carbajal, Isabel Culver, Lauren Griffiths, Gianna Jasinski, Cayla Kaplan, Rakhi Kundra, and Gabriela Tenorio. At Coastal Carolina University, we thank research assistants Kai Legette-Gideon, Taylor Repp, and Caitlin Rhodes.

We were fortunate to have received several rounds of reviews of our book that clarified our argument and improved it substantially. We thank the anonymous reviewers for their extensive feedback and support of this project. Likewise, we thank our editor Rachel Blaifeder who understood and recognized the importance of this topic and believed in its success as much as we did. We thank editorial assistant Jadyn Fauconier-Herry for helping us prepare our manuscript for publication. We would also like to thank our content managers Hannah Weber and Becky Jackaman, senior project manager Shaheer Husanne, and our copyeditor JaNoel Lowe, for their work on the book.

Kaitlin would like to thank her department chair at Coastal Carolina University, Adam Chamberlain for his support of this manuscript. She would also like to thank her husband, Ryan for his feedback, encouragement, and unwavering support of her professional goals. Kaitlin thanks her mother and her grandmother, both of whom are survivors of domestic violence. They were at the forefront of her mind as she completed this project. While writing this book, Kaitlin gave birth to her son Luca. She hopes he grows up in a world where there are far fewer victims of domestic violence – one where it fades to a distant memory as it has for his Mimi and Great-Grandmother.

Wendy would like to thank her colleagues, friends, and family for their support from the beginning of this project including Mary-Jane April, Iris Bahar, Shari Bennett, Ilene Berman, Janet Blume, Martha Few, Rachel Friedberg, Patricia Gardner, Helen Guler, Kei Hirano, Matt Levine, Hillary Maharam, Susan Moffitt, Lisa Montgomery, Eric Patashnik, Paul Testa, Emily Rauscher, Jordana Schwartz, Tiffany Trigg, Margaret Weir, Darrell West, and Miriam Wugmeister. She wants to especially thank her husband, Robert Kalunian, for his patience and endless support.

We hope our book shines a light on the policy failures present at the local, state, and federal levels of government to reveal the pathway to reform that can protect women from domestic violence. We dedicate this work and future expansion of our research to the victims of domestic violence who are too often underserved in the halls of government and in our judicial system.

Abbreviations

AB	Assembly Bill
ACA	Affordable Care Act
ACP	Address Confidentiality Program
ATF	Bureau of Alcohol, Tobacco, Firearms and Explosives
BSCA	Bipartisan Safer Communities Act
CCADV	Connecticut Coalition Against Domestic Violence
CDC	Centers for Disease Control and Prevention
COVID-19	coronavirus pandemic
DA	district attorney
DV	domestic violence
DVFL	domestic violence firearm law
DVRO	domestic violence restraining order
EHA	event history analysis
EZASHR	Easy Access to the FBI's Supplementary Homicide Reports
FBI	Federal Bureau of Investigation
FVPSA	Family Violence Protection Services Act
FY	fiscal year
GOP	Republican Party
HB	House Bill
IP	intimate partner
IPDV	intimate partner domestic violence
IPV	intimate partner violence
LGBTQ	lesbian, gay, bisexual, transgender, and queer
MCEDV	Maine Coalition to End Domestic Violence
MNADV	Maryland Network Against Domestic Violence

MSPCC	Massachusetts Society for the Prevention of Cruelty to Children
NCADV	National Coalition Against Domestic Violence
NCSL	National Council of State Legislatures
NICS	National Instant Criminal Background Check System
NNEDV	National Network to End Domestic Violence
NRA	National Rifle Association
OVW	Office of Violence Against Women
PCADV	Pennsylvania Coalition Against Domestic Violence
PD	Public Defender
PFA	protection from abuse
PTSD	post-traumatic stress disorder
SB	Senate Bill
SDVCJ	special domestic violence criminal jurisdictions
SF	Senate File
STOP	Services, Training, Officers, and Prosecutors Formula Grant Program
UCR	Uniform Crime Reporting
VAWA	Violence Against Women Act

Domestic Violence and Gender Inequality

Ferintosh Court in Matoaca, Virginia, is a quiet cul-de-sac. With less than a dozen well-kept houses, the neighbors are close and keep an eye on each other and their properties. In 2015, 1-year-old Leah Rogers lived with her mother, 34-year-old Morgan in one of the houses on the cul-de-sac. It would be the last place either of them would ever live. On Friday, May 29, both Leah and Morgan were shot and killed by Leah's father and Morgan's estranged boyfriend, Stafford L. Shaw Sr. He would die later in the day following a police pursuit during which he crashed his Corvette into 65-year-old Wendell E. Hayman and 66-year-old Ethel D. Ellis, who would both die from their injuries (Orcutt, 2015). Shaw had a serious history of domestic violence (DV). In 2008, he had violently attacked his former fiancé and was sentenced to a 24-week batterer's intervention program. In January 2015, he was arrested for attacking Morgan Rogers, resulting in "visible cuts to both sides of her nose, a mark on her forehead, a swollen right eye and... a bump on the back of her head" according to *The Progress-Index* Staff (2015). In her affidavit that awarded her a two-year protective order, Morgan had testified that some of her injuries were the result of being hit with the butt of a gun.

Neighbors of Morgan and Leah were devastated by their deaths. Neighbor James Trea would often see Leah when she would run over to pick up stones in his driveway. Trea described Morgan as a

great mother, she loved that baby dearly.... We're tight in this cul-de-sac, we watch each other's back, and when somebody goes away, we watch. There hasn't been much crime down here.... The bad part about this is that we couldn't save her, and she was a sweet lady. She was a sweet lady and her little girl was just absolutely, she was a doll." (Orcutt, 2015).

Nancye Hunter, another neighbor of Morgan and Leah said,

You don't know people's personal lives so you try not to dig in too much unless you're really close with them. I think with domestic violence situations, unfortunately these men have a way of sweet talking their way back into these women's lives. My view is you can live in a million-dollar house, neighborhood, and it can still happen right next door to you. (Orcutt, 2015)

Morgan and Leah's murders are not rare. In 2015, Morgan was one of 55 intimate partner homicides and Leah was one of 17 murders of children by a caretaker in Virginia alone (Tingley, 2015). The majority of such homicides in Virginia were committed using a firearm. DV is primarily but not exclusively a crime against women and children and occurs across generations, locations, income levels, ethnicity, and race.

One of the fundamental responsibilities of government is to protect its citizens, but it does not protect millions of women and children from DV (National Coalition Against Domestic Violence, 2019) in the United States each year. To truly understand Morgan and Leah's story and how the commonwealth of Virginia and the federal government failed them, one must understand the politics behind DV policies. In this book, we focus on the politics of DV and reveal the multiple levels of inequality under the law that are present for victims of domestic abuse – a burden affecting more women than men.

When studying equality – specifically gender equality – in the United States, most scholars investigate economic, social, political, or medical equality. Feminist scholars are among the few individuals who have studied DV in a political context, helping us understand how our patriarchal society has created and contributed to a world where violence against women is commonplace. We argue that our understanding of DV policy from an institutional perspective is underdeveloped. In particular, the focus of this work is on how political institutions and actors address DV in the United States. We ask what leads some political actors to support DV laws while others fight against them. Are the gaps left by these laws a problem of insufficient policy adoption, implementation, or both? How does the federalist system create multiple levels of gender inequality? As of this writing, the current policy landscape of DV fails to protect women. It is time to understand the politics behind this policy failure.

1.1 A THEORY OF FEDERALISM, GENDER INEQUALITY, AND DOMESTIC VIOLENCE

As political scientists, we can better understand institutional and political responses to DV that criminologists and sociologists do not study. State governments have a patchwork of legislation to try to address the DV epidemic, and local law enforcement entities try to enforce the laws. Because DV is primarily adjudicated at the state and local levels, there is tremendous variation in this policy area within the United States. Political science has done too little to shed light on both the origins and implementation of DV policies and how they affect the capacity of women to be treated equally under the law.

We also argue that the existing federal response to this widespread national problem does not successfully protect women, resulting in decreased personal safety that prevents women from living full private and public lives. More specifically, we provide a theoretical framework around different levels of inequality that have been produced and sustained by current DV laws. We argue throughout this book that there are four different layers of gender inequality produced from the federalist system and current state and federal laws. Figure 1.1 shows these layers of inequality that are nested because they build upon one another and the related outcomes.

The first layer of inequality is in human security among men and women. Morgan Rogers was much more likely to be a victim of DV because she identified as a woman; one in three women as compared to one in four men will experience some form of physical violence in their lifetime. The numbers are not much better for intimate partner violence, depicted in Figure 1.1, which shows that the outcome of inequality of women across jurisdictions (states) means women in some states are less safe than others. The foundational inequality between men and women in being a victim of DV is profound and exacerbates the gender inequality in the other domains in which women are disadvantaged compared to men. A woman may earn less money per hour than a man and suffer discrimination in the workplace as a result of her gender; imagine how that is compounded when that woman is a victim of physical, psychological, or sexual abuse at the hands of her partner.

But victims like Morgan and Leah Rogers are subject not only to more gender inequality in human security compared to men but also to inequality within their gender based upon the jurisdiction in which they live. This

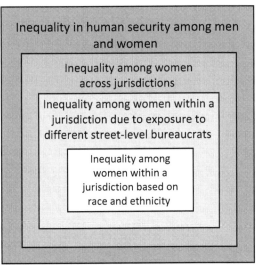

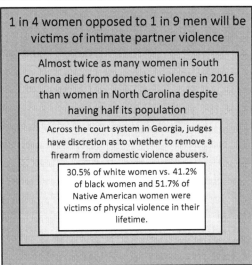

FIGURE 1.1 **Layers of DV inequalities and their outcomes**
This author-generated figure shows the relationships across levels of DV
inequalities and the examples of levels of DV inequalities in the United States.

is the second layer of inequality. Under federal law, Shaw should have had
his firearm removed from his possession. Because he and Morgan shared
a child together, he was prohibited from owning or possessing a firearm

when he was convicted of a misdemeanor of DV and had a protective order issued against him. However this law, known as the Lautenberg Amendment, was not enforced in the state of Virginia and is effective only if a state passes its own version of the law. In 2015, Virginia did not have a domestic violence firearm law (DVFL) that aligned with federal law. Other states that border Virginia, such as Maryland, West Virginia, and Tennessee, had a law enforcing the Lautenberg Amendment. Morgan Rogers was just a state away from being better protected from gun-related violence from her abuser. Not until 2021 did Virginia pass a law that would have prohibited Shaw from owning or possessing a weapon for three years following his conviction, essentially removing his access to the firearm he used to murder Morgan and Leah.[1] From a federal enforcement perspective, there is no consequence for states that do not enforce the Lautenberg Amendment, which is one federal policy on DV that is only as powerful as a state's implementation of it. This second layer of inequality based on location is embedded throughout DV policy and most acutely varies in firearm laws.

The third layer of inequality in DV policy affects women within the same jurisdiction. As a victim of DV, Morgan came into contact with many different government entities from law enforcement to members of the judicial branch. As a repeat offender, Shaw could have been subject to a range of consequences for his actions from jail time to rehabilitation and to fines. Yet despite his violent attack on Morgan that resulted in the issuance of the protective order, he was sentenced to jail time only on the weekends, which unfortunately gave him ample opportunity to commit the murders of Morgan and Leah (WWBT NBC12 News, 2015). Because judges have a considerable amount of latitude in sentencing and setting bail, Morgan and Leah might have been better protected if a different judge had sentenced Shaw. This exemplifies the inequality of women at the hands of different members of law enforcement. Whether a police officer who chooses to make an arrest, a prosecutor who chooses to file charges, or a judge who grants bail or hands down a specific sentence – each of these actors can affect how women are protected from DV where they live.

The fourth and final level of inequality within DV policy involves race and ethnicity. Justice is not served for many women of color or their families. As an African American woman, Morgan was much more likely

---

[1] **Virginia** § 18.2-308.1:8.

to be a victim of DV than women of different races and ethnicities. In addition, when she called police for help, she was more likely to be arrested at the same time as her abuser because she was a black woman. The existing inequalities that pervade the political, economic, and social systems in the United States also extend to both the incidence and prosecution of DV crimes.

1.2 SCHOLARSHIP ON FEDERALISM AND INEQUALITY

Many notable scholars have studied federalism and its ability to create inequality in the United States. Mettler, as well as Skocpol in her own work (1995), argues in *Dividing Citizens* that federalism creates inequality between the sexes (1998, p. 8) and that citizens who receive state-level benefits are treated unequally when compared to those who receive standardized, national-level benefits (p. 9).

Federalism scholars have also questioned whether federalism is gendered. Sawer and Vickers (2016) argue that federalism is gendered in multiple ways: through provisions to protect individual rights, governmental distribution, and financial resources such as taxing and spending. Gendered power distribution is maintained by the federalist structure, which often mimics the public–private divide. Central governments are typically in charge of "public" issues such as defense, security, and foreign relations, while "private" issues such as health, education, and welfare are controlled by regional governments (Watts, 2005). Areas where the federal government is powerful are typically seen as more important than others and these areas normally receive more resources as well as potential international exposure (Resnik, 2002).

In *The Costs of Federalism*, Wildavsky (1984) argues that "federalism means inequality." Inequality in public policy in a federal system has been studied across a number of issue and policy domains, including studies on entitlement programs such as Medicaid (Michener, 2018), the Affordable Care Act (Beland, Rocco, and Waddan, 2016), pension benefits (Skocpol, 1995), and welfare programs (Mettler, 1998). In their book, Daniel Béland, Phillip Rocco, and Alex Waddan use Medicaid and the Affordable Care Act (ACA) to illustrate how the federal system is composed of "many distinct policy battlefields" where variation in the implementation of the ACA can be attributed to policy legacies, institutional fragmentation, and public sentiments (p. 4).

We believe that the framework of Beland et al. (2016) can also apply to DV policy because it is a highly fragmented policy across states, has a relatively short policy legacy, and has varying levels of public support depending on the aspect of DV that a specific policy addresses. For example, public support for ending DV is generally high, but curtailing Second Amendment rights through passage of firearm laws related to DV is deeply unpopular across a number of states. Furthermore, the salience of DV can ebb and flow depending on the levels of violence in a community and the socioeconomic, racial, and ethnic characteristics of a community, whether or not a DV incident turns into a mass shooting or an external shock event, such as the COVID-19 pandemic, occurs that exacerbates it.

Michener's book *Fragmented Democracy* explores the implementation of Medicaid under a federal system and its impact on disenfranchising an already disadvantaged population of the citizenry. Using quantitative and qualitative analysis, Michener argues for an expanded understanding of what it means to participate in politics: "political life also involves more mundane actions taken by denizens seeking resources, redress, or protection from national, state, or municipal governments" (2018, p. 7). The protection citizens seek from their governments is especially important to women's political participation when they are disproportionately victims of DV. Michener writes that political capacity "encompasses the factors that bear upon citizens' willingness to take political action (efficacy, knowledge, attitudes, resources)," which is influenced via institutions such as federalism (p. 29). When a state renders a woman less safe than she should be by its failure to grant a restraining order without forcing her to testify against her accuser, to remove a firearm from her abuser, or to appropriately prosecute a case of DV abuse, women necessarily have decreased capacity to participate in civil society economically, socially, and politically.

To those who argue that men can be similarly incapacitated by inequality in policy adoption and implementation across states, we point to the crucial factor that it is a woman's gender that makes her more vulnerable to DV abuse. As we note later in our discussion, women are far more likely to be a victim of DV than men. The factors that contribute to unequal effects of policies, such as income, race, ethnicity, education, geographic location, and lesbian, gay, bisexual, transgender, and queer (LGBTQ) status, are distributed across men and women, and in some cases systematically so, but none of these factors is as disproportionate in impact as DV on women. In fact, we argue that DV is yet another factor in addition to those just identified that produce an uneven and barrier-filled policy sphere for women.

DV sits at the crossroads of the public–private divide; the violence happens within the private sphere of a family or intimate relationship, but it fundamentally concerns women's personal safety and security. In her book, *Battered Women and Feminist Lawmaking*, Schneider (2000, especially Chapters 1, 2, and 6) posits that the crime of DV against women produces gender inequality in their capacity to achieve economic and social status on the same levels as men. The fact that the law has protected DV abusers under the guise of privacy has only compounded gender inequality and helped to maintain a power structure where women are rendered perpetually subordinate to their abusers who are predominantly male. Because the key actors in the adjudication of DV cases are more frequently men, there can be a gendered bias to their interpretation of the severity of the crime, and an additional burden of proof for women to secure a remedy (Schneider, 2000, pp. 101–111; Ptacek, 1999, pp. 40–68; Epstein, 1999).

Morgan Rogers' murder provides yet another example of how federal and state laws keep violence private and thus prevent women from equal treatment under the law. The Lautenberg Amendment – even when enforced – applies only to a "current or former spouse, parent, or guardian of the victim, by a person with whom the victim shares a child in common, by a person who is cohabitating with or has cohabitated with the victim as a spouse, parent, or guardian, or by a person similarly situated to a spouse, parent, or guardian of the victim."[2] This means any abuse that Morgan Rogers was subjected to prior to the birth of Leah was not covered under federal law at the time. This "boyfriend loophole" allows abusive dating partners to keep their firearms even if they are convicted of a DV offense; 37 states include dating partners even when they are convicted of a DV offense, but only 26 states have extended some type of firearm prohibitions to dating partners who have been convicted of DV or who are under a restraining order.

The fact remains that women cannot be equal to men or to each other if they are victims of violence and if the law does not justly protect them. If women are unsafe in their personal security, they are not being treated equally under the law, which affects their civic and noncivic lives. It has been argued that women do participate in political life proportionate to their presence in the population in terms of voting, but they do not yet achieve full parity in elected or appointed office (Sidorsky, 2015, 2019).

---

[2] This is footnote 2: 18 U.S.C. § 922(g)(9).

Even then, factors such as education and income still characterize female participation in politics at every level. These same factors can also have an impact on the incidence of DV against women. Coupled with the economic losses that victims of DV suffer in terms of wages and medical costs, it is not a far leap to realize that DV depresses the equal participation of women in social, economic, and political life.

We build the case that it is essential for scholars and policymakers to address the vast federal, state, and local differences in the policies, practice, and implementation of law regarding violence against women as part of any effort to achieve gender equality under the law. The creation and application of laws pertaining to DV in the hands of multiple levels of government, mainly the state level, lead directly to women's unequal treatment and varying levels of personal safety in the United States.

1.3 DEFINING DOMESTIC VIOLENCE

Although views on DV have changed over time, researchers and advocacy groups have come to an agreement on what commonly constitutes DV crimes even if the government does not always endorse these definitions. We begin by presenting DV offenses as pictured in the Power and Control Wheel created by the Domestic Abuse Intervention Project (Figure 1.2). The most common DV is use of *physical force*, which can include anything from punching, slapping, pushing, restricting food or sleep, and harming pets or children. *Emotional abuse*, which can also be referred to as *psychological abuse*, includes name calling or belittling, isolation from family or social networks, humiliation, and extreme jealousy or possessiveness. *Sexual abuse* includes rape, harassment, or assault as well as sexual coercion. *Financial abuse* occurs when a partner controls a victim's finances in a restrictive way, such as preventing the victim from working, restricting the victim to an allowance, forcing the victim to track all spending, or denying access to any pertinent bank accounts. All of these kinds of abuse can include threats, intimidation, using children against the victim, stalking, and digital harassment or control (National Coalition Against Domestic Violence, 1996).[3]

---

[3] See also the National Domestic Violence Hotline, www.thehotline.org/is-this-abuse/abuse-defined/; National Coalition Against Domestic Violence, https://ncadv.org/signs-of-abuse; and National Research Council.

FIGURE 1.2 **Power and control wheel**
The Power and Control Wheel explains the various tactics abusers use against
their victims, including physical violence, sexual violence, and coercive control; its
explanation can be found at www.theduluthmodel.org/wheels/. Used with
permission from the Domestic Abuse Intervention Programs, 2022. www.
theduluthmodel.org.

The Power and Control Wheel is a good starting point to understand
what constitutes DV. It provides many different examples of DV that are
typically overlooked in lieu of more traditional (and potentially obvious)
physical DV. Actual DV statutes can fall far short in identifying the abuse
women can experience at the hands of their intimate partners. This means
that even when women may get some form of justice in the form of a
conviction, it may be a limited form of justice because there is no law that
can account for other kinds of domestic abuse that can be equally
damaging.

Under the federal Violence Against Women Act (VAWA), the delineation of DV is in the context of federal grant support to agencies or organizations and in some part relies on state and local definitions of DV as the following description indicates:

[domestic violence encompasses] felony or misdemeanor crimes of violence committed by a current or former spouse or intimate partner of the victim, by a person with whom the victim shares a child in common, by a person who is cohabitating with or has cohabitated with the victim as a spouse or intimate partner, by a person similarly situated to a spouse of the victim under the domestic or family violence laws of the jurisdiction receiving grant monies, or by any other person against an adult or youth victim who is protected from that person's acts under the domestic or family violence laws of the jurisdiction (Sacco, 2017).[4]

VAWA also includes sexual assault, dating violence, and stalking as crimes that can be prosecuted as stand-alone offenses whether they are committed by intimate partners or not. But as we have argued, the enforcement of these laws is constrained to a great extent by the reach of federal law that requires crossing state lines in the commission of these crimes. Consequently, most DV and associated crimes are prosecuted under state laws that vary considerably in definitions and scope of DV. Laws can be different from state to state in terms of delineation of DV, grounds for arrest, gun removal, financial punishment, and incarceration.

Which crimes constitute DV and who can be considered to be victims of DV under the law differ from state to state. For example, Minnesota Statute 609.2242 states that domestic assault is a misdemeanor for "whoever does any of the following against a family or household member: (1) commits an act with the intent to cause fear in another of immediate bodily harm or death or (2) intentionally inflicts or attempts to inflict bodily harm upon another" (Minnesota Code of Laws, 2018).[5] In Minnesota, DV becomes a felony if another act of abuse occurs "within

---

[4] See also www.govinfo.gov/content/pkg/USCODE-2017-title34/pdf/USCODE-2017-title 34-subtitleI-chap121-subchapIII.pdf.

[5] In Minnesota, a household member includes the following: spouses and former spouses; parents and children; persons related by blood; persons who are presently residing together or who have resided together in the past; persons who have a child in common regardless or whether they have been married or have lived together at any time; a man and women if the woman is pregnant and the man is alleged to be the father, regardless of whether they have been married or have lived together at any time; and persons involved in a significant romantic or sexual relationship. (2018 Minnesota Statutes, Domestic Abuse Act).

ten years of the first of any combination of two or more previous qualified DV-related offense convictions or adjudications of delinquency." Revised Code Washington 26.50.010 (2019), meanwhile, defines DV as "(a) physical harm, bodily injury, assault, or the infliction of fear of imminent physical harm, bodily injury or assault, between family or household members; (b) sexual assault of one family or household member by another; or (c) stalking... of one family or household member by another family or household member" and states that

"Family or household members" means spouses, domestic partners, former spouses, former domestic partners, persons who have a child in common regardless of whether they have been married or have lived together at any time, adult persons related by blood or marriage, adult persons who are presently residing together or who have resided together in the past, persons sixteen years of age or older who are presently residing together or who have resided together in the past and who have or have had a dating relationship, persons sixteen years of age or older with whom a person sixteen years of age or older has or has had a dating relationship, and persons who have a biological or legal parent-child relationship, including stepparents and stepchildren and grandparents and grandchildren.

In Washington, therefore, stalking is considered a DV crime while in Minnesota it is not. This is problematic because stalking can cause serious psychological as well as economic costs for victims and can be a precursor to more serious bodily harm. A misdemeanor domestic assault in Minnesota can result in imprisonment of not more than one year or a fine of more than $3,000 while in Washington, an individual charged with battery for a Class A misdemeanor could receive a prison sentence of up to nine months and a fine of up to $10,000.[6] It is alarming to consider the different impact that variations in DV punishments can have on the safety, well-being, and equality of female victims.

Judges, prosecutors, and defense attorneys can influence the implementation of state laws, substantially affecting the outcome of DV cases. Even when one state makes a concerted effort to pass more stringent DV laws for any or all of these areas, other states or local governments may do much less. In many parts of the United States, perpetrators of DV are allowed to keep their firearms, thereby increasing the risks to potential victims like Morgan and Leah Rogers.

---

[6] Minnesota Statute 609.2242; Revised Code Washington 939.51.

1.4 THE EPIDEMIC OF DOMESTIC VIOLENCE IN THE UNITED STATES

The murders of Morgan and Leah Roger are not anomalies. In the United States, DV is a serious problem facing women that cuts across age, race, ethnicity, education, and income, and their murders at the hand of a repeat DV offender is indicative of the level of gender inequality in human security that women face every day. NCADV, one of the leading organizations promoting DV prevention and education, tries to document how many women are victims of DV. They report, for example, that every 20 minutes, someone is abused by an intimate partner, equating to 10 million people a year. Furthermore, "1 in 4 women and 1 in 9 men will experience severe intimate partner physical violence, intimate partner contacts sexual violence, and/or intimate partner stalking" (National Coalition Against Domestic Violence, 1966). The US Department of Justice estimated that an average of 494,434 intimate partner violence incidents are reported to the police every year. But this figure only accounts for 56 percent of all incidents that occur each year (Reaves, 2017). Many victims did not report their attacks to the police because they believed the incident was a private matter, they wanted to protect their abuser, or they feared reprisals (Petrosky, Blair, Betz, et al., 2017).

As directed by VAWA, the US Department of Justice completed a survey of violent crimes against women from 1995 to 1996. The survey revealed some disturbing patterns. Over 17 percent of women in the survey said they were victims of rape with over 20 percent of these women having been raped before they were 12 years old (Tjaden and Thoennes, 2000a, 2000b). Native American/Alaska Native women were more likely to report being victims of violent crime than any other racial or ethnic group. This is not surprising since Alaska has been known to have a higher incidence of rape than any other state in the nation (Fuchs, 2013a, 2013b). Women from the survey were more likely to be victims of intimate partner violence than rape. Over 22 percent of the female respondents compared to just over 7 percent of the male respondents reported intimate partner violence. Furthermore, 64 percent of the women who were victims of violence were mistreated by a partner compared to 16 percent of men who reported their partners as offenders of the violence (Tjaden and Thoennes, 2000a, 2000b).

Many studies have shown the lasting health and economic effects of physical violence on victims. Because women are more likely to be victims of physical violence, they are disproportionately affected by its consequences, including the higher likelihood of post-traumatic stress disorder (PTSD), chronic pain, poor mental health, and difficulty sleeping (L. Cook, 2014). Experiencing DV in the early stages of life can also increase the likelihood of incarceration (DeHart, 2008; DeHart et al., 2014). Rothman and her co-authors (2007) find that intimate partner violence costs more than $8.3 billion per year with victims across the country losing a total of 8 million days of work every year.

Moreover, survey evidence suggests that DV does not discriminate by sexual orientation. According to the National Coalition Against Domestic Violence (2019), "43.8 percent of lesbian women and 61.1 percent of bisexual women have experienced rape, physical violence, and/or stalking by an intimate partner at some point in their lifetime, as opposed to 35 percent of heterosexual women." The vast majority of physical intimate partner violence for bisexual women was perpetrated by men, but over two-thirds of the intimate partner violence of lesbian women was perpetrated by other women (Walters, Chen, and Breiding, 2013). Over one-quarter of gay men and one-third of bisexual men have also experienced some form of DV, which means states like North Carolina that try to exclude same-sex dating relationships from DV statutes are mischaracterizing significant instances of abuse within their state. Over 90 percent of the gay men who reported abuse said it was from a male perpetrator (Walters et al., 2013). Therefore, the law has only just been adapted to provide for same-sex marriage, and in at least one of our states, same-sex partners face even stronger barriers to securing protection from a domestic abuser than opposite-sex partners.

The most severe outcome from DV is the death of the victim. Data on DV homicides have been collected by different government entities and come with gaps in reporting. For example, the National Violent Death Reporting System from the CDC reports that 9,450 women were murdered as the result of DV between 2003 and 2017 (Centers for Disease Control and Prevention, 2021a, 2021b). This number is an estimate because not every state submits its homicide data to the CDC each year. Nearly 50 percent of these homicides were conducted with a firearm.[7] These numbers are alarming in and of themselves but more so

---

[7] The National Violent Death Reporting System began collecting data in 2003 from Alaska, Maryland, Massachusetts, New Jersey, Oregon, South Carolina, and Virginia. Since that time, more states have begun reporting their homicide numbers with 35 states plus the District of Columbia reporting their violent deaths as of 2017. The numbers in Figures 1.3–1.6 include all intended injuries and intimate partners, parents, children, and other relatives by an intimate partner of a relative as the suspects. When the numbers of violent

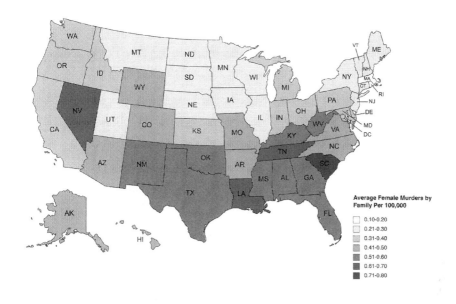

FIGURE 1.3 **Average number of female murders by family per 100,000**
(1990–2017)
Source: Author compiled from FBI Uniform Crime Reporting.

when we take into account that nearly half of the incidences of DV that occur in the United States are never even reported to the police (Bureau of Justice Statistics, 2017).

For our analysis, we collected data from the Federal Bureau of Investigation (FBI) Easy Access to the FBI's Supplementary Homicide Reports (EZASHR) from 1990 to 2016. It provides data over a longer time span than the CDC.[8] We graphically present the data; Figures 1.3 through 1.6. show the geographic patterns of female murders by a family member from 1990 to 2016, and Figures 1.3–1.5 break them down by decade. The data suggest that where a woman lives in the United States has a direct bearing on her vulnerability to, and protection from, death by DV.

---

death are below 10 in any given year in any state, the CDC withholds the cause of injury and other identifying data to preserve confidentiality. The percentage of homicides via firearm is therefore a conservative estimate.

[8] See Appendix Table A.1 for a list of the states that reported data to the FBI and in which years.

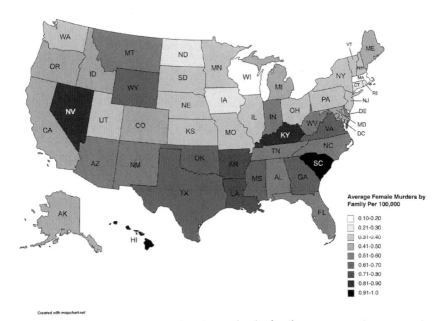

FIGURE 1.4 **Average number of female murders by family per 100,000 (1990–1999)**
Source: Author compiled from FBI Uniform Crime Reporting.

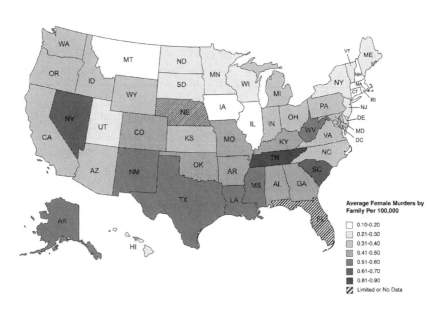

FIGURE 1.5 **Average number of female murders by family per 100,000 (2000–2009)**
Source: Author compiled from FBI Uniform Crime Reporting.

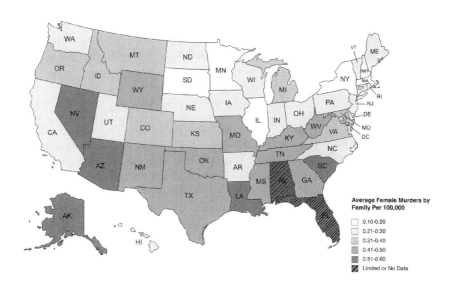

Created with mapchart.net

FIGURE 1.6 **Average number of female murders by family per 100,000 (2010–2017)**
Source: Author compiled from FBI Uniform Crime Reporting.

Several patterns emerge from these data. First is that the general trend of DV homicide has been decreasing over the last 26 years. Second, some states, specifically Florida, have become more reluctant to report their homicide data over time. Finally, there are specific regions and states within the Southern region that consistently have higher levels of intimate partner homicides despite the fact that their numbers have decreased overall. Throughout this book, we will try to explain why these state-to-state differences persist and how that reflects a more general policy failure in this area.

1.5 RACIALIZATION OF GUN VIOLENCE, REPUBLICAN PARTY IDEOLOGY, AND THE OBSTRUCTION OF DOMESTIC VIOLENCE LEGISLATION

In the past three decades, there have been significant changes in the political landscape and surrounding environment for policymaking at the federal and state levels driven by changes in party policy positioning, interest group strategy, and ideological shifts in the electorate. In Chapter 2, we discuss the emergence of DV in the public sphere in the 1980s, which was in large part due to both the women's movement and the related movement to change rape laws. Bringing DV into the public domain outside the traditional bounds of the "private" marriage household met resistance among state legislators who were far more comfortable insisting that domestic issues stay out of the public realm. Enacting laws to punish and prevent DV became part of the larger set of newer issues that gave rise to a gender gap between the two major political parties. As this book proceeds, we will show how this intensifying conservatism, especially among Republicans, came to have a direct impact on the adoption of DV laws at the federal and state levels.

By 1990, Republicans were moving more firmly in the direction of antiabortion policy and limited access to contraception and sex education and continued to resist other "women's" issues such as pay equity and the Family Leave Act. The election of Bill Clinton, a southern Democrat, in 1992 gave the Democrats unified government and the opportunity to enact women-friendly laws such as the Family and Medical Leave Act of 1993 and VAWA in 1994. Those pieces of legislation could have signaled a key turning point in bringing issues such as DV and sexual assault to the forefront, and we argue later in this book that VAWA did spur states to enact policies to combat DV.

However, the congressional elections of 1994 slowed this momentum with the victory in Georgia of Newt Gingrich's style of Republican politics, which was unabashedly conservative and confrontational. More to the point here is the fact that Gingrich built his string of victories in the formerly Democratic south on a platform that mobilized Christian conservatives and white southerners who opposed the advancement of civil rights (Seib, 2020). Gingrich did this under the banner of a smaller federal government and a promise to protect individual rights and values. Rolling back legal protections for women against discrimination, harassment, and violence were implicit and explicit parts of electoral strategy under the guise of states' rights and privacy – both in the home and the workplace. Over the next two and a half decades, Republican Party rhetoric would grow increasingly antigovernment, and the smaller pockets of the party that relied on nativist, racist, and antiwomen rhetoric grew louder and more electorally powerful as embodied in movements like the Tea Party and the Freedom Caucus (Skocpol and Williamson, 2016). The echo chamber of cable news, talk radio, and social media amplified the differences between the two major parties, increasingly so on the issues of gender and race.

Overall, Democrats lost considerable ground at the state level over this same time period. For example, in 1994, Democrats controlled 22 state legislatures outright and split control with Republicans in 12 legislatures, and Republicans controlled 15 state legislatures outright (Nebraska was nonpartisan). In 2004, Democrats controlled 19 state legislatures outright and split control with Republicans in 10 legislatures, and Republicans controlled 20 state legislatures outright. By 2020, Democrats controlled 19 state legislatures outright and split control with the Republicans in only 1 state legislature, and Republicans controlled 29 state legislatures outright.[9] Over this same time period, state policymaking became more polarized (Shor and McCarty, 2011). Regarding public policy specifically, Grumbach (2018) studied 16 distinct issue areas and found evidence of polarized public policies across the 50 states in all but two kinds of policies: education and criminal justice. He measured criminal justice with death penalty repeal, determinate sentencing, DNA motions, three strikes laws, and truth in sentencing policies, but he excluded DV legislation.

In the midst of these broader changes, states have diverged considerably on expanding gun ownership rights (Republican position) or tightening access to firearms (Democratic position). DV policies and firearm laws sit at the crossroads of public policy regarding issues of women's rights, criminal justice, and gun control. Given that firearm usage is responsible for nearly half of deaths of all women from DV, firearm policy is more than tangential to DV policy. The rise of the more conservative Republican (GOP) Party at the national and state levels was concurrent with the rise of the power of the National Rifle Association (NRA) in solidifying opposition to firearm regulation and, by extension, DV firearm regulation (Carlson, 2020; Cook and Goss, 2020; Lacombe, 2019). The NRA took full advantage of the increased use of illegal weaponry in the drug wars of the 1980s to persuade police forces that they were lacking weapons of the capacity that could counter gun violence.

In 1994, both the Republicans and Democrats supported the crime bill that nearly three decades later is acknowledged to have perpetuated a decades' long period of mass incarceration for men and women of color. Also in 1994, the Democratic-controlled Congress and President Clinton

---

[9] Data compiled from the National Council of State Legislatures. www.ncsl.org/research/about-state-legislatures/partisan-composition.aspx#Timelines

enacted a ban on assault weapons with Republican cooperation; working with the NRA, however, the GOP engineered an escape clause with a sunset provision in 2004; the ban on assault weapons has never been enacted again at the federal level. As Carlson (2020, chapters 2 and 4) demonstrates, police chiefs and officers held the racialized perceptions that men of color who possess guns are threats to public safety but "normal people" should not be restricted in access to guns or punished unnecessarily for making a one-time mistake. In Chapter 6, we discuss how the implementation and enforcement of DV laws is also affected by these racialized perceptions (e.g., women of color who call for help may be arrested with their abusers more frequently than white women or a judge refuses to insist on the surrender of a gun from a DV abuser under a restraining order because he is a middle-class white male).

Over time, the NRA and the GOP have made the politically successful argument that Americans should resist limitations on gun ownership to protect themselves from illegal gun violence, which is essentially portrayed as perpetrated by men of color. This perception exists in spite of strong evidence of mass shootings committed by white men, DV murders by white men with guns, and DV murders that evolve into larger mass shooting events. One study estimates that 53 percent of mass shootings involved the murder of an intimate partner or family member (Everytown for Gun Safety, 2021). Getting the NRA's tacit agreement not to block a bill to enact meaningful DV firearm legislation has become almost required (see Smucker, 2019). One Washington State legislator, Roger Goodman, said as much in a newspaper interview about a bill he introduced and hoped to pass in 2013. As he explained in the news interview:

In our effort to address the gun-safety issue, a no-brainer is to identify known dangerous people and prevent them from having access to firearms. And people who are ordered by the court to stay away from their victims, and who have been identified by the court as a credible threat, shouldn't be allowed to possess firearms. It's already prohibited under federal law.... We worked out the language with the NRA.... [Washington State's constitution] guarantees the individual right to bear arms to a greater degree than the Second Amendment. (Minard, 2013)

But apparently the so-called compromise worked out with the NRA was not satisfactory to some progun rights advocates in the state senate, and the bill did not pass in 2013. But according to one news media account (Bassett and Wilkie, 2014), the NRA more generally softened its opposition to laws addressing DV and gun possession over the course of 2013 and 2014. Its change in stance was apparently due to the growing support demonstrated in nationwide and state polling for greater restrictions on access to guns to individuals convicted of DV, stalking, or harassment, or under a restraining order for the threat of such actions. The NRA tacitly agreed to drop its opposition to the pared down version of the bill, which freed Republican senators to support it (Bassett and Wilkie, 2014).

In some states, Republicans have used DV shootings to expand the capacity to own and carry a gun in public. They have even harnessed the gun rights movement as a way for women to protect themselves as well. US Rep. Debbie Lesko (Republican, Arizona) pushed for a clause in a gun bill in February 2019 that would allow victims of DV to get a firearm within three days without the requirement of a background check (Spangler, 2019). Lesko, a survivor of DV and consistently endorsed by the NRA, argued that women should have access to a firearm to protect themselves from their abuser. Such a law puts women in dangerous situations because it does not prevent a woman's abuser from using the gun that the woman purchased to shoot her. We argue that the combination of the GOP alliance with the NRA on firearm regulation and the broader conservative ideology on women's rights and privacy prevalent among elected Republican Party officials has produced an inhospitable environment to address DV. In Chapter 4, we investigate whether Republican Party control in state legislatures makes it more difficult to enact laws that expand the scope of DV protections and keep firearms out of the hands of DV abusers.

1.6 RESEARCH DESIGN, DATA, AND METHODS

In this book, we chose to study DV policy at the federal and state levels with a focus on the years 1990–2017. In particular, we wanted to start the study several years before the adoption of VAWA in 1994 and end the study four years after the 2013 reauthorization of VAWA. Our goal is to bridge available data on state definitions and scope of DV, identify the policies that address the most severe form of violence resulting in the death of victims, and investigate the adjudication of DV cases at the local level.

DV can encompass significant psychological abuse without physical violence, and living in constant fear for themselves and frequently for their children damages women's capacity to excel or succeed in the social, economic, and political quadrants of their lives. We specifically include these elements of DV statutes because they speak to both the controlling nature of DV and the frequent emotional and psychological abuse that

comes with DV as described by the Power and Control Wheel in
Figure 1.2. These kinds of offenses can be much harder to prosecute
and find evidence for, yet they are important to include when writing
DV legislation.

We collected the statutory definition of DV set by Congress and the
statutory definitions compiled from the National Conference of State
Legislatures (NCSL) to assess differences in type and scope of these
laws.[10] To illustrate the differences across states in defining the scope of
DV and who is considered eligible for protection under these laws, we
tracked a subset of these DV statutes:

- Stalking
- Terroristic and/or threatening language or treatment
- False imprisonment
- Extension of DV to dating partners

We discuss these further in Chapter 3 and present the state-by-state data
in Table 3.1.

In Chapter 3, we also seek to demonstrate the dynamic of policymaking in this arena at the state level. To do so, we selected six states:
Georgia, Montana, Pennsylvania, West Virginia, Alaska, and
Minnesota. We constructed brief case studies on the evolution or devolution of DV laws over time to highlight three key factors: conservative
ideology on gun rights, the impact of DV homicides, and vertical policy
diffusion. These case studies also provide examples of the policy feedback
loop in action and set the stage for a quantitative analysis predicting the
adoption of DV firearm laws at the state level presented in Chapter 4.

To address the lethality of DV as a result of firearms, we constructed a
data set of DVFLs across all 50 states from 1990 to 2017, the incidence of
firearm deaths by state and year, and the demographic, political, and
policy factors that can explain the conditions under which those laws
were passed. We chose to focus on eight categories of laws that we
analyze in greater depth in Chapter 4:[11]

- Prohibiting domestic violence misdemeanants from buying or possessing firearms or ammunition

---

[10] We used the NCSL database www.ncsl.org/research/human-services/domestic-violence-
domestic-abuse-definitions-and-relationships.aspx as a starting point and followed up
with each statute on each state's Code of Laws website.

[11] In compiling this list of laws, we consulted the 2015 Institute of Women's Policy Research
report on the Status of Women, Table B7.3, p. 260. See Hess et al. (2015).

- Prohibiting subjects of domestic violence restraining orders (DVROs) issued after notice and hearing from purchasing or possessing firearms
- Prohibiting dating partners convicted of domestic violence misdemeanors from purchasing or possessing a firearm
- Prohibiting stalking felons from buying or possessing firearms
- Providing gun surrender for those with permanent restraining orders
- Restricting ex parte restraining orders
- Prohibiting stalking misdemeanants from buying or possessing firearms
- Prohibiting misdemeanants of DV or stalking conviction or under a DVRO to obtain concealed carry permits

There is an issue regarding cohesive law enforcement implementation of state law by local and state prosecutors. When they respond to a DV scene, law enforcement officers use their own discretion when making an arrest. In the same way, a police officer can give a lower traffic offense for a person who is speeding, so too can a police officer decide not to charge a person with DV but with assault, battery, or similar charges. In states with mandatory arrest for DV, a police officer can either encourage the victim to press charges for the crime as a DV offense or be persuaded by the victim that the offense does not require that categorization so the offender would not be subject to mandatory arrest. Even if law enforcement within a state were to respond consistently to all calls of DV, prosecutors involved with cases that make it that far may charge or plea bargain the offense to a different crime.

In her work cited earlier, Epstein argues that a "law is only as good as the system designed to deliver on its promises" (1999, 13). This is because the implementation of laws can change the intent behind the law itself. Most criminal and civil DV cases are prosecuted under state law, and each state has developed its own definitions of crimes associated with DV and resulting punishments. Furthermore, individual prosecutors can select other categories under which to prosecute DV, such as simple or misdemeanor assault, which takes the case out of the purview of DV law. Because every jurisdiction is unique and prosecutors have discretion over whom to charge and what to charge, there is differential defense representation of DV offenders. One of the consequences of this is varying outcomes for DV offenses with the only difference being where the crime occurred and thus which state laws are being applied. For work on the efficacy of the implementation of state laws, see Browne and Williams (1989) and Dugan (2002).

The actions of victims, advocacy organizations, and street-level bur-
eaucrats such as law enforcement, prosecutors, and public defenders
combine to increase or decrease the incidence of DV well before a case
goes to court. From our earlier research, we know there is a great deal of
variation – indeed latitude – in how DV cases are handled in local
jurisdictions. Dugan, Nagin, and Rosenfeld (2003) studied homicide rates
and found mixed results regarding the impact of specific enforcement and
prosecution policies at the local level among married and unmarried
intimate partners from 1976 to 1996. Specifically, they found that removing the abuser from the home, typically through mandatory arrest and
warrantless arrest policies, decreased intimate partner (IP) fatalities in the
case of both married and unmarried couples. However, when prosecutors
chose to enforce a no-contact order, IP female homicides increased among
married and unmarried couples. The authors also found that lower economic and educational levels were associated with higher intimate partner
violence (IPV) but had different results according to race and marital
status. Other researchers have tried to assess the effect of local policies
on referrals to counseling programs on rearrest rates and have found that
when IPV cases are ignored, rearrest rates are highest, but they are lower
for individuals who attended a counseling program (Wooldredge and
Thistlethwaite, 2002; Bergen, Edleson, and Renzetti, 2011).

In order to assess the variation in how domestic laws are adjudicated
across states, we designed and conducted an original survey of public
defenders and prosecutors asking them about the DV cases they defend or
prosecute and the specific conditions and outcomes associated with those
cases. The difficulty in amassing the contact information for public
defenders and prosecutors presented obstacles to implementing the survey
in all 50 states. Instead, we selected a random sample of 16 states that we
describe in more detail in Chapter 5.[12]

---

[12] As with any study of multiple dimensions of policymaking, data can be either unavailable
or scattered across multiple sources. DV is a highly under-reported crime where even the
violence that is being reported is just a fraction of the violence that is actually occurring.
Also, national law enforcement organizations such as the FBI do not collect data on all
acts of violence against women (or if they do, do not share it publicly). The Uniform
Crime Reporting (UCR) Program is used by the FBI to collect data on criminal offenses at
the state level from almost every state. Although states participate to varying degrees
across our period of study, only Florida failed to report gun homicide data from 1996 to
the present day. The UCR provides access to information about a homicide that is
committed by a family member, but there is no distinct category of "homicide by
domestic violence." Not all murders, rapes, or assaults are domestic violence related
but without a separate category, it is very difficult to gauge the true extent of violence

1.7 BOOK ROADMAP

We use a multimethod approach to understand how federalism and policy diffusion affect the adoption and implementation of DV statutes. The book proceeds from here as follows:

Chapter 2: Federal Action on Domestic Violence. In this chapter, we present the federal response to violence against women. We begin the chapter with a brief overview of the history of DV in the United States. We then analyze the response of Congress to the DV epidemic compared to the Supreme Court's response. These detailed case studies reveal the gaps federal law has created by leaving states the option to enforce federal law and that nearly all of the enforcement of DV law is relegated to local authorities. Chapter 2 underscores the role and limits of federal policy in remedying the inequities among women in their personal protection from DV. The lack of a cohesive federal response contributes to all four levels of gender inequality in DV policy.

Chapter 3: Policymaking in the States: Domestic Violence Statutes. Here we explore the policy feedback process and describe how state policies have evolved or devolved in the specific issue area of firearm laws and DV. This chapter is meant to demonstrate how and when states respond to the need for reform in their DV laws and show how key actors in that process, including legislators and interest groups, affect the content of the policy that is adopted. The chapter includes examples of states that vary in the definition and scope of DV law and contrasts the laws with each other and with federal law. We present six case studies of states that differ in their legislative histories on DV laws to identify key factors that can explain this variation; we test these factors in the quantitative analysis presented in Chapter 4.

Chapter 4: Explaining and Predicting the Adoption of State Domestic Violence Gun Laws. Using quantitative data, we construct an explanation for the adoption of policies that address the intersection of firearm and DV. Our focus on DV gun laws stems from the direct link between the presence of a gun in a DV relationship and the incidence of DV homicide. Removing guns from perpetrators of DV, including DV among unmarried couples, decreases intimate partner deaths (Zeoli et al., 2018). Beyond the

---

against women more generally. This leads back to the problem that states define domestic violence in different ways even if the FBI were to collect that data in that category. This means that in some states, a husband's physical attack on his wife could be prosecuted as aggravated assault, while in other states, it could be considered domestic violence.

very positive effects that laws on DV gun ownership can have on making women safer, we have also seen an increase in the sponsorship and passage of these laws over the last 30 years.

With our original dataset of DVFL enactments, we analyze the circumstances under which states adopt these laws. Law regarding DV firearms is one vehicle for understanding DV policy adoption at the state level. Although existing research has revealed the positive impact that such laws can have on reducing DV homicides, not every state has adopted them; even when states have similar laws in place, they do not implement them equally. We find evidence that state and federal factors influence policy adoption employing a set of political and demographic indicators as independent variables; in particular, the number of gun-related homicides, partisan control of the legislature, citizen ideology, federal legislation, and election years influence the likelihood of DVFL enactments. We find support for the effects of vertical policy diffusion but not for horizontal policy diffusion across states. We found no effects associated with support for gun ownership or the percent of women state legislators.

Chapter 5: The View from the Courtroom: Inconsistent Implementation of Domestic Violence Policy at the Local Level. In this chapter, we move from the adoption of DVFLs at the state level to the ways in which DV cases are adjudicated at the local level. Using this vantage point, we analyze the gap between DV public policies and how such cases are prosecuted and defended in the courtroom. The public defenders and district attorneys we considered in the State Public Defender and District Attorney survey are on the front lines of DV cases as they enter courtrooms; nearly 25 percent of their caseload was DV cases and of those, about 50 percent involved repeat offenders. Including public defenders and district attorneys in our analysis allows us to capture both the passage of laws and their implementation in the judicial system; we argue that each is important to truly understand women's equality via DV. We utilize the information from these public defenders and prosecutors to understand what kinds of DV cases they see, who the victims are, and what happens to those who are convicted of such crimes. We also analyze the reported outcomes of DV cases to see whether specific DV laws have any influence on the punishment of DV offenses. In short, with these data, we are able to present the first-hand perspectives of some of the individuals who are involved with DV cases on a daily basis.

In particular, we find that DV public policies, such as mandatory arrest and gun removal, are implemented inconsistently across states, and we demonstrate that differing policies and implementation practices lead to diverse outcomes of DV cases in the courtroom. We emphasize that there are vast disparities among policies in terms of how they are implemented in the courtroom that depend on a combination of state laws, local laws, caseloads, and characteristics of public defenders and district attorneys including ideology and race.

Chapter 6: The Costs of Inequality in Domestic Violence Policies. Here we consider the personal and political costs of varying DV policies in the United States, and we describe the challenges women face for civic participation due to being DV victims. Unfortunately, no dataset contains questions asking voters if they were DV victims. But there is ample evidence that DV can be a barrier to voting and political participation for women – particularly women of color. We also discuss disparities in different communities based on race, ethnicity, and immigration status in terms of the investigation and prosecution of DV crimes and how DV laws have used criminalization as an answer to DV, especially in communities of color. Women of color are much more likely to be accused of DV instead of being seen as victims. These victims who are treated as offenders have to live with a conviction on their record, and in most states have their most fundamental right to vote removed while they serve their sentence or are on probation. In the last part of this chapter, we delve more deeply into the current system in place to protect women in light of public health crises such as the COVID-19 pandemic.

Chapter 7: Pathways for Improving Women's Human Security. We conclude our book by summarizing our findings and discussing their implications. We circle back to where we began: violence against women remains a significant and serious impediment to achieving equal status for women in all dimensions of their lives. We offer suggested reforms for how DV laws and policy implementation can be improved at the federal and state levels while recognizing the federal government's limits in dealing with what is essentially a very localized problem. The reality is that federalism creates unequal conditions for women's human security across state lines. We end this chapter with proposed avenues of future research that explore more holistically the ways that communities deal with DV. In expanding attention to DV as a source of suppressed citizen participation by women in the United States, we hope to encourage the discipline of political science, as well as policymakers and practitioners to address DV more consistently and effectively.

2

Federal Action on Domestic Violence

The documentary *Private Violence* follows the story of Deanna Walters, a victim of severe domestic violence (DV) at the hands of her husband Robbie Howell.[1] Like many stories of intimate partner violence (IPV), Walters described Howell as initially sweet and nice. Unfortunately, he changed just a few months into their relationship. He took control of her money, questioned her past relationships, and belittled her. In 2008, Walters gathered her courage and separated from her husband, although she often saw him for shared events with their young daughter. On Halloween, Walters invited her husband to go trick-or-treating with their 2-year-old daughter Martina. It was a decision that would come with lifelong consequences.

Howell became jealous while he watched Walters take Martina trick-or-treating, and while the child slept in the back seat, he pulled Walters out of the car in a hospital parking lot and beat her. He then forced Walters and Martina to join him and his cousin (and codriver) on a cross-country truck trip during which he repeatedly beat Walters with a flashlight and refused to feed Martina because her mom was "not telling him the truth" about cheating on him. Walters never cheated on her husband. The trip took the family all the way from North Carolina to California and back with the worst beating on the return trip to North Carolina occurring in Oklahoma where Howell beat and smothered Walters until she started having seizures. On November 6, an Oklahoma patrol deputy

---

[1] Deanna Walters' story was detailed in the Criminal Discourse Podcast on May 4, 2020, which was used to construct this vignette; see https://criminaldiscoursepodcast.com/deanna-walters/.

stopped the truck after the trucking company that operated it reported that it had two unauthorized passengers. Because of Walters' condition, she was taken to the hospital where she was treated for six days – her husband was not arrested by Oklahoma police.

Walters experienced horrific abuse; she was beaten, burned, suffocated, bitten, and urinated on by her husband. Even though Howell admitted to the abuse to the North Carolina police, he was still not arrested, and the local district attorney wanted to charge him only for misdemeanor assault on a female with a maximum sentence of 150 days in jail. It took over a year before a federal prosecutor agreed to press charges of kidnapping and interstate DV, the latter charge created under the Violence Against Women Act (VAWA). In 2011, Howell was found guilty of kidnapping and interstate DV and sentenced to 21 years in federal prison. Walters came very close to losing her life at the hands of someone who was supposed to love her. Howell almost got away with his crimes with little to no penalty. If not for the creation of VAWA and the federal government's addressing the epidemic of DV, Walters' case might have been ignored, and Howell might never have been prosecuted.

But Walters was one of the rare victims of DV crime who was covered by federal law. This is not the case for the majority of women who are abused; they will see their abusers receive little to no punishment or rehabilitation for their actions. In this chapter, as well as the book as a whole, we assess the role the federal government has played in addressing DV. We argue that the federal government's reach has been limited and because the federal government has left much of the actual policy response on DV to state and local governments, federal laws are not particularly effective in keeping women safe. Nowhere is this more glaring than in the area of DV abuse committed with a firearm. Political opposition to gun control grew far more intense during the same period that laws addressing DV in other ways have become more expansive such as being extended to dating partners in some states. While it appears that more public energy is devoted to protecting women from domestic abuse, the real effects of federal and local policies are less than they could be. Despite repeated attempts by some members of Congress, no reauthorization of VAWA ever included a provision that limited the purchase and ownership of guns by dating partners who committed domestic violence abuse. Republican members of Congress, in conjunction with the NRA, sustained intense opposition to this provision in VAWA. It was not until 2022 when the BSCA was passed that dating partners were covered under federal law. Without reauthorizing legislation, money for programs authorized by VAWA is contingent on the extension of funding in appropriation bills (US Department of Justice FY Budget 2022 Request). The next section of this chapter depicts the early history of DV policy at the federal, state, and local levels. Until 1984, it is a very short story.

2.1 DECADES OF SILENCE ON DOMESTIC VIOLENCE

In her book *Women and Justice for the Poor: A History of Legal Aid, 1863–1945*, Batlan documents the history of the availability of legal services to protect women from physical harm at the hands of their husbands. Batlan (2015, p. 62) writes that some of the earliest advocacy for women was provided by the Chicago Protective Agency for Women and Children, founded in 1885:

The Chicago Protective Agency accepted cases of wage claims as well as what we would now call domestic violence.... Adequate laws, however, did not exist to protect a wife and children when her husband was an abusive drunk who failed to support the family. This recognition of, and focus on, domestic violence was unusual for the period, although leaders of the agency primarily imagined that domestic violence occurred only in poor and working-class homes rooted in lower-class men's depravity and lack of self-discipline. In its early years, the agency handled wage claims... but by the turn of the century domestic relations cases surpassed those of wage claims.

Divorce was not common in the late 1800s; many legal aid organizations refused to handle divorce requests from women even if they were abused. At the same time, women were just beginning to gain some control over their own finances or at least not be held responsible for their husbands' debts. In the mid-nineteenth century, some states passed married women's property acts, but these were not consistently adopted and did little to help women who were abused by their spouse (Speth, 1982). It took until 1911 for Chicago to establish a separate court, known as a domestic relations court, which "dealt primarily with desertion cases, failure to support, bastardy, and abuse" – the kinds of case that the agency [Chicago Protective Agency for Women and Children] had long handled for women (Speth, 1982, p. 71). The growing profession of social work produced advocates for women who worked to persuade the male-dominated judicial system that "divorce could be a narrative of new beginnings rather than a tragedy"(Batlan, 2015, p. 207). It would take nearly 30 additional years before legal aid organizations across the country recognized that divorce was a better option than asking women to stay in violent homes and began systematically (though on a limited basis) offering women legal representation to secure a divorce.

Gordon's book, *Heroes of Their Own Lives: The Politics and History of Family Violence: Boston, 1880–1960*, delves deeply into the history of legal and social policy on DV. Gordon (1988, pp. 254–256, 264) reviews the earliest efforts to punish "wife-beaters" starting in the 1870s, even though what is now referred to as DV was outlawed in most states by then and was to some extent tied to the temperance movement and new ideas about how men should behave. Poor and generally uneducated women who sought protection from their husbands were much more concerned about financial support for them and their children. However, when the Depression caused economic opportunity to dwindle, women who asked for help began to rely more equally on the dual arguments of economic insecurity and protection of themselves and their children from violence. There is a particularly striking passage in Gordon's book (p. 272) about a woman from the 1920s on this point:

Mrs. O'Brien, for example, changed her mind repeatedly about how she wanted to deal with her problem, and her seeming ambivalence reflects the lack of options she and so many others had. Living with a husband so brutal even the police advised her to have him arrested, she told them, speaking for thousands, "She does not want to lose her chn. [children] however and the little money which she does receive from fa. [father] enables her to keep her home together." Instead, she tried to get the MSPCC [Massachusetts Society for the Prevention of Cruelty to Children] agent to "scare" him into treating her and her children "right."

Pleck (1989, pp. 39–40) notes that while society was becoming more concerned with protecting children in abusive situations, the same was not true for women being abused: "In the nineteenth century, there were hundreds of societies to protect children from cruelty but only one society to protect wives from cruelty. Children were innocent and helpless; women were not."

It took more than 50 years before there was anywhere for women like Mrs. O'Brien to go to escape the violence of their homes, even temporarily, as the creation of emergency shelters for DV victims was a slow process starting in the late 1970s. According to Schechter (1982), the increased attention to the female victims of DV grew out of the battered women's movement and broader advocacy efforts for women in multiple issue areas such as social welfare, divorce laws, and the antirape movement. The growth of DV shelters was integral to the battered women's movement and in helping lawmakers, social workers, law enforcement, and psychologists understand family violence and battered women more specifically. Schechter explains that before the growth of shelters, many people viewed battered women as passive, dependent, or aberrant. Shelters offered the supportive framework through which thousands of women turned "personal" problems into political ones, relieved themselves of self-blame, and called attention to the sexism that left millions of women violently victimized.

Even medical professionals' understanding of DV for much of the mid-twentieth century was incredibly lacking. Not one study in the *Journal of Marriage and the Family* referenced violence between 1939 and 1969. One article in the *Archives of General Psychiatry* studied intimate partner violence but never condemned it. In fact, the study blamed the wife for the husband's abusive actions and claimed the wives who were beaten were "aggressive, efficient, masculine, and sexually frigid" (Schechter, 1982, 22). It is not difficult to see how victim blaming, either by the victim herself or society writ large, became such a challenge to ending the cycle of abuse and getting these victims the resources they needed. In fact, until the early 1980s, police could not act on DV even at the misdemeanor charge level, unless the officers themselves had "witnessed a part of the action" (Browne and Williams, 1989, p. 78). Restraining orders against husbands were virtually impossible to obtain without simultan-eously filing for divorce and were not issued on any emergency basis; moreover, one incident was not sufficient grounds for divorce (Browne and Williams, 1989, p. 78).

The 1980s would see an increase in the number of shelters and DV hotlines, and states passed laws addressing the aforementioned gaps in protections for abused women. According Schechter, "as late as 1976, New York City, with a population estimated at more than 8 million people, had 1000 beds for homeless men and 45 for homeless women" (1982, 11). Browne and Williams (1989) argue that without any recourse, women were more likely to kill their spouses or partners; using an index of resources for abused women, including shelters and hotlines, Browne and Williams (1989, pp. 88–90) found that such resources had a statistic-ally significant impact on reducing the number of female murders of male spouses or partners. In contrast, they found no such impact for state-level DV laws. In her work on the efficacy of state laws pertaining to protective orders, Dugan (2002) found that most protective orders were associated with lower levels of DV incidents with the exception of custody awards that were associated with higher levels. She also found that in jurisdictions with mandatory arrest policies, the reporting of DV incidents decreased.

There is also an extensive network of nongovernmental organizations including interest groups and community groups devoted to aiding victims of DV and working with abusers to reduce recidivism. As Orloff and Feldman (2017) describe, the network began to emerge at the local and then national level. Pennsylvania formed the first statewide coalition against DV in 1976, and the national coalition was formed just two years later. Over the next decade, organizations at the local level formed to address the specific needs of ethnic, racial, and immigrant communities (Orloff and Feldman, 2017). By 1997, the Women of Color Network, Inc. was founded as a national organization to address the needs of women from across these communities.[2] In the 2000s, additional groups arose to provide services to Muslim women, immigrant women, and women who had been victims of human trafficking (Sokoloff, 2008).

Today, nearly 100 years after Mrs. O'Brien's pleas for help, there is a much more extensive network of support for victims of DV at the local, state, and national levels. But even with those changes over a relatively short period of time, DV crimes still generate daily headlines, and they are increasingly costing additional human lives in the form of collateral damage from DV committed with firearms. Just one look at the website for the National Coalition Against Domestic Violence (NCADV) confirms that women face many of the same bad options that Mrs. O'Brien did; its front page has topics entitled "8 Steps that Explain 'Why She Doesn't Leave'" and "When Women Must Choose between Abuse and Homelessness"; the website also has a Safety Exit box to allow users to "quickly exit the site if in danger.[3]" Despite the enormous strides that women have made on many other dimensions, including education, income, and professional success, the gendered patterns of DV abuse still leave too many women unable to fully participate in society as equal human beings.

2.2 CONGRESS STEPS IN

The Civil Rights Act of 1964 for the first time established a national guarantee of equality under the law regardless of race, color, religion, sex, or national origin. In doing so, it set the precedent for the federal government to step in and try to remedy the lack of protection for citizens by state governments. However, at that time, there was no consistent national policy on DV, and it would take 30 more years before Congress acted to pass the VAWA, which is the most comprehensive federal law to

[2] Women of Color Network, Inc. http://wocninc.org/about/.
[3] www.ncadv.org/.

combat violence against women, specifically by an intimate partner. Figure 2.1 traces the evolution of federal action both legislatively and in the judicial system on DV–related policy.

Despite the considerable activism of the 1960s on the federal government's part, there was no action on DV until the late 1970s. On June 6, 1977, Sen. Wendell Anderson (Democrat, Minnesota) took the first step to introduce the Domestic Violence Prevention and Treatment Act.[4] It had eight original cosponsors (two Republicans and six Democrats), one of whom was Sen. Ted Kennedy (Democrat, Massachusetts). The bill directed:

the Secretary of Health, Education, and Welfare, acting through the Director of the National Institute of Mental Health, to establish a grant program designed to support projects which: (1) develop methods for the identification, prevention, and treatment of domestic violence; and (2) provide for family rehabilitation and support, and for emergency shelter and protection for individuals who are threatened by domestic violence. Directs the Director to establish a national information and resource clearinghouse to collect, analyze, prepare, and disseminate information relating to domestic violence. Requires the Director, in cooperation with the Administrator of Law Enforcement Assistance and the head of any other Federal agency involved with domestic violence, to study State laws, practices, and policies relating to domestic violence. Requires the Director to annually review the effectiveness of projects carried out under this Act and to report the findings to the Secretary. Directs the Secretary to transmit each such report to the President and to each House of Congress.[5]

The *St. Louis Post-Dispatch* wrote about DV, including the new Anderson and Kennedy bill, on July 1, 1977. The article stated that battered women are hidden victims in society and "those who do report the attack encounter obstacles that have sprung from official unwillingness to deal with the problem, as for example, the informal 'stitches rule' used by some police departments that requires a woman to have a certain number of stitches as a result of the beating before her husband can be arrested" ("Hidden Problem," 1977, p. 32).

Just three months later, freshman Rep. Barbara Mikulski (Democrat, Maryland) introduced the Family Violence Prevention and Treatment Act with six cosponsors (five Democrats and one Republican). At the time, there were only 18 women serving in the House; 6 of those women had their names on this bill. It called for the creation of a coordinating council

---

[4] The corresponding bill was introduced by Reps. Lindy Boggs and Newton Steers Jr. in the House.
[5] www.congress.gov/bill/95th-congress/senate-bill/1728?r=5&s=3.

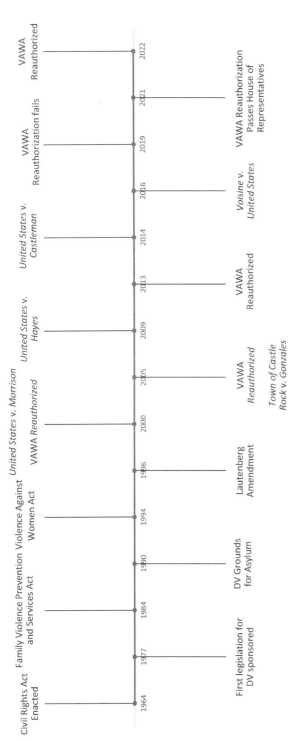

FIGURE 2.1 **Timeline of federal action on DV**
This figure presents the timeline of federal legislation and Supreme Court decisions that influence DV policy.
Source: Author.

on family violence that would "(1) identify, assess, and coordinate all Federal programs related to problems of family violence in order to eliminate duplication of effort, inefficient use of resources, and lack of strategic objectives and priorities and (2) stimulate new programs within member agencies of the Council where necessary to fill gaps in services, funding, research, or demonstration programs."[6] The bill also proposed the establishment of the National Center for Community Action Against Family Violence and devoted resources toward researching the effects of the bill. It, like its predecessor, never made it out of committee.

It took seven years for a version of the Anderson and Kennedy and Mikulski bills to be enacted into law. The Family Violence Prevention and Services Act (FVPSA) of 1984 provided federal funds to "assist states in preventing incidents of family violence and to provide shelter and related assistance to victims and their dependents" (Sacco, 2019, p. 1). This infusion of federal money was sorely needed, because until this legislation, there was very little funding or coordination among shelters; they mainly relied on private charities and donations. The law also created the DV hotline to help victims navigate their options when trying to get out of an abusive relationship. While the federal government certainly lagged behind states in enacting its legislation (states were starting to pass their own DV legislation in the 1970s), it was attempting to address the issue, albeit with little success.

The only other notable federal legislative action on DV between the FVSPA and VAWA was a provision in the Immigration Act of 1990 that granted a waiver to immigrant spouses of US citizens to enable them to become permanent legal residents without their spouse's "knowledge, consent, or cooperation" (Orloff and Feldman, 2017, p. 4). Around the same time, the Immigration and Naturalization Service (now called the US Citizenship and Immigration Services) put in place a policy to "recognize domestic violence as grounds for asylum in the U.S." (p. 5).

In 1990, Sen. Joe Biden (Democrat, Delaware) introduced the VAWA, but it would take four years before it was debated on the Senate floor, passed by Congress, and signed into law by President Bill Clinton. The VAWA was technically passed as part of the Violent Crime Control and Law Enforcement Act of 1994. This law was supported by 95 senators (53 Democrats, 42 Republicans), but 4 senators (2 Republicans and 2 Democrats) voted against it, and it passed via voice vote in the House.

[6] www.congress.gov/bill/95th-congress/house-bill/8948?r=6&s=3.

During the floor debate in the Senate, then-freshman Sen. Barbara Boxer (Democrat, California) stated:

What we do know is that the criminal justice system is guilty because it routinely turns its back on this form of brutality and leaves too many women out in the cold. Mr. President, beating is beating. Blood spilled is blood spilled. Whether it occurs at the hands of a stranger or a family member, there should be no difference in the way it is viewed. It is time for action to prevent violence in the home. The excuse that "This is just a family matter" is no longer acceptable. "I love her so much that I lost myself" are words that must be seen as a cry for help from both spouses in the relationship. (*Congressional Record*, p. 13658)

The VAWA established the Office of Violence Against Women (OVW) in the US Department of Justice and provided grant money to law enforcement and states that would help to prevent DV, provide services for DV victims, better investigate and prosecute DV crimes, and increase arrests of DV offenses. Additionally, VAWA "authorized the grant for the National Domestic Violence Hotline and. . . reauthorized funding for battered women's shelters" as well as "authorized research and education grants for judges and court personnel in federal court circuits to gain a better understanding of the nature and the extent of gender bias in the federal courts" (Sacco, 2019). The next section details these grants and the gaps they leave in requiring stronger state compliance with federal law.

2.2.1 Grant Programs Funded through the Violence Against Women Act

As of 2021, the OVW had 19 grant programs: 4 are formula and 15 are discretionary. Each grant has its own set of eligibility criteria, with some grants going only toward state, local, or tribal governments, some available only to nonprofit or nongovernmental organizations, and others allowing both governmental and nongovernmental organizations to apply. Although each program is different, generally the grant money goes to train staff, law enforcement, judges, and prosecutors on the best ways to address DV or handle actual cases. Other grants provide better housing opportunities for victims or educate children on how to recognize and understand violence toward women. Yet others are geared toward specific demographics, such as violence toward those with disabilities, Native Americans, elderly abuse victims and violence that occurs in rural areas. In 2020 the OVW awarded nearly $500 million dollars to 773 grant recipients.

Two of the awardees in 2020 were the Alaska Native Justice Center ($750,000 grant) and Itasca County Minnesota ($292,0000 grant) that were both funded via a Rural Sexual Assault, Domestic Violence, Dating Violence and Stalking Assistance Program grant. This discretionary grant "enhances the safety of rural victims of sexual assault, domestic violence, dating violence and stalking and supports projects uniquely designed to address and prevent these crimes in rural area. Eligible applicants are states, territories, Indian tribes, local governments, and nonprofit entities, including tribal nonprofit organizations" (US Department of Justice, 2016). In 2020 this program provided a total of 57 grants of over $32.2 million worth of funding (US Department of Justice, 2021).

By far the largest grant from the OVW is from the Services, Training, Officers, and Prosecutors Formula Grant Program (STOP), which awarded 56 grants totaling over $150 million in 2020. This grant is:

Awarded to states and territories, enhances the capacity of local communities to develop and strengthen effective law enforcement and prosecution strategies to combat violent crimes against women and to develop and strengthen victim services in cases involving violent crimes against women. Each state and territory must allocate 25 percent for law enforcement, 25 percent for prosecutors, 30 percent for victim services (of which at least 10 percent must be distributed to culturally specific community-based organizations), 5 percent to state and local courts, and 15 percent for discretionary distribution.[7]

Table 2.1 lists the OVW grants that state, local, and tribal governments are eligible for with the number of state/local grant awardees, the funding from each grant that went to a governmental organization, and the total amount of grant money that was awarded in total from each program regardless of which organization it went to. More than half ($266,200,390) of all the grant money that state, local, and tribal governments were eligible for went to those organizations.

2.2.2 The Importance of the Lautenberg Amendment

Sen. Frank Lautenberg (Democrat, New Jersey) was a staunch supporter of gun control having attempted to get guns out of the hands of violent offenders even before the passage of VAWA (see S.2304, Stop Arming

---

[7] The state that received the largest STOP grant in 2020 was California ($14,772,775) followed by Texas, ($11,000,634) and Florida ($8,303,925). www.justice.gov/ovw/page/file/914131/download.

TABLE 2.1. *Office on Violence Against Women grants for state, local and tribal governments*

Grant	Grant Type	Number of State/Local Government Awards 2020	Funding to State/Local Governments 2020	Total Funding Awarded from Grant 2020
STOP Violence Against Women	Formula	56	$152,993,041	$152,993,041
Sexual Assault Services	Formula	56	25,825,000	25,825,000
Consolidated Grant Program to Address Children and Youth Experiencing Domestic and Sexual Assault and Engage Men and Boys as Allies*	Discretionary	1	500,000	8,475,841
Enhanced Training and Services to End Abuse in Later Life	Discretionary	7	3,105,476	3,805,476
Grants to Support Families in the Justice System	Discretionary	12	6,377,983	13,074,625
Grants to Tribal Governments to Exercise Special Domestic Violence Criminal Jurisdiction*	Discretionary	10	3,266,458	3,266,458
Improving Criminal Justice Responses to Sexual Assault, Domestic Violence, Dating Violence, and Stalking	Discretionary	38	26,694,374	29,694,374
Legal Assistance for Victims*	Discretionary	4	2,117,458	36,543,406
Rural Sexual Assault, Domestic Violence, Dating Violence and Stalking Assistance	Discretionary	6	3,710,066	32,237,326

(continued)

TABLE 2.1. (*continued*)

Grant	Grant Type	Number of State/Local Government Awards 2020	Funding to State/Local Governments 2020	Total Funding Awarded from Grant 2020
Training and Services to End Violence Against Women with Disabilities	Discretionary	1	325,000	4,359,657
Transitional Housing Assistance Grants for Victims of Sexual Assault, Domestic Violence, Dating Violence, and Stalking	Discretionary	6	2,969,775	40,490,820
Tribal Governments Program*	Discretionary	50	35,976,584	39,070,734
Tribal Sexual Assault Services Program*	Discretionary	8	2,339,175	2,662,939
Total		255	$266,200,390	$392,499,697

*Tribal governments are eligible for this grant; state and local governments are not. The money to Legal Assistance for Victims Grant Program awardees went to three public universities and one Native American tribe.

Felons [SAFE] Act in 1992).[8] VAWA was part of larger legislative attention being paid to firearm violence and crime in the early 1990s to prevent
individuals with a restraining order from possessing a gun. Federal law at
the time also prevented some felons from owning firearms. Lautenberg, a
supporter of VAWA, recognized that many DV offenders were going to
slip through the cracks of federal law. On March 21, 1996, he sponsored
S.1632 that would "prohibit persons convicted of a crime involving
domestic violence from owning or possessing firearms." The bill included
both misdemeanor and felony crimes of violence that were:

Committed by a current or former spouse, parent, or guardian of the victim, by a
person with whom the victim shares a child in common, by a person with is
cohabitating or has cohabitated with the victim as a spouse, parent or guardian, or
by a person similarly situated to a spouse, parent or guardian of the victim under
the domestic or family violence laws of the jurisdiction in which such felony or
misdemeanor was committed. (Stop Arming Felons Act, 1992)

Lautenberg's bill had 10 cosponsors in the Senate (all Democrats); its
companion bill in the House was sponsored by Rep. Robert Torricelli
(Democrat, New Jersey) and cosponsored by 24 representatives (21
Democrats and 3 Republicans). A local New Jersey newspaper reported
on the bill and noted how New Jersey had some of the toughest DV laws
in the nation, which is in part why the senator and representative from
New Jersey wanted to pass this firearm restriction bill (Piore, 1996a).
    The NRA pushed back against the Lautenberg Amendment; when its
spokeswoman Elizabeth Swasey was asked about the bill, she said, "We
should be taking domestic violence seriously and prosecuting it vigorously
rather than going off on side issues like this bill" (Piore, 1996a). To shore
up support for the bill, Lautenberg attached it as an amendment to an
antistalking law sponsored by Republican Kay Bailey Hutchison (Texas).
This bill made stalking across state lines a federal offense and was
extremely personal to Hutchison, who had been a stalking victim in the
1970s. Lautenberg's amendment stalled Hutchinson's bill, which had
robust Republican Party support. A *Denver Post* article in July 1996 high-
lighted the political quandary facing lawmakers with Lautenberg's move
to tie the two bills together. Lawmakers were "not eager to choose
between offending the powerful National Rifle Association, which
opposes the gun proposal, and voting against legislation aimed at curbing
domestic violence" (Dewar, 1996). In the end, Hutchinson's bill with

---

[8] Lautenberg sponsored this bill in 1992, 1993, and 1995.

Lautenberg's amendment passed with overwhelming approval in the Senate. Lautenberg's amendment also had the support of President Bill Clinton, who was seeking his second term in office. Despite this approval, the Lautenberg amendment was removed from the stalking bill in the House where the NRA became more vocal in its opposition, claiming it was an overreach by the federal government and that states were better equipped to handle the issue at the local level (Piore, 1996b). Hutchinson's stalking bill would end up becoming law on its own in September 1996.

Sen. Lautenberg was not deterred in trying to remove firearm access for DV offenders. In his third attempt to enact this law, he submitted it as an amendment to an entirely unrelated bill concerning appropriations to the US Post Office, the Executive Office of the President, and other independent agencies (H.R. 3756; Congressional Record, US Senate, 1996). The bill with his amendment would pass with a 97–2 Senate majority. Although the Republican Party majority leadership had refused to pass Lautenberg's amendment just weeks earlier, Speaker of the House Newt Gingrich (Republican, Georgia) came out in favor of the bill, saying on *Meet the Press*: "I'm very much in favor of stopping people who engage in violence against their spouses from having guns. I think that's a very reasonable position" (Associated Press, 1996a, 1996b). The appropriations bill with the Lautenberg amendment was passed on September 28, 1996, despite continued NRA disapproval. Reports at the time attributed the shift in policy position to the Republican Party's desire for a better record on women's issues in the upcoming 1996 presidential election. The most important part of this story is that the Republican Party of the 1990s was generally more willing to change its position on a firearm-related federal law than the Republican Party of today.

The Lautenberg Amendment has an interesting policy history because most lawmakers and reporters at the time felt it was a dead-on-arrival bill. The House of Representatives was controlled by the Republican Party, and the NRA lobbied against it. But in reality, it took only six months from Lautenberg's original sponsorship to his amendment's adoption on an appropriations bill. Furthermore, Lautenberg was able to turn the discussion of the federal DV firearms ban into a national conversation. He along with three other senators wrote a letter to Republican presidential nominee (and former Senate majority leader) Bob Dole, urging him to help pass the legislation. Dole had been instrumental in negotiating with the Clinton administration and the NRA on the assault weapon ban that passed in 1994, insisting on a sunset provision. Dole decided to support the Lautenberg Amendment because he could argue it was a reasonable but limited policy designed to keep women safe (Associated Press, 1996b). The Lautenberg Amendment was the first major revision of a portion of federal law on DV, but it would not be the last. We detail the VAWA reauthorizations in the next section.

However, there was a significant disconnect between the criteria for receiving federal grant money under VAWA and adoption and enforcement of the Lautenberg Amendment at the state level. In the Solicitation Program Guide, the OVW states, "OVW does not fund activities that jeopardize victim safety, deter or prevent physical or emotional healing for victims, or allow offenders to escape responsibility for their actions" (Office of Violence Against Women, 2021). The guide then lists the activities that jeopardize victim safety for each program, but it never requires a state to follow federal DV law. No federal grant program from the OVW requires states to enforce the Lautenberg Amendment.

A striking example of a lack of coercive mechanism in VAWA is the program Improving Criminal Justice to Response to Sexual Assault, Domestic Violence, Dating Violence, and Stalking. The US Department of Justice describes the program as encouraging state, local, and tribal governments "to treat domestic violence, dating violence, sexual assault, and stalking as serious violations of criminal law requiring the coordinated involvement of the entire criminal justice system" (Office of Violence Against Women, 2020b). In 2020 the program awarded 41 grants valued at over $29 million (refer to Table 2.1). The program lists 24 areas eligible for funding that range from implementing "proarrest programs and policies in police departments, including policies for protection order violations and enforcement of protection orders across state and tribal lines," to centralizing and coordinating "police enforcement, prosecution, or judicial responsibility for domestic violence, dating violence, sexual assault, and stalking cases in teams or units of police officers, prosecutors, parole and probation officers, or judges," to developing and promoting "best practices for responding to the crimes of domestic violence, dating violence, sexual assault, and stalking, including the appropriate treatment of victims" (US House of Representatives, 2022). While the passage of DV firearm laws would certainly fall within many of the purposes of the grant program, none of them explicitly requires passing DV firearm laws as a goal of the program.

In 2021 the Justice Department under the Biden Administration issued a FY2021 Solicitation Companion Guide and included a list of activities that would prevent the funding of a grant because they compromised victim safety and recovery or undermined offender accountability. Any of these activities, such as policies that compromise victim privacy or policies that offer "anger management programs for offenders as a substitute for batterer intervention programs," disqualify the state, tribe, or city applying for the Improving Criminal Justice grant (Office of Violence Against Women, 2021). Despite the potential to use these grants as a persuasive tool to encourage states to enact legislation in this area, no state is disqualified for not having DV firearm laws compatible with the Lautenberg Amendment. Kansas and Wisconsin each received a $1 million grant under this program in 2019 despite the fact that Kansas had only two domestic violence firearm laws (DVFLs) and Wisconsin had only three. Prior years followed the same pattern: South Dakota received a $750,000 grant in 2016 despite having only one DVFL, Wisconsin received a $900,000 grant in 2016 despite not having a law that prohibits DV misdemeanants from buying or possessing firearms, and Montana received almost $850,000 in 2014 under this same program despite actively trying to protect gun owners' rights even if they had been convicted of a DV offense (Office of Violence Against Women, 2020b). The states of Georgia, Mississippi, Montana, and Wyoming have not passed any DVFLs at all (see Chapter 3 for a more detailed discussion of DV laws in Georgia and Montana). However, the governments of these states have received a combination of more than $11 million from a mixture of federal OVW formula and discretionary grant programs in 2020.

Table 2.2 details the amount of grant money each state received and its overall ranking in the number of DVFLs that it has in place (we discuss these laws in depth in Chapter 4). States are ranked by population, starting with California, the largest. We included the per capita grant data for each state for better comparison.

Although a full quantitative analysis of these federal OVW funding patterns is beyond the scope of this book, it does appear that they reflect the overall level of DV per capita in a given state. Alaska has very high levels of violence against women as well as a large Native American population, and it receives more money per capita than any other state in the country, almost double that of Indiana, which is the next most funded state. In fact, states that have high levels of Native American populations (e.g., Wyoming, North Dakota, South Dakota, and Oklahoma) are all in the top 10 states for per capita governmental grant funding.

In Table 2.2, we also break down federal funding for governmental and nongovernmental organizations in order to illustrate the

TABLE 2.2. *States by population size, number of DV gun laws, and grants (2020)*

State	Number of DV Gun Laws, 2017	Total Governmental Organizations Grant Amount	Per Capita Governmental Organization Grants	Total Nongovernmental Organization Grant Amount	Per Capita Nongovernmental Organizations Grants
California	8.0	$13,095,476	0.34	$13,413,259	0.34
Texas	8.0	13,593,114	0.49	5,151,402	0.18
Florida	1.5	11,568,933	0.55	8,350,312	0.40
New York	5.5	15,202,345	0.76	12,681,016	0.63
Illinois	8.0	9,750,650	0.75	8,881,434	0.68
Pennsylvania*	7.5	5,766,346	0.44	7,568,436	0.58
Ohio	1.0	8,123,914	0.74	4,764,944	0.43
Georgia	0.0	6,042,321	0.60	3,941,699	0.39
Michigan	3.0	11,027,100	1.10	6,171,254	0.62
North Carolina	5.0	7,283,391	0.73	2,808,597	0.28
New Jersey*	7.5	4,296,787	0.48	3,831,919	0.43
Virginia	4.5	6,248,882	0.74	3,847,560	0.45
Washington	8.0	8,015,550	1.10	3,152,178	0.43
Arizona	7.0	6,893,759	0.98	3,221,282	0.46
Massachusetts	7.0	5,463,764	0.80	4,675,706	0.69
Tennessee	5.0	3,827,098	0.57	4,430,486	0.66
Maryland	6.5	4,393,361	0.72	3,470,583	0.57
Missouri	1.0	6,060,848	1.03	4,965,543	0.84
Wisconsin	3.5	7,670,962	1.32	3,852,234	0.66
Colorado	5.0	5,371,651	0.96	3,343,813	0.60

(*continued*)

TABLE 2.2. (*continued*)

State	Number of DV Gun Laws, 2017	Total Governmental Organizations Grant Amount	Per Capita Governmental Organization Grants	Total Nongovernmental Organization Grant Amount	Per Capita Nongovernmental Organizations Grants
Minnesota	6.0	7,244,242	1.34	7,806,214	1.45
South Carolina*	1.0	2,897,082	0.58	2,197,391	0.44
Alabama*	5.0	2,805,031	0.57	543,619	0.11
Louisiana*	4.0	2,954,259	0.64	2,122,850	0.46
Kentucky	1.0	3,141,756	0.70	1,588,962	0.35
Oregon	2.0	7,151,154	1.74	4,396,855	1.07
Oklahoma	1.0	9,435,136	2.42	2,596,924	0.67
Connecticut*	7.0	2,510,756	0.70	1,991,500	0.55
Iowa	4.0	4,016,068	1.30	4,068,070	1.31
Utah*	3.5	2,168,729	0.70	3,541,138	1.14
Arkansas	1.0	2,597,980	0.87	1,418,619	0.47
Kansas	2.0	3,227,100	1.11	2,516,369	0.87
Mississippi	0.0	4,421,019	1.52	1,581,919	0.55
Nevada	4.0	3,857,936	1.33	2,071,119	0.71
New Mexico	2.0	4,152,509	1.98	4,802,931	2.29
Nebraska	4.0	3,515,828	1.85	3,286,825	1.73
West Virginia	5.5	2,120,545	1.18	643,619	0.36
Idaho	1.0	4,073,201	2.40	1,493,563	0.88
Hawaii*	5.0	1,497,615	1.07	1,068,619	0.76

Maine	5.5	3,140,951	2.42	2,520,983	1.94
New Hampshire*	4.5	1,476,560	1.14	2,262,483	1.74
Montana	0.0	4,032,385	3.67	4,786,813	4.35
Rhode Island	7.0	0	0.00	793,619	0.72
Delaware*	6.5	1,331,866	1.39	521,119	0.54
South Dakota	1.0	2,198,459	2.52	3,646,339	4.18
North Dakota	3.5	3,527,807	4.71	2,112,234	2.82
Alaska	3.5	6,738,664	9.48	7,825,784	11.01
Indiana	5.5	3,824,707	5.79	693,619	1.05
Vermont	3.5	2,762,932	4.44	3,376,420	5.42
Wyoming	0.0	2,953,871	5.10	2,243,619	3.88
Average	**4.04**	**$5,309,448**	**1.60**	**$3,860,876**	**1.28**

*Indicates that these states received funds only from formula grants, not discretionary funding. Grant recipients include state governments, local governments, public colleges and universities, public schools, and tribal governments. States are marked as having half of a DVFL if a law leaves the removal of a firearm up to the discretion of individual judges rather than mandating that judges order the removal of a firearm in all cases.

Source: Author compiled from Office of Violence Against Women data. Office of Violence Against Women (2020a, 2020b).

fragmentation that exists within states in addressing DV. Most states depend on nongovernmental organizations, such as those that operate DV shelters, as part of their overall service delivery infrastructure in this issue arena. One could argue that the mere existence of so many non-governmental organizations suggests a failure by states and the federal government to adopt a comprehensive approach to this problem.

While many women in these states will benefit from the federal grant money, it does not come with a requirement that a state enforce federal law, which is a significant gap in policy implementation. In fact, there is seemingly no penalty whatever for a state that does not follow federal law on DV, leaving thousands of women vulnerable to deadly abuse because of the state in which they live. This absence of state accountability has created inequality under federal law. The Lautenberg Amendment was passed in part to remedy a loophole that DV offenders could exploit to keep their firearms under federal law. However, without states' legislative action and active enforcement, this remedy has failed to live up to its potential to keep women safer.

2.2.3 Violence Against Women Act Reauthorizations in Congress

As previously noted, the original VAWA passed with overwhelming bipartisan support in both the House and the Senate in 1994. There was still bipartisan support for VAWA in 2000 and 2005 when it was reauthorized. The political environment was different in 2013 with a Democratic president, a Democratic-controlled Senate, and a Republican-controlled House of Representatives. Under President Barack Obama, there was a controversy over provisions concerning immigrant women and protection for same-sex couples (Weisman, 2012), but even so, the 2013 reauthorization bill passed with bipartisan support. Again, none of the reauthorizations in 2000, 2005, or 2013 included expanding the firearm provisions first established by the Lautenberg Amendment.

Table 2.3 provides an overview of the three successful reauthorizations of VAWA as well as the failed 2019 reauthorization. This policy history has a few important patterns. First, sponsorship of the 2000 and 2005 reauthorizations was bipartisan. In fact, both of those bills were originally sponsored by Republicans in the House, potentially demonstrating the bipartisan nature of addressing violence against women so long as firearm restrictions were not expanded. Second, both the 2000 and 2005 reauthorizations had bipartisan support in passage of the law; only one representative voted against the 2000 reauthorization in the House, and a

TABLE 2.3. *VAWA reauthorization overview*

Year	Institutional Context	Number of Sponsors in the House	Additions to VAWA	Partisan Distribution of Votes on Reauthorization
1994	President: Clinton (D) House: 176 R, 258 D; 1I Senate: 43 R, 57 D	225 (186 D, 38 R, 1 I)	Original law: • Created OVW • Funded numerous grants to help training of law enforcement, prosecutors, and judges handling DV cases. • Provided grants on education on VAWA. • Immigration provisions for battered immigrants. • Funded federal research on violence against women.	House: Voice Vote Senate: 95–4 • Yay: 42R, 53D • Nay: 2R, 2D
2000	President: Clinton (D) House: 221 R, 208 D, 2 I Senate: 54 R,46 D	37 (17 D, 19 R, 1I)	• Additional protections for battered non-immigrants • New program for DV victims • Transitional housing for victims of dating violence, sexual assault, and stalking • New grant requirements • Programs for elderly, disabled women • Funds exclusively for rape prevention and education programs • Amended interstate stalking and DV laws	House: 371–1 • Yay: 187 R, 182 D, 2I • Nay: 1 R Senate: 95–0 • Yay: 53 R, 42 D
2005	President: Bush (R) House: 231 R, 202 D Senate: 55 R, 44 D, 1I	19 (10 D, 9 R)	• Protections for battered and/or trafficked nonimmigrants. • Programs for Native Americans. • Programs to improve public health response. • Increased penalties for stalking • Expanded stalking to include cyberstalking • Amended interstate stalking definition	House: 415–4 • Yay: 225 R, 189 D, 1I • Nay: 2 R, 2 D Senate: Unanimous
2013	President: Obama (D) House: 232 R, 200 D Senate: 45 R, 53 D, 2I	200 (200 D, 0 R)	• Consolidated grant programs • Added new provisions for grant programs, including one on discrimination	House: 286–138 • Yay: 87 R, 199 D • Nay: 138 R, 0 D

(continued)

TABLE 2.3. (continued)

Year	Institutional Context	Number of Sponsors in the House	Additions to VAWA	Partisan Distribution of Votes on Reauthorization
			• Revised numerous definitions including DV to include intimate partners. • New accountability provisions for grants • Strengthened audit requirements for sexual assault evidence backlog • Allowed tribes to create their own special DV criminal jurisdiction courts • Expanded grants to underserved populations • Added housing rights for victims of DV, dating violence, sexual assault and stalking • Requirements for higher education institutions to report data on DV, dating violence, and stalking • Required victims in higher education receive written notification of the services available to them • Increased grants to states that had laws that protected a victim who had a child conceived from rape to "seek court-ordered termination of the parental rights of her rapist"	• Senate: 78–22 • Yay: 53 D, 2I, 23 R • Nay: 22 R, 0 D
2019	President: Trump (R) House: 198 R, 235 D Senate: 53 R, 25 D, 2I	167 (166 D, 1 R)	• Extended prohibition on gun possession for DV offenders to those who commit dating violence and stalking • Increased funding for grants for community resources • Expanded housing protections for survivors, particularly transgender women • Protected employees from being fired because they are victims of DV • Allowed tribes to have more access to federal crime information databases to help protect Native American women	• House: 263–158 • Yay: 33 R, 230 D • Nay: 157 R, 1 D • Senate: Never brought to a vote

Year	Political context	Cosponsors	Key provisions	Votes
2021	President: Biden (D) House: 211 R, 222 D Senate: 50 R, 48 D, 2I	186 (184 D, 2 R)	• Reaffirmed special DV criminal jurisdiction courts in tribes to hold non-Native American offenders accountable for offenses against Native Americans • Extended the Lautenberg Amendment firearm prohibitions to include dating partners • Addresses deficiencies in the Special Domestic Violence Criminal Jurisdiction Program created in the 2013 reauthorization • Increased funding to address DV	House: 244–172 • Yay: 29 R, 215 D • Nay: 172 R, 0 D • Senate: Never brought to a vote
2022	President: Biden (D) House: 211 R, 222 D Senate: 50 R, 48 D, 2I	N/A	• Failed to extend Lautenberg Amendment firearm prohibitions to include dating partners; that provision is later enacted via the Bipartisan Safer Communities Act • Required the Attorney General to notify state, local, or tribal law enforcement in cases of failed background checks • Extended Special Domestic Violence Criminal Jurisdiction Program to previously ineligible tribes • Included Bree's Law, which addresses teen dating violence • Expanded definitions of DV, including "abuse in later life," "forced marriage," and "female genital mutilation or cutting," etc.	House: 218–204 • Yay: 0 R, 218 D • Nay: 202 R, 2 D • Senate: 68–31 • Yay: 18 R, 48 D, 2I • Nay: 31 R, 0 D

There was bipartisan support for the 2012 reauthorization in the Senate; 61 senators including 7 Republicans sponsored the law. The 2022 reauthorization was passed via continuing resolution.

Source: Author compiled from Congress.gov as well as the Congressional Research Service (crsreports.congress.gov).

Republican president signed the 2005 reauthorization into law with only four representatives voting against it.

By 2019, polarized politics intersected more forcefully with efforts to combat DV and Congress failed to pass the 2019 VAWA reauthorization. The Democrats had regained control of the House, and the Republican Party (GOP) won the presidency and kept the Senate. The sponsors of the reauthorization wanted to expand the Lautenberg Amendment to dating partners, thereby closing the "boyfriend loophole" to make it federal law to prohibit dating partners who are convicted of DV charges from owning or possessing firearms. Jason Ouimet, NRA executive director of lobbying, said the inclusion of expanding firearm provisions was done to make Second Amendment rights advocates look bad: "Speaker Pelosi and anti-gun lawmakers chose to insert gun control provisions into this bill in 2019 to pit pro-gun lawmakers against it so that they can falsely and maliciously claim these lawmakers don't care about women" (Davis, 2021). Rep. Bob Good (Republican, Virginia) argued that "this legislation makes it clear that Democrats consider gun ownership a second-class right" (Davis, 2021), and Rep. Doug Collins (Republican, Georgia) said Democrats "sought at every turn to make this bill into a political weapon, rather than a critical resource for victims and tools to support law enforcement" (Kolinovsky, 2019). Although the 2019 VAWA reauthorization bill was passed by the House, it was met with such strong opposition by GOP members that it was not brought to a vote in the Republican-controlled Senate.

In the 117th Congress, Reps. Sheila Jackson Lee (Democrat, Texas), Jerry Nadler (Democrat, New York), and Brian Fitzpatrick (Republican, Pennsylvania) together introduced a bill to reauthorize VAWA on March 8, 2021, which was International Women's Day. The bill contained a firearm purchase prohibition for individuals convicted of misdemeanor stalking and made it "illegal for a person to transfer or sell a firearm or ammunition to a person they believe has been convicted of misdemeanor stalking" (Duster, 2021). The House subsequently passed the VAWA reauthorization on March 17, 2021, by a vote of 244–172; only 29 Republicans voted for it along with the entire Democratic caucus.[9] The bill would have expanded jurisdiction on tribal lands to prosecute non-Native American assailants for sexual violence, and it would have closed the boyfriend loophole.

---

[9] https://clerk.house.gov/Votes/202186.

The 2021 House version of VAWA reauthorization bill never made it through the Senate. Almost a year after the House passed it, another VAWA reauthorization bill was introduced in the Senate on February 9, 2022. Sens. Lisa Murkowski (Republican, Alaska), Dianne Feinstein (Democrat, California), Joni Ernst (Republican, Iowa) and Dick Durbin (Democrat, Illinois) introduced the reauthorization bill that would support the programs and grants to address violence against women through 2027 with a few expansions.[10] The bill was hailed as a bipartisan success, mainly because the new reauthorization dropped the controversial boyfriend loophole. As news reports noted at the time, "The gun provision was the biggest sticking point in the Senate, where most Republicans simply refused to support a VAWA bill that included any kind of restrictions on gun access. The National Rifle Association, among other gun rights groups, made it clear they opposed the provision" (Bendery, 2022).

The reauthorization did include one new firearm provision, the Denial Notification Act, a bipartisan measure that strengthened the National Instant Criminal Background Check System (NICS). According to the bill, the US attorney general is required to notify state, local, or tribal law enforcement and prosecutors within 24 hours if an individual is denied purchasing a firearm because of the person's background check. Such notification would allow law enforcement to reach out to the individual who attempted to purchase the firearm, giving the agency time to intervene before a situation turns deadly (Brownlee, 2022). The bill makes it illegal for a person who is not allowed to buy a gun to attempt to do so and lie on the federal background check form. Prior to the 2022 VAWA reauthorization, the Federal Bureau of Investigation (FBI) did not have to notify state or local law enforcement when this happened although police could ask for that information. Very few of such cases were investigated at the federal level, mainly because the federal government did not have the resources to do so. Evidence suggests that state and local law enforcement were better equipped to handle these cases; Pennsylvania, Oregon, and Virginia investigated and prosecuted "thousands of denials,

[10] United States Senator for Alaska Lisa Murkowski. 2022. "Murkowski and Colleagues Introduce Bipartisan Bill to Reauthorize Violence Against Women Act." www.murkowski.senate.gov/press/release/murkowski-and-colleagues-introduce-bipartisan-bill-to-reauthorize-violence-against-women-act.

significantly higher than the number investigated at the federal level" (Brownlee, 2022). We discuss Pennsylvania's attempts to pass state-level DV firearm laws more extensively in Chapter 3.

Over time, polarized politics has intensified, and the extent of bipartisan cooperation on DV at the federal level has diminished significantly. Part of this trend can be explained by the increasingly conservative tenor of the Republican Party and the increased emphasis on Second Amendment rights. Republican opposition to closing the boyfriend loophole finally decreased after the tragic shooting in Uvalde, Texas in May 2022. The shooting began with the assailant shooting his grandmother in an act of DV, and it became that rare event that had the power to overcome high levels of polarization around gun control at the federal level. Congress subsequently enacted the Bipartisan Safer Communities Act and included a provision to close the boyfriend loophole; enough GOP Senators supported the bill to allow passage, although a majority of Republican Senators voted against it.

2.3 THE SUPREME COURT AND DOMESTIC VIOLENCE LAWS

At the same time that Congress has become increasingly divided over VAWA due to firearm restrictions, the Supreme Court has upheld challenges to the Lautenberg Amendment on three occasions. The divergence between congressional action and Supreme Court action on DV, particularly with firearms, showcases the lack of cohesion and the overall fragility of federal intervention. It also illustrates the Court's belief in constitutional protections of firearm restrictions for DV abusers. Despite this judicial support, as we noted earlier in this chapter, Democrats in Congress have not been able to extend these protections to dating partners because of Republican opposition to new gun control measures. We next discuss more broadly the role of the Supreme Court in federal DV policy.

The Supreme Court issued one of its first rulings in a civil DV case *(U.S. v. Dixon)* in 1993. (Table 2.4 provides the summaries for the Supreme Court cases concerning DV.) The decision was about two cases, one of which involved an individual named Michael Foster who was accused of threatening his wife while under an order of protection. He was convicted of contempt of court for violating that order and subsequently indicted for assault for the same threats he made. Foster argued he was protected from being prosecuted twice for essentially the same crime, but the

TABLE 2.4. *Case summaries of Supreme Court DV decisions*

Year	Case	Question	Outcome	Vote	Impact
1993	U.S. v. Dixon	Can a defendant be prosecuted for criminal charges for the same actions that had previously held the person in contempt of court?	Yes, double jeopardy does not preclude being prosecuted again if the offenses include different elements.	5–4	Provides protection for victims under a restraining order while also being able to convict the offender for the crimes that led to the order
2000	United States v. Morrison	Can VAWA provide a federal civil remedy for victims of gender-motivated violence under the Commerce Clause?	No, the Commerce Clause does allow Congress to provide a federal civil remedy that can be provided only by the states.	5–4	Weakens VAWA
2005	Town of Castle Rock v. Gonzales	Can an individual who has a obtained a restraining order sue the local government for failing to enforce the order as a procedural due process claim?	No, the state of Colorado did not create an entitlement to the benefit of enforcing a restraining order and therefore did not create a property interest.	7–2	Limits DV victims' recourse for police failure to enforce a restraining order
2009	United States v. Hayes	Do generic charges of battery and or assault that are not specifically DV offenses fall under Lautenberg firearm restrictions under Lautenberg when the offense is between domestic partners?	Yes, Lautenberg does not require that the offense the person was charged with to be a DV charge but that the crime used or attempted "physical force, or threatened use of a deadly weapon," and was committed by someone who had a domestic relationship with the victim.	7–2	Affirms scope of Lautenberg Amendment

(continued)

TABLE 2.4. (*continued*)

Year	Case	Question	Outcome	Vote	Impact
2014	*United States v. Castleman*	Do state misdemeanor domestic assault laws count as a misdemeanor DV crime under federal law?	Yes, the state law incorporates a common law meaning of violence, including the use of physical force, which is consistent with the federal statute.	9–0	Affirms scope of Lautenberg Amendment
2016	*Voisine v. United States*	Does a misdemeanor DV crime that includes recklessness as a cause qualify as a misdemeanor crime of federal DV law?	Yes, reckless behavior that leads to DV qualifies under federal law as long as the cause was not a true accident.	6–2	Affirms scope of Lautenberg Amendment

Source: Case summaries adapted from Cornell Law School's Legal Information Institute and Oyez.org.

Supreme Court reversed the lower appeals court decision and ruled that double jeopardy did not apply.[11] As Orloff and Feldman (2017) stated, this decision was important for victims of DV who would seek enforcement of an order of protection for their temporary safety and seek to convict their abusers of the underlying crimes for which they sought the order of protection in the first place (Orloff and Feldman, 2017, p. 6).

Not long after the *Dixon* decision, VAWA passed with bipartisan support. Most of VAWA has survived legal scrutiny with the exception of the Supreme Court ruling in *United States* v. *Morrison* in 2000. In this case, the Court struck down the part of VAWA that allowed civil remedies in gender-based crimes. That ruling had a considerable effect on the federal response to DV that may have made justice more equal for victims. For now, the only kind of DV that is covered by federal courts (outside of the Lautenberg Amendment) involves crimes that cross state boundaries like the crimes committed against Deanna Walters. These kinds of DV crimes are less common and more difficult to prove and prosecute. It took over a year for a federal district attorney to take Walter's case, which already had an admission of guilt and a considerable amount of evidence. The idea that women can suffer violence in private but cannot seek civil redress against her perpetrators unless allowed by state law limits the set of remedies that are available to DV victims.

The next Supreme Court case regarding DV did not concern VAWA or Lautenberg but reaffirmed the discretion afforded to local government in enforcing DV laws.[12] The Supreme Court ruled 7 to 2 in *Town of Castle Rock* v. *Gonzales* (2005) against a woman whose estranged husband violated a restraining order and kidnapped and murdered their three children before he died in a gunfight with police. Jessica Gonzales argued that the town of Castle Rock infringed upon her due process rights under the 14th Amendment by failing to respond to her request to pursue her husband after he had taken their children from their home, which was in violation of the restraining order. Gonzales argued that she was entitled to civil remedies for the police's lack of action. However, as Quester

---

[11] *United States* v. *Dixon* (1993). www.oyez.org/cases/1992/91-1231.

[12] The Supreme Court decision in *Crawford* v. *Washington* (2004) Supreme Court cases related to domestic violence *Crawford* v. *Washington* (2004) *n* can be interpreted as weakening the capacity to prosecute DV abusers in cases where their victim is either too afraid to testify in person or has been murdered. Rather than allowing testimony given to police to be used as evidence, the ruling held that using testimony without allowing cross-examination violates the Sixth Amendment's "Confrontation Clause." www.oyez.org/cases/2003/02-9410.

(2007) explains, the Court decided that there was no explicit contract between Gonzales and the police department that required it to enforce the restraining order in a specific way and therefore no "property" had been taken from her for which to be compensated. This ruling essentially claimed that enforcement of the restraining order was entirely a matter of the local police and the state of Colorado in its statute. Quester goes on to argue that judicial rulings such as this one actively undermine the capacity for victims of DV to seek protection from injury and recourse for it from their abusers or from those who are responsible for preventing the abuse. *Town of Castle Rock* v. *Gonzales* exemplifies the limitations that policy-makers face at the national level in standardizing both punishments for and protection from DV.

Unlike portions of VAWA, Lautenberg has been strengthened on three separate occasions by the Supreme Court. In *United States* v. *Hayes* (2009), the Court ruled that an offender did not have to be convicted of a specific DV offence for it to qualify as a DV misdemeanor under federal law. In the majority opinion, Justice Ginsburg wrote:

Practical considerations strongly support our reading of [Lautenberg]'s language. Existing felon-in-possession laws, Congress recognized, were not keeping firearms out of the hands of domestic abusers, because "many people who engage in serious spousal or child abuse ultimately are not charged with or convicted of felonies" 142 Cong. Rec. 22985 (1996) (statement of Sen. Lautenberg). By extending the federal firearm prohibition to persons convicted of "misdemeanor crime[s] of domestic violence," proponents of [the Lautenberg Amendment] sought to "close this dangerous loophole." *Id.*, at 22986. Construing [Lautenberg] to exclude the domestic abuser convicted under a generic use-of-force statute (one that does not designate a domestic relationship as an element of the offense) would frustrate Congress' manifest purpose. Firearms and domestic strife are a potentially deadly combination nationwide.... Yet, as interpreted by the Fourth Circuit, [Lautenberg] would have been "a dead letter" in some two-thirds of the States from the very moment of its enactment.[13]

In 2014 the Court unanimously affirmed the scope of Lautenberg again in *United States* v. *Castleman*. In this case, the defendant argued that his misdemeanor conviction of DV in Tennessee should not qualify toward the federal ban on firearm possession for DV misdemeanants because his crime did not include the use of force, which is written into Lautenberg. Justice Sotomayor argued in the Court's majority opinion that DV is a unique set of crimes. She wrote:

---

[13] *United States* v. *Hayes*, 555 U.S. 415 (2009).

Whereas the word "violent" or "violence" standing alone "connotes a substantial degree of force," id., at 140, [4] that is not true of "domestic violence." "Domestic violence" is not merely a type of "violence"; it is a term of art encompassing acts that one might not characterize as "violent" in a nondomestic context.... Indeed, "most physical assaults committed against women and men by intimates are relatively minor and consist of pushing, grabbing, shoving, slapping, and hitting." DOJ, P. Tjaden & N. Thoennes, Extent, Nature and Consequences of Intimate Partner Violence 11 (2000). Minor uses of force may not constitute "violence" in the generic sense. For example, in an opinion that we cited with approval in Johnson, the Seventh Circuit noted that it was "hard to describe... as 'violence'" "a squeeze of the arm [that] causes a bruise." Flores v. Ashcroft, 350 F. 3d 666, 670 (2003). But an act of this nature is easy to describe as "domestic violence," when the accumulation of such acts over time can subject one intimate partner to the other's control. If a seemingly minor act like this draws the attention of authorities and leads to a successful prosecution for a misdemeanor offense, it does not offend common sense or the English language to characterize the resulting conviction as a "misdemeanor crime of domestic violence."[14]

Both of these opinions demonstrate that the Court was aware of the unique nature of DV as well as the intent behind the Lautenberg Amendment to remove firearm access from DV abusers. In both opinions, the Justices noted that they intended to close the loophole in federal law that originally did not take away firearms from domestic abusers. Justice Kagan reaffirmed the Court's understanding of the Lautenberg Amendment in the most recent Supreme Court case on this issue in *Voisine* v. *United States* (2016). She ended the majority opinion by saying:

The federal ban on firearms possession applies to any person with a prior misde-meanor conviction for the "use ... of physical force" against a domestic relation. §921(a)(33)(A). That language, naturally read, encompasses acts of force under-taken recklessly—i.e., with conscious disregard of a substantial risk of harm. And the state-law backdrop to that provision, which included misdemeanor assault statutes covering reckless conduct in a significant majority of jurisdictions, indi-cates that Congress meant just what it said. Each petitioner's possession of a gun, following a conviction under Maine law for abusing a domestic partner, therefore violates [Lautenberg].[15]

Table 2.3 and our explanation of the case history regarding DV demon-strates how a federal institution other than the Executive Branch and Congress has a mixed record on VAWA but has been consistent on strengthening the key firearm provision in the Lautenberg Amendment. This has been true for liberal and conservative justices. Justices Alito and

---

[14] *United States v. Castleman.* 572 U.S. 157 (2014).
[15] *Voisine v. United States.* 579 US (2016).

Thomas were in the majority for *Hayes,* all of the conservative justices (Roberts, Scalia, Alito, and Thomas) upheld the Lautenberg Amendment in *Castleman,* and Roberts and Alito were in the majority for *Voisine.* Perhaps even more interesting is the fact that until 2022, as Congress became more polarized around the issue of gun control, its ability to pass DV laws decreased while an increasingly conservative Supreme Court supported the one federal law prohibiting gun access to DV misdemeanants. The lesson to be learned from this policy history is that partisanship has affected Congress's ability to address DV but has not yet affected the Supreme Court in the same way.

2.4 CONCLUSION

The federal government's history on DV is more complicated than the way it is often depicted. The conventional wisdom is that VAWA was the federal government's first foray into DV policy. This overlooks the many representatives and senators who sponsored DV legislation in the late 1970s and the FVPSA, which was the first federal legislation in this policy arena. The true story of DV and federal government response is that it was on the radar of congressional members for nearly two decades before VAWA was passed.

Each branch of the federal government, Congress, Executive, and the Judicial, has addressed DV laws. Although advocates for DV policy might say that it was slow to start, Congress was able to enact the VAWA in 1994 and reauthorize it four times in 2000, 2005, 2013, and 2022 despite increasing disagreement between the parties. The Lautenberg Amendment was enacted in a year – 1996 – that both houses of Congress were controlled by Republicans who worked with a Democratic president to enact it. Liberal and conservative Supreme Court justices have upheld the Lautenberg Amendment on three separate occasions via three separate legal questions. Most states have responded to federal action in this arena by initiating new programs to address and prevent DV that are funded through the VAWA. Far fewer states have taken steps to pass their own firearm laws to conform with the firearm provisions in the Lautenberg Amendment. We include federal action as an explanatory variable in our model of state adoption of DV firearm laws presented in Chapter 4 and find support for the impact of vertical diffusion. However, as we discuss next, adopting a law is not the same as adequately and effectively enforcing it.

Party differences on policies toward the VAWA only begin to truly derail congressional responsiveness when it more forcefully tried to include expanded gun control measures. This one policy area is so divisive as to be able to nearly kill the reauthorization of a publicly popular piece of legislation and serves as one example of how increasing polarization has also affected the representatives' capacity to enact federal DV laws. Additionally, the Executive Branch, through its funding of grants via the OVW, has not taken any steps to enforce the one federal firearm prohibition that is on the books – the Lautenberg Amendment. Instead, the executive branch continues to provide grants to states that ignore federal law.

The Lautenberg Amendment and other laws that remove firearms from abusers save lives. By not fully enforcing this law or more forcefully encouraging states to adopt their own conforming laws, the federal government has made women less safe when compared to men who are not as at risk of DV homicide. This has also contributed to inequality among women across states and within jurisdictions. Because states can decide to flout Lautenberg, women are more vulnerable in states that do not mandate that judges order the collection or surrender of firearms from DV abusers. Although some states have given judicial authority to issue such orders, not all judges do so. Again, as we noted in Chapter 1, that means that a victim's security – even life – depends on whether the judge who presides over her case believes in limiting firearm access to abusers.

Ultimately, the passage of VAWA was landmark legislation that was sorely needed to address a widespread policy problem, but this legislation has fallen short; there is still much the federal government can do on its own and in conjunction with state governments to address DV in the United States. The sheer inadequacy of the enforcement of current federal law, specifically the Lautenberg Amendment, has sustained the four levels of inequality outlined in Chapter 1: between women and men, between women across states, between women within the same state but in different legal jurisdictions, and between white women and women of color. In Chapters 3 and 4, we discuss and analyze the variation in the passage of DVFLs at the state level and argue that such variation highlights the inconsistency in the protections afforded to women based upon where they live.

3

Policymaking in the States

Domestic Violence Statutes

In this chapter, we aim to show the broader issue of inconsistency in punitive laws against domestic violence (DV) and firearm possession by DV abusers across states and across time. A woman in one state who is a DV victim might see her perpetrator forced to stay in jail or released on bail and/or relinquish his or her gun or be allowed to keep it. A dating partner in one state may fall under restraining order protections but not in another state; a stalker or cyberstalker in one state may be included in the category of DV assailant but not in another state. If a DV perpetrator is required to relinquish his or her gun in one state under certain conditions but not in a neighboring state, we argue that women are necessarily rendered unequal in their personal safety across state lines. Our goal is to demonstrate how and when states respond to the need for reform in their DV laws and who the key actors are in that process.

We will also show the evolution or devolution in state DV policy over time. In one way, the trajectory of DV policy in the states illustrates what Mettler and SoRelle (2014, pp. 163–164) identify as two elements of the policy feedback process: problem definition and partisan issue ownership (also see Petrocik, 1996, pp. 825–850). As we discussed in Chapter 2, the first challenge in drawing scholars to the issue of DV was to take it from the home to the public sphere. In the 1990s, the federal government put DV squarely on the public agenda and put in place federal definitions related to the problem:

- *Domestic violence.* Felony or misdemeanor crimes
- *Sexual assault.* Any nonconsensual sexual act proscribed by federal, tribal, or state law including when the victim lacks capacity to consent

- *Dating violence.* Violence committed by a person who is or has been in a social relationship of a romantic or intimate nature with the victim

This federal policy expanded the scope of DV policy by extending the general prohibitions on gun ownership or possession for a felony or misdemeanor crime to individuals convicted of DV. The consequence of that policy adoption was to transform DV, an issue that was at one time about safety for women and children, into a policy that provoked battles over Second Amendment gun rights and became vulnerable to the intensifying Republican Party opposition to firearm regulation. Consequently, attempts by advocates and legislators to expand policies such as mandatory surrender of firearms when subject to protective orders or to include dating partners in the category of DV abusers (which would by definition expand firearm restrictions to a larger population) were met with opposition from members of groups such as the National Rifle Association (NRA) and Republican legislators. By seeking to strengthen protection to victims of DV from gun violence, policymakers at the federal and state levels mobilized groups to oppose measures to decrease DV when they might not have otherwise done so.

The discussion unfolds as follows. First, we present state-by-state data on specific aspects of DV that are included in state laws both in the realm of the scope of what constitutes DV and in terms of firearm regulation. We follow with a set of case studies to illustrate the policy feedback process at the state level and demonstrate how different variables appear to shape the adoption and implementation of DV policies. In Chapter 4, we present a quantitative analysis of the factors that influence the adoption of domestic firearm laws specifically. In Chapter 5, we present an analysis of the implementation of DV policy in the form of explaining the outcomes of cases of DV in local judicial systems.

The lesson we learn from DV policy in the United States is that women are at a disadvantage at every step of the process. Not only are women more likely to be abused but also the lack of uniform laws renders women unequal under the law. Domestic violence policies illustrate how women's basic personal safety is more at risk based upon where they live.

3.1 STATE VARIATION IN THE DEFINITION OF DOMESTIC VIOLENCE

As we referenced in Chapter 1, four legal provisions related to behaviors are explicitly considered DV offenses in some states but not others. We summarize DV statutes across four categories in Table 3.1.

TABLE 3.1. *DV offenses*

State	DV Definition Includes Stalking	DV Definition Includes Threatening Language or Threats	DV Definition Includes False Imprisonment	DV Definition Includes Actions by Dating/Intimate Partners
Alabama	Yes	No	Yes	Yes
Alaska	No	Yes	No	Yes
Arizona	No	No	No	Yes
Arkansas	No	No	No	Yes
California	No	No	No	Yes
Colorado	Yes	Yes	No	Yes
Connecticut	Yes	Yes	No	Yes
Delaware	No	Yes	Yes	Yes
Florida	Yes	No	Yes	No
Georgia	Yes	No	No	No
Hawaii	No	Yes	No	Yes
Idaho	No	No	No	No
Illinois	No	No	No	Yes
Indiana	No	Yes	No	No
Iowa	No	No	No	Yes
Kansas	No	No	No	Yes
Kentucky	Yes	No	No	Yes
Louisiana	No	No	No	No
Maine	No	Yes	No	Yes
Maryland	Yes	No	Yes	No
Massachusetts	No	Yes	No	Yes
Michigan	No	No	No	Yes
Minnesota	No	Yes	No	Yes
Mississippi	Yes	Yes	No	Yes
Missouri	Yes	Yes	Yes	Yes
Montana	No	No	No	Yes
Nebraska	No	Yes	No	Yes
Nevada	Yes	Yes	Yes	Yes
New Hampshire	No	Yes	No	Yes
New Jersey	Yes	Yes	Yes	Yes
New Mexico	Yes	Yes	No	Yes
New York	Yes	No	No	Yes
North Carolina	No	No	No	Yes*
North Dakota	No	No	No	Yes
Ohio	No	Yes	No	No
Oklahoma	No	Yes	No	Yes
Oregon	No	Yes	No	No

State	DV Definition Includes Stalking	DV Definition Includes Threatening Language or Threats	DV Definition Includes False Imprisonment	DV Definition Includes Actions by Dating/Intimate Partners
Pennsylvania	No	No	Yes	No
Rhode Island	Yes	Yes	No	Yes
South Carolina	No	Yes	No	No
South Dakota	No	No	No	Yes
Tennessee	No	No	No	Yes
Texas	No	Yes	No	Yes
Utah	No	No	No	No
Vermont	Yes	No	No	Yes
Virginia	Yes	Yes	Yes	No
Washington	Yes	No	Yes	Yes
West Virginia	Yes	Yes	No	Yes
Wisconsin	No	No	No	No
Wyoming	No	Yes	No	Yes
Total (Yes)	18	25	10	37

*Applies only to heterosexual couples only.

Source: Author-generated data using the National Council of State Legislatures database as a starting point and confirmed with each statute on each state's code of laws website. These are the definitions of the state's DV laws as of June 13, 2019. See www.ncsl.org/research/human-services/domestic-violence-domestic-abuse-definitions-and-relationships.aspx.

- *Stalking.* California passed the first antistalking law in 1990, and while the vast majority of states have some kind of stalking law, only 18 states consider stalking a DV offense. In fact, the vast majority of stalking definitions focus much more closely on physical offenses, such as murder, assault, battery, and sexual violence.
- *Terroristic and/or threatening language or treatment.* 25 states specifically mention that terroristic threats or threatening language or behavior are considered DV offenses.
- *False imprisonment.* Only 10 states consider false imprisonment as a DV offense.
- *Actions by dating partners.* This appears to be the only element of the four we examine here that the majority of states (37) have acted on, although not entirely in a uniform way. This extension to dating partners in recent years may not be totally surprising. Given that rates of cohabitation are rising among young people who are delaying

marriage and older couples, there has been a necessity to consider the danger posed by DV in dating relationships. With the decline or delay in traditional marriage, more couples across income strata and in same- or opposite-sex relationships are outside the bounds of traditional legal jurisdiction over married couples. And for individuals who choose not to share the same domicile or physical living space, there is still the possibility of ongoing violence, and it can persist even after the dating relationship has ended. In our time frame of study, DV offenses extend to dating partners in 37 states, but only 26 states include dating partners when limiting access to owning or possessing firearms.

Certain states stand out as having limited definitions of DV. Arizona, for example, extends DV to dating partners but has not adopted any of the provisions related to the four behaviors. Arizona was also one of the states with the highest consistent levels of intimate partner homicide we discussed in Chapter 1. Four states have not extended legal provisions to cover any of these behaviors: Idaho, Louisiana, Utah, and Wisconsin. With the exception of Louisiana, which had significant Democratic influence in the governor's mansion and state house from 1990 to 2010, these states are conservative and tend to lean toward Republican partisan control. This is particularly true for Idaho and Utah.

On the other end of the spectrum, only three states have adopted all four of these DV related to these behaviors: Missouri, Nevada, and New Jersey. Both parties have controlled state institutions there during the time period of this study, but these states may have expanded their statutes to address the levels of DV. Nevada has some of the highest levels of intimate partner homicide, and our analysis of the Lautenberg Amendment revealed that New Jersey had some of the most stringent DV laws on the books dating back to the 1990s.

3.2 FACTORS IN ADOPTING STATE DOMESTIC VIOLENCE POLICIES

In this section, we present examples of the ways that the factors identified in the previous section might support or block policy adoption in the DV arena. Although we do not describe every state's evolution on DV policymaking, we use specific states to exemplify factors that we argue have either stalled or promoted DV legislation over the past 30 years. These case studies are designed to illustrate the constant interplay among state legislators, DV policy advocates, and firearm rights groups as well as the policy feedback process across states in this issue arena. These case studies show DV policy construction at different stages in each state; some states have a solid foundation of laws that define DV and restrict access to firearms for DV abusers and continue to build on these laws. Other states have taken very little action in this area of DV policy or have considered but dropped firearm restrictions while adopting other policies, such as registration of protective orders that are not related to firearms, designed to reduce DV injury or death.

We propose that these policy adoptions or contractions are driven by three core factors: conservative ideology surrounding gun rights, increases in gun violence over time, and action taken by the federal government. Our first factor is conservative ideology with a specific emphasis on Second Amendment rights. We use Georgia and Montana to show how the growth in conservative opposition to firearm restrictions has spilled over into opposition to legislated DV protections.

Our second factor is the rise in levels of DV, and we use Pennsylvania and West Virginia to exemplify the role that this factor plays in the passage of DV laws. In these two states, a policy problem such as an increase in DV draws public attention to the failure of the government to address or remedy the problem and spurs interest groups and legislators to act. These states show that years of high rates of DV can push legislators to pass laws that go against the grain of state ideology. The commonwealth of Pennsylvania also shows that sometimes the only thing needed is a policy proposal that encourages activism from proponents and silent acquiescence from powerful interest groups in order to get specific legislation passed. The NRA's lack of pushback of state domestic violence firearm laws (DVFLs) led Pennsylvania to become one of the states with the strongest DV firearm laws.

Our third factor is the role of vertical policy diffusion where the federal government can exert pressure on states to adopt certain policies (Gray, 1973) via either mandate or financial incentives. The other mechanisms of policy diffusion include competition between governments, innovation and learning, and normative pressures (we expand on this discussion in Chapter 4). The passage of the Violence Against Women Act (VAWA) in 1994 and the Lautenberg Amendment in 1996 were powerful forces that led to the adoption of many DVFLs at the state level. We present case studies of Alaska and Minnesota as two states that adopted DVFLs in conjunction with this federal legislation. The legal definitions and scope of DV at the federal level and in these states are presented in Table 3.2.

TABLE 3.2. *DV law definitions and scope*

State	Statute	Domestic Abuse/Violence Definition	Relationship between Victim and Perpetrator
United States	29 34 U.S.C. §12291(a)(8). 34 U.S.C. §12291(a)(29). 34 U.S.C. §12291(a)(10)	DV: Felony or misdemeanor crimes Sexual assault: Any nonconsensual sexual act proscribed by federal, tribal, or state law, including when the victim lacks capacity to consent Dating violence: Violence committed by a person who is or has been in a social relationship of a romantic or intimate nature with the victim	Violence committed by a current or former spouse or intimate partner of the victim, by a person with whom the victim shares a child in common, by a person who is cohabitating with or has cohabitated with the victim as a spouse or intimate partner, by a person similarly situated to a spouse of the victim under the domestic or family violence laws of the jurisdiction receiving grant monies, or by any other person against an adult or youth victim who is protected from that person's acts under the domestic or family violence laws of the jurisdiction. VICTIM. An individual who is related to the person who commits an act of abuse in any of the following ways: a. Is related by marriage to the defendant, including a common law marriage. b. Had a former marriage or common law marriage with the defendant. c. Has a child in common with the defendant regardless of whether the victim and defendant have ever been married and regardless of whether they are currently residing or have in the past resided together in the same household. d. Has or had a dating relationship with the defendant.

e. Is a current or former household member. A household member is a person maintaining or having maintained a living arrangement with the defendant where he or she is in, or was engaged in, a romantic or sexual relationship.

f. A relative of a current or former household member as defined in paragraph e. who also lived with the defendant.

g. An individual who is a parent, stepparent, child, or stepchild and who is in or has maintained a living arrangement with the defendant.

(3) DATING RELATIONSHIP.

a. A significant relationship of a romantic or intimate nature characterized by the expectation of affectionate or sexual involvement over a period of time and on a continuing basis during the course of the relationship.

b. A dating relationship includes the period of engagement to be married.

c. A dating relationship does not include a casual or business relationship or a relationship that ended more than 12 months prior to the filing of the petition for a protection order.

(4) "Family or household members" means past or present spouses, persons who are parents of the same child, or other persons living or formerly living in the same household.

Georgia	Ga. Stat. Ann. § 19-13-10	(5) "Family violence" means the commission of the offenses of battery, simple battery, simple assault, assault, stalking, criminal damage to property, or criminal trespass between family or household members.

(continued)

TABLE 3.2. (*continued*)

State	Statute	Domestic Abuse/Violence Definition	Relationship between Victim and Perpetrator
Montana	Mont. Code § 45-5-206	(1) A person commits the offense of partner or family member assault if the person: (a) purposely or knowingly causes bodily injury to a partner or family member; (b) negligently causes bodily injury to a partner or family member with a weapon; or (c) purposely or knowingly causes reasonable apprehension of bodily injury in a partner or family member.	(2) For the purposes of Title 40, chapter 15, 45-5-231 through 45-5-234, 46-6-311, and this section, the following definitions apply: (a) "Family member" means mothers, fathers, children, brothers, sisters, and other past or present family members of a household. These relationships continue regardless of the ages of the parties and whether the parties reside in the same household. These relationships include relationships created by adoption and remarriage, including stepchildren, stepparents, in-laws, and adoptive children and parents. These relationships continue regardless of the ages of the parties and whether the parties reside in the same household. (b) "Partners" means spouses, former spouses, persons who have a child in common, and persons who have been or are currently in a dating or ongoing intimate relationship.
Pennsylvania	Penn. Cons. State. tit. 23, § 6102	"Abuse." The occurrence of one or more of the following acts between family or household members, sexual or intimate partners or persons who share biological parenthood: a) Attempting to cause or intentionally, knowingly or recklessly causing bodily injury, serious bodily injury, rape, involuntary deviate sexual intercourse, sexual assault, statutory sexual assault, aggravated indecent assault, indecent assault or incest with or without a deadly weapon. b) Placing another in reasonable fear of imminent serious bodily injury.	"Family or household members." Spouses or persons who have been spouses, persons living as spouses or who lived as spouses, parents and children, other persons related by consanguinity or affinity, current or former sexual or intimate partners or persons who share biological parenthood.

c) The infliction of false imprisonment pursuant to 18 Pa. C.S. § 2903 (relating to false imprisonment).

d) Physically or sexually abusing minor children, including such terms as defined in Chapter 63 (relating to child protective services).

e) Knowingly engaging in a course of conduct or repeatedly committing acts toward another person, including following the person, without proper authority, under circumstances which place the person in reasonable fear of bodily injury. The definition of this paragraph applies only to proceedings commenced under this title and is inapplicable to any criminal prosecutions commenced under Title 18 (relating to crimes and offenses).

West Virginia	W.V. Code § 48-27-202 W.V. Stat. § 48-27-204	"Domestic violence" or "abuse" means the occurrence of one or more of the following acts between family or household members, as that term is defined in section 204 of this article:	"Family or household members" means persons who:

"Domestic violence" or "abuse" means the occurrence of one or more of the following acts between family or household members, as that term is defined in section 204 of this article:

a) Attempting to cause or intentionally, knowingly or recklessly causing physical harm to another with or without dangerous or deadly weapons;

b) Placing another in reasonable apprehension of physical harm;

c) Creating fear of physical harm by harassment, stalking, psychological abuse or threatening acts;

d) Committing either sexual assault or sexual abuse as those terms are defined in articles eight-b and eight-d, Chapter 61 of this code; and

e) Holding, confining, detaining or abducting another person against that person's will.

"Family or household members" means persons who:

a) Are or were married to each other;

b) Are or were living together as spouses;

c) Are or were sexual or intimate partners;

d) Are or were dating: Provided, that a casual acquaintance or ordinary fraternization between persons in a business or social context does not establish a dating relationship;

e) Are or were residing together in the same household;

(continued)

TABLE 3.2. (*continued*)

State	Statute	Domestic Abuse/Violence Definition	Relationship between Victim and Perpetrator
			f) Have a child in common regardless of whether they have ever married or lived together;
			g) Have the following relationships to another person:
			1) Parent;
			2) Stepparent;
			3) Brother or sister;
			4) Half-brother or half-sister;
			5) Stepbrother or stepsister;
			6) Father-in-law or mother-in-law;
			7) Stepfather-in-law or stepmother-in-law;
			8) Child or stepchild;
			9) Daughter-in-law or son-in-law;
			10) Stepdaughter-in-law or stepson-in-law;
			11) Grandparent;
			12) Step grandparent;
			13) Aunt, aunt-in-law or step aunt;
			14) Uncle, uncle-in-law or step uncle;
			15) Niece or nephew;
			16) First or second cousin; or
			17) Have the relationships set forth in paragraphs (A) through (P), subdivision (7) of this section to a family or household member, as defined in subdivisions (1) through (6) of this section.

State	Statute	Definition
Alaska	Alaska Code §18.66.990	"Domestic violence" and "crime involving domestic violence" mean one or more of the following offenses or an offense under a law or ordinance of another jurisdiction having elements similar to these offenses, or an attempt to commit the offense, by a household member against another household member. Includes a) A crime against the person under murder in the first degree; b) Burglary; c) Criminal trespass; d) Arson or criminally negligent burning; e) Criminal mischief; f) Terrorist threatening; g) Violating a protective order; h) Harassment; i) Cruelty to animals. "Household Member" includes: a) Adults or minors who are current or former spouses; b) Adults or minors who live together or who have lived together; c) Adults or minors who are dating or who have dated; d) Adults or minors who are engaged in or who have engaged in a sexual relationship; e) Adults or minors who are related to each other up to the fourth degree of consanguinity, whether of the whole or half blood or by adoption; f) Adults or minors who are related or formerly related by marriage; g) Persons who have a child of the relationship h) Minor children of a person in a relationship that is described in (a)–(g).
Minnesota	Minn. Stat. § 518B.01	"Domestic abuse" means the following, if committed against a family or household member by a family or household member: a) Physical harm, bodily injury, or assault; b) The infliction of fear of imminent physical harm, bodily injury, or assault; or "Family or household members" means: a) Spouses and former spouses; b) Parents and children; c) Persons related by blood; d) Persons who are presently residing together or who have resided together in the past;

(continued)

TABLE 3.2. (*continued*)

State	Statute	Domestic Abuse/Violence Definition	Relationship between Victim and Perpetrator
		c) Terroristic threats, within the meaning of section 609.713, subdivision 1; criminal sexual conduct, within the meaning of section 609.342, 609.343, 609.344, 609.345, or 609.3451; or interference with an emergency call within the meaning of section 609.78, subdivision 2.	e) Persons who have a child in common regardless of whether they have been married or have lived together at any time; f) A man and woman if the woman is pregnant and the man is alleged to be the father, regardless of whether they have been married or have lived together at any time; and g) Persons involved in a significant romantic or sexual relationship.

Source: National Council of State Legislatures (2019).

3.2.1 Conservative Ideology as a Factor Blocking Domestic Violence Firearm Laws: The Cases of Georgia and Montana

3.2.1.1 *Georgia*

Georgia was a Democratic-controlled state from 1992 to 2002 and then a completely Republican-controlled state from 2005 to 2021.[1] Why did Georgia fail to pass DV firearm legislation following the passage of VAWA and the Lautenberg amendment when the state was governed by the Democratic Party? Part of the answer to this question involves the vestiges of party realignment that started in the 1960s. Democrats may have controlled the Georgia government following the passage of federal DV legislation, but it was certainly not the same Democratic Party that was passing DVFLs in states such as New York and California. As we noted in Chapter 2, the rise of Newt Gingrich (Republican, Georgia) in the 1980s and 1990s and his brand of Republican conservatism came from the heart of Georgia. His triumph in winning back control of the US House (and the Senate) in 1994 essentially capped the tide that turned conservative Democratic voters into Republicans across the deep South. The conservative ideology that successfully blocks many women's rights and gun control laws today is an important factor that explains many states' inability to pass DV legislation.

The state of Georgia took limited action in this policy arena between 1990 and 2020. In 2001, the legislature successfully passed and the governor signed an amendment to the Georgia code of laws that would "create a registry of protective orders as a centralized data base for protective orders... to provide for standard forms for protective orders; to provide for electronic transmittal and maintenance of orders."[2] This bill was sponsored by five legislators: – four Democrats and one Republican – and had bipartisan support. Two years later, Georgia enacted an amendment to its DV laws that extended the length of temporary restraining orders, again with bipartisan sponsorship and support.

Four years later, Republican Rep. John Lunsford from Georgia District 110 sponsored a DV firearm law that would not allow a person to retain a license for a pistol or revolver if that person was under a restraining order for "harassing, stalking, or threatening an intimate partner of such person or child of such intimate partner or person, or engaging in other conduct that would place an intimate partner in reasonable fear of bodily injury to

---

[1] Ballotpedia's States section at ballotpedia.org/States#State_governments.
[2] www.legis.ga.gov/legislation/2647.

the partner or child. . . [and] any person [who] has been convicted in any court of a misdemeanor crime of DV."[3] Unfortunately, all of the clauses related to taking firearms away from DV offenders were removed by the Georgia House Committee on Non-Civil Judiciary; the remainder of the bill created a database for protective orders and streamlined the protective order process. The updated law without firearm provisions successfully made it through the Georgia House with unanimous support and near unanimous support in the Senate and went into effect by July 2006. We could not find any specific reasons in the legislative record why the firearm provisions were dropped. This is one of the few major aspects of the legislation that is missing from the original version of the bill that became law. Since then, Georgia has not enacted any DV laws or DVFLs.

In 2016, the *Atlanta Journal-Constitution* reported that 139 people were killed in Georgia due to DV in 2015, including 20 people who had obtained protective orders (Cook, 2016). Despite these homicide numbers, Georgia does not have any DVFLs on the books, a rationale that judges offered when they were issuing protective orders without prohibiting firearm access. In fact, the *Atlanta Journal-Constitution* also found that each judge used different standards when attempting to remove firearms from abusers. Chief Judge William Prior Jr. stated that his standard (as well as that of his fellow judges on his circuit) was to remove the gun if the claimant, frequently a woman, was threatened with a gun but not if she was "just threatened with physical violence" (Cook, 2016). Douglas County Sheriff Bobby Holmes stated that "our judges do not, as a rule, put that [firearm restriction] in" (Cook, 2016). Western Judicial Circuit Chief Judge David Sweat said, "When we have someone applying for a family violence protective order we will inquire as to whether there are firearms, pistols or whatever in the home and will then direct the sheriff to take possession of guns pending resolution. Just to make sure everybody stays safe" (Cook, 2016).

The Georgia Commission on Family Violence (GCFV) created and funded by the Georgia General Assembly has argued for firearm restrictions in the state. Judge Sweat served on this commission, which may in part explain his more proactive stance of firearm restrictions. According to the GCFV, 59 percent of the deaths from DV in Georgia involved the use of a firearm from 2005 to 2018 (Georgia Commission on Family Violence, 2018). In its second of 10 goals to reduce DV fatalities, the

---

[3] www.legis.ga.gov/legislation/2647.

commission stated that the state "failed to comprehensively address the fundamental issue that would reduce the number of deaths in our communities: abuser access to firearms" (Georgia Commission on Family Violence, p. 23). The commission's report (p. 25) went on to say:

Keeping guns out of the hands of abusers is essential to protecting victims. The Project's ongoing finding of firearms as the leading cause of death in reviewed cases underscores our repeated recommendation for use of all legal means possible to remove firearms from the hands of domestic violence abusers. . . . In fact, each state bordering Georgia – Alabama, Tennessee, Florida, North Carolina and South Carolina – has adopted measures to prohibit those convicted of qualifying misdemeanor crimes of domestic violence from possessing a firearm, but Georgia has neglected to take this important step towards supporting victim safety. State officials can only enforce the prohibition if there is a state law mirroring the federal prohibition, leaving many community stakeholders feeling like their hands are tied.

Removing firearms from abusers not only saves the lives of their victims but can also protect the lives of responding police officers. The 2018 report of the Georgia Commission on Family Violence notes that DV incidents were the deadliest situations a police officer could respond to and each one of the law enforcement deaths attributed to DV was caused by the use of a firearm.

Some legislators have taken note of the importance of protecting victims from abusers, but only bills that do not restrict firearms appear to succeed in Georgia. The 2017–2018 session of the Georgia General Assembly considered and passed one DV bill, HB 834. It was a nonfirearm-related law that successfully passed both chambers with bipartisan support. It allows victims to terminate a rental or lease without penalty as long as they could provide a restraining order to the landlord. This law increases a victim's safety because it provides the financial freedom for the person to leave an abusive situation without having to worry about fees or trying to juggle two rents until the original lease has ended.[4] In the February 2019 session, a bill that would allow for the issuance of extreme risk protection orders was introduced by six representatives, all Democrats.[5] Commonly known as a "red flag law," 19 states have enacted such laws; they have been proposed in 10 other states (Campbell, Yablon, and Mascia, 2021). After reviewing committee hearing recordings, we found that the bill did not appear to have been considered by the full committee. A group of these same representatives

---

[4] www.legis.ga.gov/legislation/52509.   [5] www.legis.ga.gov/legislation/55318.

sponsored the same bill again in February 2021, but as of September 2022, the bill had not been enacted.[6]

Although the Lautenberg Amendment should result in the removal of firearms from those who have been convicted of a DV misdemeanor, there is no process for federal authorities to remove the weapons. This means that states like Georgia that have no state-level law written to follow the Lautenberg Amendment essentially provide no protection to women who have partners with firearms. Because less than half of the state's circuit courts actually have protocols to follow in regard to firearm removal, women in the state of Georgia have differing levels of protection based upon where they live. Additionally, some judges do not even follow protocols if they exist in their circuit, a fact that may be attributed to the election of the judges (Cook, 2016). Attorney John Monroe, representing GeorgiaCarry.org argued that taking firearms away would be unconstitutional because "you have an obligation to divest yourself of them (guns) but it's however you choose. They are your property and you would be deprived of the right to sell them" (Cook, 2016). In Georgia, the issue of Second Amendment rights becomes paramount when the issue of firearm surrender arises and, in the process, prevents the adoption of consistent standards for gun removal from DV abusers.

3.2.1.2 *Montana*

From 1995 to 2004, the Republican Party had control of both chambers of the Montana state legislature as well as the governor's mansion. The past 15 years have seen the Democratic Party's candidate become governor from 2005 to 2020, and the Democratic Party controlled the state senate from 2005 to 2008. Despite Democratic control of the governor's office for 15 years and Democratic influence in the state senate and house during that time, Montana remains ideologically conservative, especially on the issue of gun rights.[7] The legislature has failed to enact legislation to address DV or deaths by firearms committed during DV in the time period of our study; this is in spite of the fact that 72 percent of the DV homicides from 2000 to 2018 in Montana were committed with a firearm (Montana Domestic Violence Fatality Review Commission, 2020). In fact, the only legislation that has passed the legislature was designed to undermine federal firearm regulations. Since 2003, the state has had a Domestic Violence Fatality Review Commission whose charge is to review closed

---

[6] www.legis.ga.gov/legislation/59351.
[7] In 2005–2006 and 2009–2010, the state house had split control.

DV homicide cases and provide recommendations to the legislature on how the law could be changed to better protect victims.[8] There is also a specific team dedicated to Native American DV homicides in the state.

However, between 2018 and 2021, there was a small uptick in attempts to pass DV firearm laws. In November 2018, Democrat Robert Farris Olsen of District 79 sponsored HB 718, a red flag bill that would make possessing a firearm illegal for a person who had been issued "an extreme risk protective order" and that would terminate a concealed weapon permit.[9] Farris Olsen made a concerted effort to convince committee members that this law was not an infringement on Second Amendment rights:

I know we have talked a lot about guns in this committee, this really isn't a firearms control bill. It's not seeking to control or to limit access to purchasing guns, it's just is used in those situations where you know something is about to go wrong and it allows law enforcement to intervene and remove those firearms or stop you from purchasing new firearms until that risk is removed. And this isn't a new type of legislation. In fact, yesterday the Senate, the U.S. Senate Judiciary Committee, held a hearing on these types of laws, and in doing so Lindsey Graham noted that "there are lots of people who may be worried, is the government going to come take your guns? The answer is no." So, this law isn't about limiting guns or infringing upon your second amendment rights. He [Graham] continued in that hearing, and he noted that he hopes one day there could be a federal process for law enforcement or family members to be able to petition a court signaling someone is quote "about to blow." So again, that's what this is about. This is about those situations where you know someone, perhaps, is having a mental breakdown and there is a risk that they may use the firearm to die by suicide. And so, this gives the family member or the law enforcement officer the ability to go in and seek an extreme order of protection. This type of law has been enacted in 14 different states around the country, including five that are run by Republican governors, such as Indiana and Florida. (Montana House Judiciary Committee, 2019)

Child safety organizations that were concerned about suicide by teenagers as well as citizens testified in support of this bill. One of those citizens was Christl Domina of Billings, Montana, who testified:

Grandma had been making plans to come live with us to escape her abusive spouse. When she told him she was leaving him, he got the rifle they used for "varmints" on the farm, chased her out into an alfalfa field, shot her three times and then turned the gun on himself. Fast forward forty years. Tommy was my best

---

[8] https://dojmt.gov/victims/domestic-violence-fatality-review-commission/.
[9] https://leg.mt.gov/bills/2019/billpdf/HB0718.pdf; data for all states is current to February 2021.

friend... when Tommy turned 35, he started to exhibit some signs of mental illness. He also became abusive towards his partner. We begged him to get help, but he, clouded by illness, did not see a problem. His wife decided to leave him. As she got in her car to drive off, he jumped in the passenger seat with one of his handguns. We will never know what was said between the two of them, we just knew he murdered her, and then put the gun to his own head.... Being affected by gun violence, and being a survivor of domestic violence myself, has spurred me to action. I am the Local Lead for the Billings Chapter of Moms Demand Action for Gun Sense.... Red flag laws protect individuals from not just harming others, but from harming themselves.[10]

Despite Rep. Farris Olsen's sponsorship of the bill, it did not make it out of committee. As theories of the policy feedback process might predict, intertwining the issue of child safety and victim protection became intertwined with the separate issue of Second Amendment rights engendered opposition.

In January 2021, Republican Rep. Jedediah Hinkle from Montana District 67, who was consistently endorsed by the NRA, sponsored HB 258 that has been introduced seven times in the Montana legislature, having passed successfully through both chambers three times only to be vetoed by the governor each time.[11] This bill would stop "the enforcement of a federal ban on or regulation of firearms, magazines, ammunition, ammunition components, or firearm accessories" both immediately and retroactively.[12] The bill was first submitted by Hinkle in December 2020 with the provision that it did not apply to "the enforcement of any federal or state law prohibiting a person convicted of a misdemeanor offense of domestic violence from possessing a firearm," which means this would still allow local and state law enforcement to enforce the Lautenberg Amendment.[13]

Hinkle's bill was reported out of the Montana Judiciary Committee on February 24, 2021; it did not include the exception for the Lautenberg Amendment. It passed the Montana House on a party line vote of 66 Republicans to 33 Democrats, 1 absent on February 27, 2021, passed the Senate on a vote of 30 Republicans to 20 (Democrats and 1 R) on

---

[10] https://leg.mt.gov/bills/2019/Minutes/House/Exhibits/juh63a06.pdf.

[11] One of the last times this bill passed the legislature was as House Bill 203 in 2015 first sponsored by Republican Rep. A. Wittich. This bill passed the House with a 58 to 42 vote, passed the Senate with a 27 to 22 vote, and was vetoed by Democratic Gov. Steven Bullock in March 2015. A similar law (HB 381) died in process in April 2011.

[12] https://leg.mt.gov/bills/2021/HB0299//HB0258_2.pdf.

[13] https://leg.mt.gov/bills/2021/HB0299//HB0258_1.pdf.

April 1, 2021, and the governor signed it into law on April 23, 2021.[14] This law effectively eliminates the one DV firearm protection the victims of DV in Montana have by prohibiting law enforcement from enforcing the Lautenberg Amendment.

Georgia and Montana's legislative histories on DV tell us something about the factors that keep these states from acting to prevent DV injury and death. First, the narrative in them almost always circles around Second Amendment rights at the expense of DV victims' rights. Legislators in these states often rely on the Second, Ninth, and Tenth Amendments in their arguments against DVFLs. Second, high levels of gun homicides are not enough of a motivation to restrict domestic abusers' firearm access; we explore this dynamic more fully in Chapter 4. Finally, Montana has not only failed to pass DV firearm restrictions but has in fact actively tried to bolster access to firearms for those convicted of DV offenses and to repeal the permit to carry concealed firearms. Georgia and Montana reveal the roadblocks that conservative ideology can present to block the passage of DV laws that seek to provide adequate personal safety protections for DV victims. In these states, the goal of reducing victimization in DV became dominated by a different issue – firearm rights.

Next we describe how interest group advocates and legislators successfully used that attention to generate momentum for policy change.

3.2.2 Increases in Domestic Violence Rates as a Prompt for State Action: The Cases of Pennsylvania and West Virginia

In contrast to Georgia and Montana, Pennsylvania and West Virginia, have adopted DV firearm restrictions and expanded their scope of DV laws, although those efforts have faced more resistance in recent years. Pennsylvania's legislative actions in this arena show how interest group advocacy coupled with strategically minimizing the opposition can produce laws that restrict access to firearms by DV abusers. For both Pennsylvania and West Virginia, the impact of firearm violence is also key, although not in the form of a sudden shock event like a mass shooting. In West Virginia where the majority of women who are murdered are killed by guns by intimate partners, the legislature passed firearm restrictions and expanded the definition of DV to dating partners (Office of the Chief Medical Examiner, 2016). The cumulative buildup of

---

[14] https://legiscan.com/MT/bill/HB258/2021.

DV deaths pushed the legislature in both states to act. These actions serve as examples of what can happen in the policy arena when a spotlight shines on a specific problem.

3.2.2.1 Pennsylvania

The Republican Party had a considerable hold on Pennsylvania state government from 1992 to 2021. The Democratic Party has held the majority in the state senate for only one year (1993) and controlled the state assembly sporadically for 7 of the 29 years. This might suggest that Pennsylvania would be like Georgia and Montana with a conservative ideology that blocks DV legislation. But as we will show, increasing levels of DV in Pennsylvania encouraged the state to adopt DV firearm laws.

As we noted in Chapters 1 and 2, the issue of DV was gaining national attention even before VAWA was enacted at the federal level in 1994. Three years before it was first enacted, Pennsylvania required law enforcement to remove firearms from a situation in which a DV event had occurred.[15] In 1992, two years before VAWA, the state enacted a law that prevented individuals who were convicted of stalking from owning or possessing firearms.[16] However, it would be 12 years until Pennsylvania acted again in the area of DV and firearms.

No one single act of gun violence created momentum for action in the Pennsylvania legislature in 2005; however, several high-profile DV murders had occurred in the preceding year (Burling, 2005). In 2004, the Pennsylvania Coalition Against Domestic Violence (PCADV) reported that 110 people in that state had died in 2004 as a result of DV including 63 women, 9 children, and 38 men; 71 were shot to death. There were 34 identified perpetrators who died by suicide, 4 killed by law enforcement, 3 killed in gun crossfire, and 2 killed in cases that were subsequently ruled justified (Pennsylvania Coalition Against Domestic Violence, 2005).

In 2005, Republicans controlled both chambers of the legislature, working with Democratic Governor Ed Rendell. State Assemblywoman Katie True (Republican, Lancaster) introduced House Bill 1717, the Protection from Abuse Act, which gave judges the authority (but did not mandate) in DV cases to demand the surrender of all weapons and ammunition held by a DV abuser who was under a restraining (protection from abuse) order within 24 hours, not just the weapon he or she might

---

[15] 18 Pa. Cons. Stat. § 2711(b).
[16] 18 Pa. Cons. Stat. § 106(b)(6); 18 Pa. Cons. Stat. § 2709(B), (C).

have threatened to use in the abuse case. The bill covered a wide range of guns including rifles and long guns. Individuals had to surrender them to law enforcement or a third party who agreed to be legally responsible for the guns, and the individuals could not possess a weapon for the life of the restraining order; advocates also succeeded in extending the maximum length of restraining orders to 36 months from 18 months. The law allowed individuals to petition in writing for the return of the weapon (s) after the expiration of the order, and a hearing was required to determine whether the weapons would be returned. The bill also called for a statewide registry of all DV protection orders under the direction of the state police so that courts and local law enforcement would be able to access it. Lastly, the bill prohibited a person who had been convicted of a DV offense from possessing or owning a firearm for a period of at least five years from the conviction or the end of time served and/or probation associated with the offense.

Assemblywoman True explained that she was asked to sponsor the bill because of her favorable stance toward the NRA and her work as an advocate on women's issues. In her words, "We were not trying to take away anyone's rights. ... If someone is doing something with a gun to threaten someone, they don't deserve a gun" (Worden, 2005). Rep. True amassed support from 137 of her colleagues by ensuring that the bill did not infringe on gun ownership rights. HB1717 passed both the House (199 to 1) and Senate (48 to 2). Supporters of the bill made compromises with gun rights advocates, which included a new and more efficient permit process for weapon purchase and ownership and provisions to punish individuals who make false claims regarding DV. Ultimately, the bill was supported by both DV advocates and gun rights groups; the NRA did not take an official position despite a process of compromises that in one legislator's words was "painful." When the bill passed, Rep. True said that she believed it was successful because "enough people finally understood what happened to some women because of firearms"(Worden, 2005).

Whereas one could have described Pennsylvania as a policy innovator in 2005, per Hays (1996), in the 2017–2018 legislative session, polarization and a more resurgent Second Amendment gun rights movement put additional pressure on state legislators to reassure gun rights voters that the bill would not take away their legally owned weapons for no reason. One legislator, Jay Costa (Democrat, Alleghany) summarized the challenge of passing gun safety bills when they are framed as safety versus gun rights in this way:

Mr. President, it seems like every week we come to the Senate floor and we see these types of things occurring across our country. I believe that it is time for us to begin to have a conversation on addressing some of the reasonable and responsible things we can do here in Pennsylvania along those lines as it relates to how we manage the gun control conversation here in Pennsylvania. . . . Let me be clear, I am not looking to take anyone's guns away or violate their Second Amendment right. . . . (Costa, 2018)

In particular, Sen. Tom Killion (Republican, Delaware/Chester) began a new push to close what he saw as loopholes in the 2005 legislation. Specifically, Killion's bill (SB501) was part of a package of bills that passed the Pennsylvania Senate seeking to (1) limit the definition of acceptable third party to exclude family members and friends who can take possession of a gun from an individual who is under a protection from abuse (PFA) order, (2) mandate that judges order the surrender of guns from individuals under PFA orders within 24 hours, (3) require that individuals convicted of a DV crime surrender their firearms within 48 hours rather than the 60-day time period that was current law, and (4) make failure to relinquish firearms a misdemeanor crime (Levy, 2018). Sen. Killion's Republican colleague, Sen. Camera Bartolotta (Republican, Beaver/Green/Washington), introduced SB449, which clarified risk assessment and would give the courts additional powers to restrict the movement and gun ownership of individuals who are deemed likely to commit violence. In her words, the bill was prompted by the kidnapping and murder in the senator's home district of a woman by her estranged husband even though he was under a PFA order and house arrest with an ankle monitor (Pennsylvania State Senate, 2016). It was notable that the Republicans whose party by at the time of the crime had full ownership of the issue of Second Amendment firearm rights chose to present these bills as being distinct from that issue and instead related to DV as a public safety matter.

Although these bills did not pass the legislature, a different bill, HB2060 was enacted in October 2018; Rep. Marguerite Quinn, a Republican from Bucks County, introduced the bill that had bipartisan cosponsorship. It accomplished some of the aims of the Killion and Bartolotta bills by further expanding prohibitions of domestic abusers from possessing or owning firearms.[17] HB2060 prohibits "abusers who have been issued a final protection from abuse orders issued after a contested hearing or conviction for misdemeanor crimes of domestic

---

[17] https://trackbill.com/bill/pennsylvania-house-bill-2060.

violence from possessing firearms and requires them to turn in their guns to law enforcement agencies immediately while the order is in effect..." (Wolf, 2018). HB2060 extends the prohibition on firearms to dating partners who are under restraining orders and prohibited individuals who were convicted of misdemeanor DV from owning or possessing firearms. Pennsylvania's actions on DVFLs in 2018 reflect a common pattern across states whereby legislatures address multiple aspects of DV law by packing provisions into one omnibus law. These actions also show the complexity of negotiations to reach consensus on addressing women's safety so as to avoid being perceived to infringe on Second Amendment rights.

3.2.2.2 West Virginia

At first glance, West Virginia would be an unlikely candidate for having active policies to address DV committed with firearms; US Senate candidates in the state are known to run ads with themselves shooting guns to show they are committed to Second Amendment rights (Thomas, 2018). Still, DV is a significant issue in West Virginia in terms of incidents reported, arrests, and related homicides (*Charleston Gazette*, 2006). The Democratic Party controlled the state government for the majority of the years of this study. Only in the last six years has the Republican Party become the more powerful party in the state. Over the time period of this study, West Virginia has taken a number of incremental steps in the area of DV and firearms that have put it in line with federal law, expanded the definition of what constitutes DV, and widened the scope of DV firearm prohibitions to include dating partners. As *The Charleston Gazette* (2002) put it, "Time after time, the West Virginia Legislature has toughened laws in an attempt to protect women and kids from husbands, ex-husbands, boyfriends and ex-boyfriends who go into deadly rages."

Around the time that VAWA was first introduced in 1990, DV homicides in West Virginia represented between 30 and 36 percent of all homicides occurring there (Associated Press, 1998). In 1996, the state enacted a law that banned individuals under DV restraining orders from carrying concealed firearms or obtaining a concealed carry permit. Two years later, the state passed a law requiring law enforcement to remove firearms from the location of a DV event.[18] In 2000, West Virginia passed

---

[18] W. Va. Code § 48-2A-12(e)(1).

a law that banned all individuals who are under a DV restraining order from owning or possessing firearms.[19]

In 2001, five years after the passage of the Lautenberg Amendment, West Virginia enacted a law that was in line with federal law in that individuals who are convicted of a misdemeanor DV are banned from owning or possessing firearms; it also extended the ban on dating partners to individuals under temporary restraining orders from owning or possessing firearms. Four years later, and just one year before the 2005 reauthorization of VAWA, West Virginia passed a law prohibiting individuals convicted of DV against dating partners from carrying concealed weapons and getting a concealed carry permit.[20] In 2009, the state used federal money to establish an electronic database for DV protective orders, and in 2012, the state clarified its policy on firearms and restraining orders by making it a condition of a temporary or final restraining order that the accused be prohibited from owning or possessing a gun or ammunition and that the accused be informed of that prohibition when that order is put in place.[21]

But enforcing that law proved difficult, and there is still too big a gap between laws that are in place and their inconsistent implementation. According to Tonia Thomas of the West Virginia Coalition Against Domestic Violence, West Virginia has enacted laws

that protect victims of domestic violence, but enforcement of the laws varies by county.... In some counties, law enforcements officers will seize guns, while others use an "honor system."... Some will allow the person convicted of domestic violence or subject of a protective order to give their guns to a third party, such as a family member, or hold them at a pawn shop. (Bech, 2014)

Indeed, there are other aspects of DV prosecutions, such as requiring victims to testify in front of their abusers and the right of prosecutors not to drop charges ("no drop") even without the victim's willingness to move forward, that West Virginia has not yet consistently addressed. One recent example involved a 24-year-old man who had been arrested for DV but whose wife refused to appear in court to testify against him so the charges were dropped; he eventually shot her and their 5-year-old to death, injured their 1½-year-old, and then killed himself with his gun (Brautigan, 2021). States cannot prevent all types of DV, but the failure to

---

[19] W. Va. Code § 61-7-7(a)(7).
[20] W. Va. Code § 61-7-7(a); W. Va. Code § 61-7-4(a)(6).   [21] www.wvlegislature.gov/.

implement and enforce DV policy cohesively and remove guns from abusers continues to cost lives.

As with other states, West Virginia has adopted other nonfirearm-related DV laws that also can affect whether an assailant can procure or possess a firearm. In 2014, West Virginia changed its definition of battery to a stand-alone offense; in the context of DV, this indirectly stands at the intersection of DV and firearm law. There had been a court case in which a defendant convicted of simple battery against a family member was arrested for possessing a firearm; he challenged that arrest and ultimately won his case. That case revealed a significant loophole in West Virginia law both in conforming with federal law and in terms of DV and firearm violence. Prior to 2014, simple battery could be a crime without any physical harm and in that case would not qualify as a misdemeanor assault or DV crime. Changing the definition of domestic battery to include "force capable of physical pain or injury" essentially made it a violent offense that would be prosecuted under federal law and would carry with it a prohibition against owning or possessing firearms (Moore, 2015).

Pennsylvania and West Virginia have adapted public understanding of DV by passing laws that made it harder for DV abusers who were under restraining orders to own or possess guns and made it easier for law enforcement and judges to order the removal of guns from the home of a DV abuser. West Virginia was the most aggressive state in expanding the reach of DV firearm prohibitions to dating partners whether they were under restraining orders or they had applied for a concealed carry permit. Both Pennsylvania and West Virginia exemplify the continuous competition for definition in the policy arena between advocates for increased protections from DV committed with firearms and opponents of restrictions on access to firearms.

3.2.3 The Influence of Vertical Policy Diffusion in Adopting Domestic Violence Laws: The Cases of Alaska and Minnesota

To this point, we have focused on how conservative ideology on firearm regulation can prevent states from passing DV laws and how DV crimes that are highly publicized in a state can lead to the adoption of DV statutes. Our final two case studies of Alaska and Minnesota illustrate the role of vertical policy diffusion in motivating states to adopt DV statutes. To be clear, neither Alaska nor Minnesota has adopted a full range of DV firearm laws. But the laws they have adopted follow federal action in DV. Alaska, like the states we have discussed in this chapter so far, has mainly been controlled by the Republican Party while Minnesota has had more shifts in party control of state government.

3.2.3.1 Alaska

Alaska is a state whose general resident population faces DV and grapples with its higher rate found among Native American populations. In the latter case, the state has limited jurisdiction to address the issue; we address this more fully in Chapter 6.

In 1996, two years after the enactment of VAWA, Alaska enacted the Domestic Violence Prevention and Victim Protection Act. One of the leading Republican sponsors of the bill was Sean Parnell, a state representative who represented Anchorage and would go on to serve as governor of Alaska from 2009 to 2014.[22] In the bill, domestic violence crimes were defined more broadly to include:

(A) a crime against the person under [section 11.41 of the Alaska Statutes, which includes homicide, assault, stalking, reckless endangerment, kidnapping, custodial interference with parental rights, sexual assault, exploitation of minors, indecent exposure, robbery, extortion, and coercion]; (B) burglary...; (C) criminal trespass...; (D) arson or criminally negligent burning... [which includes negligently damaging the property of another by fire, regardless of the value of the property]; (E) criminal mischief... [which includes tampering with the property of another regardless of the value and intentionally damaging property worth $50 or more]; (F) terrorist threatening...; (G) violating a protective order...; or (H) harassment under sections 11.61.120(a)(2)–(4) of the Alaska Statutes, which include telephoning with intent to impair the ability of the other party to place or receive calls, making repeated phone calls at inconvenient hours, and making an anonymous or obscene telephone call or communication.[23] (Clark, 2010)

The Domestic Violence Prevention and Victim Protection Act allowed for mandatory arrest within the first 12 hours of the commission of a DV offense; the rationale for this provision was that mandatory arrest was necessary to prevent imminent danger to the victim of the original assault from recurring. Moreover, the law also provided courts with the authority to demand the surrender of a firearm that was "in the actual possession of or used by the defendant during the commission of a crime involving domestic violence" (Laws of Alaska, 1996). Police were also

---

[22] Parnell is quoted as explaining provisions of the bill on the House floor; see www.legis
.state.ak.us/basis/Meeting/Detail/?Meeting=HJUD%201996-01-22%2013:05:00&Bill=
HB%20326.

[23] The original law can be found at www.akleg.gov/basis/Bill/Text/19?Hsid=HB0314E

authorized to "seize a deadly weapon in plain view" and if a deadly weapon was used in the DV crime, they could seize all deadly weapons in the possession or ownership of the individual accused of the crime (Laws of Alaska, 1996, Section 27).

Additionally under this law, DV victims could seek a protective order from the court that would require the surrender of firearms by the alleged offender if a firearm was used in the offense (Laws of Alaska, 1996, Section 28 [7]). The law added a prohibition against granting a concealed carry permit to an individual who had been convicted of a DV crime in the preceding five years and required the suspension of an individual's concealed carry permit if that person is currently under a protective order. Finally, the law clarified what it meant to violate a restraining order; the law in effect at that time barred the subject of a restraining order from communicating with the victim but would allow the subject to enter a vehicle with the victim so long as the subject of the restraining order remained silent. The transcript of committee consideration of the bill reported as follows:

REPRESENTATIVE PARNELL said currently, if you violate a domestic violence restraining order, a violation is defined in statute as merely communicating directly or indirectly with the other party. A violation does not include getting into a car with somebody. CSHB 314 attempts to mirror those elements that are generally included in a domestic violence restraining order. Representative Parnell informed the committee members it is more of a technical change, but it is an important one. For instance, with the domestic violence restraining order, there are some judges that will apply the statute very literally which means that if there is no communication, technically he is not in violation of a statute. Representative Parnell said what he is trying to do is to get an even application of the violation of the domestic violence restraining order.[24]

Key to Rep. Parnell's statement is the acknowledgement that even when a law is in place at the state level, individual judges may interpret it differently and reduce the effectiveness in protecting women from their abusers (see Chapter 5 for more discussion on judicial discretion in DV cases).

Backing up Parnell's emphasis on consistent interpretation of what constitutes a violation of a restraining order, an advocate against DV reinforced the inherent weakness of the law if it is not properly enforced. In her testimony to the committee in favor of the bill, Lauree Hugonin, executive director of the Alaska Network on Domestic Violence and

---

[24] www.legis.state.ak.us/basis/Meeting/Detail/?Meeting=HJUD%201996-01-22%
2013:05:00&Bill=HB%20326.

Sexual Assault, argued that injunctions work only when abusers see them as enforceable:

Domestic violence injunctions are tools which can be used to provide some protection to victims. Injunctions are designed to deny the abuser access to the victim which hopefully decreases an elevated risk of violence, allows the victim to be safe in her home, and keeps the abuser from jeopardizing her employment and personal support. Domestic violence injunctions only work when abusers see them as enforceable. When abusers see [that] the risks to breaking them outweigh the benefits they chose to not violate the restraining order. If we do not have enforceable domestic violence injunctions, then the victim is placed in greater risk and [we] have condoned the abusers' actions. Currently, communication is the only item in a domestic violence injunction for which someone can be criminally sanctioned. Gaining access to the victim, and further domestic violence should also be criminally sanctioned.[25]

Alaska did not take any other meaningful legislative steps in this arena until 10 years later when VAWA was reauthorized in 2005 with greater emphasis on expanded definition of and penalties for stalking, adding cyberstalking specifically. Alaska responded to these expansions in 2006 by extending protections to victims of stalking and sexual assault even when the alleged perpetrator was not accused of DV per se. These protective measures included getting an order of protection against the alleged assailant and requiring police officers to inform victims of sexual assault of the remedies and services available to them.[26] Alaska's expansion of the scope of coverage under domestic policy at the state level directly reflects the actions taken one year earlier at the federal level. The Alaska legislature also passed a law in 2006 that made harassment, including unwanted verbal and electronic communication, and physical contact a crime and included the possession of a deadly weapon while conducting harassment as a crime. There is nothing in this provision, however, that enables law enforcement to make an argument for deadly weapon removal upon conviction of harassment by someone who is not accused of DV (Laws of Alaska, 2006a). As of 2021, Alaska had not enacted any major legislation related to DV or gun possession in particular.

---

[25] www.legis.state.ak.us/basis/Meeting/Detail/?Meeting=HJUD%201996-01-22%
2013:05:00&Bill=HB%20326.

[26] Orders of protection issued under the Alaska's 1996 DV law also carried with them the requirement to surrender firearms if used in the initial attack, but there is no specific mention of firearm surrender in sexual assault cases in these amendments; see Laws of Alaska (2006b), "Protective Order for Sexual Assault/Abuse."

3.2.3.2 Minnesota

The DV firearm policy history in Minnesota is less straightforward than that in Alaska. Minnesota has responded to federal action by extending the scope of DV policy to stalking, but it was slower than the federal government to restrict DV abusers from having firearms. It has also extended the scope of DV to dating partners. Studying Minnesota's DV firearm policies illustrates how the adoption of a policy does not guarantee effective implementation, especially if the people tasked with carrying it out react negatively to it.

From 1992 to 2021, Minnesota's government was mainly divided with the Democratic Party typically controlling the Senate and party control switching for the House and governor's office every few years. In 1994 and 1995, Minnesota enacted changes to its concealed carry laws when it extended its restriction on securing a permit to carry concealed weapons to dating partners and those who are convicted of stalking (Everytown for Gun Safety). Ten years later, Minnesota revisited the concealed and open carry laws to prohibit any person other than a police officer from carrying a pistol in public unless that person carries a valid permit to do so. That same year, 2005, Minnesota passed a law that categorized strangulation as a key indicator of future domestic homicide. This set of more recent laws in combination led to a rise in general DV convictions. The state also inched closer to conforming with the Lautenberg Amendment by making individuals who were convicted of a misdemeanor in DV subject to penalties if caught carrying a "dangerous weapon" (Heim, 2011). In 2010, five years after the 2005 VAWA reauthorization that broadened penalties for stalking as a DV crime, Minnesota expanded penalties for DV and broadened the definition of stalking as a DV crime but took no specific action regarding the use or possession of firearms as related to DV (Heim, 2011).

Finally, in 2014, in line with the 2013 revision of VAWA, Minnesota passed HF3238, legislation requiring individuals under restraining orders for having committed DV or being convicted of a misdemeanor DV charge to surrender their firearms was extended to rifles and shotguns; it also extended that requirement to individuals accused of certain types of stalking. This in effect put Minnesota in line with the Lautenberg Amendment, 22 years after it was enacted. Furthermore, Minnesota extended the definition of intimate partners to dating relationships for domestic abuse for the purposes of restraining orders. The bill was introduced by a Democrat, Dan Schoen, from District 54A, and it had a progun rights Republican legislator, Tony Cornish, from District 23B as a primary cosponsor. At the time the bill passed the state House, Schoen said, "I know this bill will not save every life, but this is an action that I believe will save lives.... This bill does not target the Second Amendment rights of law-abiding citizens" (Cook, 2014b). His Republican colleague Cornish described as an "avid gun rights supporter" added, "We put as much protection for gun owners as we possibly could, and also protect a woman or a man from getting shot and killed" (Cook, 2014b). These remarks highlight the continued need for legislators across states to provide reassurances to gun rights advocates that DV firearm laws will not encroach upon their legal right to possess or own a gun.

At the time it was enacted, HF3238 was lauded as a significant step forward for Minnesota whose scope on DV laws had traditionally been narrow (Helgeson, 2014). During the consideration of the bill, members of law enforcement questioned how it could be successfully implemented, saying that it would be hard to enforce because of the increased administrative responsibilities with firearm confiscation, storage, and eventual return to owners:

Jim Franklin, executive director of the Minnesota Sheriffs' Association, raised law enforcement concerns, including the extra storage space needed to store the weapons, more property clerk work and liability concerns about weapon release. "If it's a judge's order to get in, does it then require a judge's order to go back out?" Law enforcement agencies and firearms dealers would be permitted to charge "a reasonable fee" to accept firearms, and would have the right to refuse them altogether (Cook, 2014a).

Sheriff Franklin's comments directly address DV policy implementation, which involves the additional responsibilities that these laws may place on law enforcement personnel. The addition of the responsibility of securing and processing weapons is intended to keep victims safer from abusers, but without the support of the personnel who would carry out the policy, it seems destined to make the law ineffective or to fail altogether. Indeed, in Minnesota, one report that followed the implementation of the surrender provisions of the 2014 law claimed it was not effectively enforced and that relatively few guns were surrendered by individuals under restraining orders for domestic abuse (Associated Press, 2018). One can view this as an unintended consequence of a policy advancement designed to reduce DV firearm injuries and deaths; the policy appeared to engender negative feedback by those tasked with implementing it.

While Alaska and Minnesota were responsive to some federal legislation enacted in the DV arena and even went beyond the federal government on expanding DV to include dating partners, it took Minnesota over
two decades to conform to the Lautenberg Amendment on prohibiting
firearm ownership and possession for DV misdemeanants, and Alaska has
never passed a similar law. The cases for each state illustrate the ever-
present challenges in DV policymaking and implementation in a federal
system. States can be proactive on a number of dimensions to keep
women safe from their abusers, but inconsistent implementation by
police, judicial discretion, and a reluctance to both pass and implement
firearm restrictions keeps the level of danger for women far higher than it
would otherwise be.

3.3 CONCLUSION

In this chapter, we have described the evolution of the definition of DV
from a private to a public issue at both the federal and state levels. By
enacting VAWA, the federal government met the basic challenge of
defining DV as a national issue, but shared sovereignty with state governments has created a patchwork of state laws that undermine the efforts to
implement a coherent national policy. In the six case studies presented
here, we have tried to open a window into the policy feedback process
that governs the adoption of, or failure to adopt, DV firearm policies.

We illustrated how conservative ideology, particularly around Second
Amendment rights, effectively stalls DV legislation and how publicized
instances of DV can draw attention to the issue and can prompt action by
state legislatures. Our case studies show just how dependent conservative
legislators, in particular Republican legislators, are on the NRA's
approval or tacit acceptance of restrictions on gun access for DV abusers.

Our qualitative evidence points to initial findings that can explain both
the progress and the limitations of policy diffusion and DV law in the
United States. At the state level, lawmakers work within the confines of
their institutional structures and personnel who are responsible for implementing the law. The enforcement and implementation of these laws is a
vital part of ensuring women's human security, and the variation in states'
capacity and willingness to do that also contributes to inconsistent and
uneven protection under the law.

The cases we presented underscore how women who live very close to
one another geographically are subject to substantially different laws in
regard to their personal safety. We discussed the active policy of the states

of Pennsylvania and West Virginia, but we did not showcase their neighboring state of Ohio because there was little to say. These three states border each other, which means that thousands of women are living within miles of each other but are subject to differing protections simply by their address. Dating partners convicted of a DV misdemeanor cannot purchase or possess a firearm in West Virginia or Pennsylvania, but they can in Ohio. Pennsylvania prohibits stalking misdemeanants from buying or possessing firearms, West Virginia authorizes courts to do so only in certain cases, and Ohio allows stalking misdemeanants to buy and/or possess firearms. This is despite the fact that DV crimes in and of themselves are no different in one state versus another.

The extent of DV also can serve as an impetus to adopt broader related laws. In some cases, a single precipitating event or multiple DV shootings received significant media attention and seemed to strike a chord with a wide base of the public, possibly because the number of casualties was high and the events involved the murders of bystanders unrelated to the original DV dispute. It is very difficult to arrive at a systematic assessment of when and why specific DV-related shootings resonate with the larger public, but it is more than plausible that it has an immediate impact on the impetus to take legislative action. In Chapter 4, we use quantitative analysis to test for the impact of factors including gun violence, vertical and horizontal policy diffusion, partisanship, ideology, support for gun control, and state legislative elections on the adoption of DV firearms laws.

4

Explaining and Predicting the Adoption of State Domestic Violence Gun Laws

The Battered Women's Movement born of the Feminist Movement of the 1960s adopted the mantra "we will not be beaten" to shine a light on an epidemic that had been ignored for far too long (National Center on Domestic and Sexual Violence, 2008). As we discussed in Chapter 2, the federal government as well as state governments had done very little to address the millions of women who were abused by intimate partners. Recognizing the precarious position of these victims, advocates rallied in support of policies that would make divorce easier and provide shelters and related services for victims of domestic violence (DV). Even though it took more than a decade, the movement drew sufficient attention to the issue that the federal government took action and enacted the Violence Against Women Act (VAWA) in 1994. As we describe in Chapters 1 and 2, VAWA was landmark legislation that recognized DV as an acute policy problem worthy of national attention. In particular, VAWA included provisions to limit access to guns for DV abusers; it banned individuals who are convicted of a felony and any spouse or former spouse who was under a permanent restraining order from owning or possessing a firearm.

Building on the qualitative evidence from Chapter 3, we constructed a unique dataset of domestic violence firearm laws (DVFLs) across all 50 states to predict their adoption at the state level. Our results complement what we learned from Chapter 3: that state ideology and vertical policy diffusion influence the likelihood of adopting these laws and in unique ways. This chapter highlights the inequality among women across states in DV policy.

4.1 IMPACT OF FEDERAL AND STATE DOMESTIC VIOLENCE FIREARM LAWS

It bears repeating that nearly 50 percent of women who are murdered as a result of DV are killed by a firearm (Centers for Disease Control and Prevention, 2021). Other studies find that when there is an available firearm, women's vulnerability to murder increases by 500 percent (Campbell et al., 2003). In 2021, the gun safety organization Everytown for Gun Safety asserted that each month, 57 women are murdered by gun by a domestic partner and that these types of violent crimes were on the rise.

As we discussed in Chapter 2, the Lautenberg Amendment sponsored in 1996 by Sen. Frank Lautenberg (Democrat, New Jersey) expanded VAWA prohibition on firearm access to misdemeanors, specifically "anyone convicted of a "misdemeanor crime of domestic violence" (US Department of Justice, 2014). A key component of the Lautenberg Amendment was that it could be applied to individuals who had committed DV before it became law. Consequently, individuals who had already been convicted of misdemeanor DV assaults or a previous general assault against a DV victim were not allowed to own or possess a firearm. Both the 1994 VAWA legislation and the 1996 Lautenberg Amendment failed to extend their provisions to dating partners, a policy omission that took Congress 26 years to address. Simultaneous to and following the passage of VAWA and the Lautenberg Amendment, states began passing a variety of DVFLs that restricted firearm access by abusers, which put state laws more closely in line with federal policies.

DV policy and firearm regulation intersect in a way that is different from many other policy issues. DV is typically subsumed into the category of policy addressing women's physical safety and security and is meant to apply to women from all backgrounds. Issues regarding safety and security are typically supported by elected officials who hold a range of ideological and partisan positions. In contrast, limiting access to firearms is seen as a type of gun regulation. Since the initial passage of VAWA and the Lautenberg Amendment, politics has become increasingly fraught over the issue of gun control, and DV measures have become more entangled in polarized politics. For example, VAWA was enacted in 1994 with bipartisan votes in the both houses of the US Congress and the same was true of the Lautenberg Amendment two years later (US Congress, 1997).

Contrast that range of political support with what happened in 2021 in the US House of Representatives where the Democrats had majority control considered VAWA reauthorization. In the vote, 172 Republicans opposed the reauthorization because it would expand limitations on firearms to individuals who had committed violence against victims they were dating (as opposed to being married, living together, or formerly married or living together). According to the Center for Disease Control and Prevention, intimate partner violence is defined as "physical violence, sexual violence, stalking and psychological aggression (including coercive tactics) by a current or former intimate partner (i.e. spouse, boyfriend/girlfriend, dating partner, or ongoing sexual partner)" (Walters, Chen, and Breiding, 2013). For purposes of classification, couples who are of the "same or opposite sex" qualify as intimate partners. Additionally, couples who have a "child in common and a previous relationship but no current relationship, then by definition they fit into the category of former intimate partner" (Walters et al, 2013). As we noted earlier, closing the "boyfriend loophole" would not likely have been controversial except for the fact that it was portrayed by gun rights groups at the time as further limiting Second Amendment rights (Obeidallah, 2021).

Several studies have shown that laws that limit access to guns for abusers are effective in reducing mortality associated with DV. Raissian (2016) demonstrates that the Lautenberg Amendment diminished women's deaths from intimate partner violence (IPV) and lowered the deaths of male children from DV. Diez et al. (2017) and Zeoli et al. (2018) both found that coupling firearm restrictions with restraining orders and ordering gun removals from individuals under restraining orders reduced intimate partner deaths. Zeoli et al. (2018) also showed that federal misdemeanor DV firearm prohibitions did lower firearm-related intimate partner homicides.[1] Little research on DV deaths considers the collateral damage that such violence produces for children who witness the death of their mother and for the bystanders who might be injured or killed by stray bullets from a domestic abuser's gun. Taking guns out of the hands of DV abusers can help to prevent fatal injury of their victims who are mostly women and children in addition to enforcement personnel who are called to the scenes of these incidents. According to one study, one of the most dangerous situations that law enforcement members face can be in responding to domestic disturbances (Georgia Commission on Family Violence, 2018).

---

[1] This reflects the updated analysis Zeoli et al. (2018) published in the retraction of their original article.

In this chapter, we explain the policy adoption of DVFLs from 1990 to 2017, shedding light on the limitations of vertical policy diffusion on a policy area that has become increasingly partisan and polarized. Specifically, we analyze the variation in state laws on gun possession or ownership for individuals who have threatened DV, been arrested for DV, or been convicted of a DV-related crime. We do this by providing an analysis of state adoption of DVFLs in the eight categories that follow across all 50 states from 1990 through 2017; the number in parenthesis indicates how many states adopted the law. We list each state and its DVFLs in Table 4.1.

1. *Prohibit domestic violence misdemeanants from buying or possessing firearms or ammunition (28).* The 1996 Lautenberg Amendment at the federal level intended to stop those convicted of DV crimes from buying or owning guns. However, the law applies only to misdemeanor DV offenses when it "includes an element requiring proof of the use or attempted use of physical force, or the threatened use of a deadly weapon against the victim. The offender must be a current or former spouse, parent, or guardian of the victim; a person with whom the victim shares a child; a person with whom the victim has cohabitated or is cohabitating as a spouse, parent, or guardian; or a person 'similarly situated' to a spouse, parent, or guardian of the victim" (Halstead, 2001, p. 2). Because the law was narrowly written, it has many loopholes, most obviously that it rests almost entirely on physical violence when we know there are many nonphysical forms of DV that can be equally damaging if not more so. Through 2018, 27 states had passed their own prohibitions on buying or possessing a firearm or ammunition for those convicted of domestic abuse.

2. *Prohibit subjects of domestic violence restraining orders (DVROs) that are issued after notice and a hearing from purchasing or possessing firearms (35).* Protective orders, also referred to as restraining orders, are essential parts of DV civil remedies. They "can direct a batterer to avoid any kind of contact with a victim and to refrain from assaulting or threatening her. In addition, these orders may contain directives concerning custody, visitation arrangements, child support, and access to housing" (Goodman and Epstein, 2008, p. 79). It is important to remember that protective order laws vary from state to state and are meant to be flexible according to the victims' needs. Despite the benefits these protective orders can provide, they are still not enforced well by

TABLE 4.1. *DVFLs by state (2017)*

State	Prohibit DV Misdemeanants from Buying or Possessing Firearms or Ammunition	Prohibit Subjects of Permanent DVROs Issued after Notice and Hearing from Purchasing or Possessing Firearms	Dating Partners Convicted of DV Misdemeanors Not Allowed to Purchase or Possess a Firearm[a]	Prohibit Individuals Convicted of Felony Stalking from Buying or Possessing Firearms
Alabama	Yes	Yes	No	Yes
Alaska	No	Authorize courts in certain cases	Yes	No
Arizona	Yes	Authorize courts in certain cases	Yes	Yes
Arkansas	No	No	No	Yes
California	Yes	Yes	Yes	Yes
Colorado	Yes	Yes	Yes	Yes
Connecticut	Yes	Yes	Yes	No
Delaware	Yes	Yes	Yes	Yes
Florida	No	Yes	No	No
Georgia	No	No	No	No
Hawaii	No	Yes	Yes	Yes
Idaho	No	No	No	No
Illinois	Yes	Yes	Yes	Yes
Indiana	Yes	Authorize courts in certain cases	Yes	Yes
Iowa	Yes	Yes	No	No
Kansas	No	No	No	No
Kentucky	No	No	No	Yes
Louisiana	Yes	Yes	Yes	No
Maine	Yes	Yes	No	No
Maryland	Yes	Yes	No	Yes
Massachusetts	Yes	Yes	Yes	Yes
Michigan	No	Under certain conditions	Yes	No
Minnesota	Yes	Yes	Yes	No
Mississippi	No	No	No	No
Missouri	No	No	No	No
Montana	No	No	No	No
Nebraska	Yes	Under certain conditions	No	No

(continued)

TABLE 4.1. (*continued*)

State	Prohibit DV Misdemeanants from Buying or Possessing Firearms or Ammunition	Prohibit Subjects of Permanent DVROs Issued after Notice and Hearing from Purchasing or Possessing Firearms	Dating Partners Convicted of DV Misdemeanors Not Allowed to Purchase or Possess a Firearm[a]	Prohibit Individuals Convicted of Felony Stalking from Buying or Possessing Firearms
Nevada	Yes	Yes	Yes	No
New Hampshire	No	Yes	Yes	No
New Jersey	Yes	Yes	Yes	Yes
New Mexico	No	No	No	No
New York	No	Yes	Yes	No
North Carolina	No	No	Yes*	No
North Dakota	Yes	Authorize courts in certain cases	No	No
Ohio	No	No	No	No
Oklahoma	No	No	No	No
Oregon	Yes	Yes	No	No
Pennsylvania	Yes	Yes	Yes	Yes
Rhode Island	Yes	Yes	Yes	Yes
South Carolina	No	No	No	Yes
South Dakota	Yes	No	No	No
Tennessee	Yes	Yes	No	No
Texas	Yes	Yes	Yes	Yes
Utah	Yes	Yes	Yes	No
Vermont	Yes	Authorize courts in certain cases	Yes	Yes
Virginia	No	Yes	No	No
Washington	Yes	Yes	Yes	No
West Virginia	Yes	Yes	Yes	No
Wisconsin	No	Yes	Yes	Yes
Wyoming	No	No	No	No
Total (Yes)	28	35	26	20

[a]This is known as closing the boyfriend loophole: federal law did not extend prohibitions to owning or purchasing a firearm to dating partners until June 2022.

TABLE 4.1. *DVFLs by state (2017) (continued)*

State	Gun Surrender Provision for Permanent Restraining Orders	Restriction for Ex Parte Restraining Orders	Prohibit Stalking Misdemeanants from Buying or Possessing Firearms	Prohibit Concealed Carry Permits for Domestic Violence or Stalking Conviction, or under a DVRO
Alabama	No	No	Yes	Yes
Alaska	Yes	No	No	Yes
Arizona	Yes	Yes	Yes	Yes
Arkansas	No	No	Yes	Yes
California	Yes	Yes	Yes	Yes
Colorado	Yes	No	Yes	Yes
Connecticut	Yes	Yes	Yes	Yes
Delaware	Yes	Yes	Yes	Yes
Florida	Yes	No	No	No
Georgia	No	No	No	No
Hawaii	Yes	Yes	Yes	No
Idaho	No	No	No	Yes
Illinois	Yes	Yes	Yes	Yes
Indiana	Yes	No	Yes	Yes
Iowa	Yes	No	No	Yes
Kansas	No	No	No	Yes
Kentucky	No	No	No	Yes
Louisiana	Yes	No	No	Yes
Maine	Yes	Yes	No	Yes
Maryland	Yes	Yes	Yes	Yes
Massachusetts	Yes	Yes	Yes	Yes
Michigan	No	No	No	Yes
Minnesota	Yes	No	Yes	Yes
Mississippi	No	No	No	No
Missouri	No	No	No	Yes
Montana	No	No	No	No
Nebraska	No	No	No	Yes
Nevada	Yes	No	No	Yes
New Hampshire	Yes	Yes	No	Yes
New Jersey	Yes	Yes	Yes	Yes
New Mexico	No	No	No	Yes

(*continued*)

TABLE 4.1. (*continued*)

State	Gun Surrender Provision for Permanent Restraining Orders	Restriction for Ex Parte Restraining Orders	Prohibit Stalking Misdemeanants from Buying or Possessing Firearms	Prohibit Concealed Carry Permits for Domestic Violence or Stalking Conviction, or under a DVRO
New York	Yes	Yes	Yes	Yes
North Carolina	Yes	No	Yes	Yes
North Dakota	Yes	No	Yes	No
Ohio	No	No	No	Yes
Oklahoma	No	No	No	Yes
Oregon	No	No	No	No
Pennsylvania	Yes	Yes	Yes	Yes
Rhode Island	Yes	Yes	Yes	Yes
South Carolina	No	No	Yes	Yes
South Dakota	No	No	No	No
Tennessee	Yes	No	Yes	Yes
Texas	No	Yes	Yes	Yes
Utah	No	Yes	No	No
Vermont	No	No	Yes	Yes
Virginia	No	Yes	Yes	Yes
Washington	Yes	Yes	Yes	Yes
West Virginia	No	Yes	No	Yes
Wisconsin	Yes	No	Yes	Yes
Wyoming	No	No	No	No
Total	27	19	26	40

Source: Laws compiled from Giffords Law Center, https://lawcenter.giffords.org/gun-laws/policy-areas/who-can-have-a-gun/domestic-violence-firearms/#state; Everytown for Gun Safety, "Gun Law Navigator: Domestic Violence" (2021); Zeoli et al. (2018).

law enforcement and often assume that women want to end a relationship with their abuser, which may not be possible or wanted (Goodman and Epstein, 2008). Many states prohibit those who have restraining orders against them from owning or purchasing a firearm; 29 states have an outright ban and an additional 7 states have a ban under certain conditions.

3. *Dating partners convicted of domestic violence misdemeanors cannot purchase or possess a firearm (26).* As mentioned previously, one of the most glaring omissions of federal DV gun prohibitions is that they do not extend to dating partners. Just over half of the states have passed some kind of law that closes the boyfriend loophole. Some states have extended this prohibition to dating partners under protective orders as well.

4. *Prohibit stalking felons from buying or possessing firearms (20).* As we discussed in Chapter 3, stalking is not always included in DV statutes despite being a common and deadly form of abuse. More states have begun adding these prohibitions in recent years; to date, fewer than half of the states have some form of gun prohibitions on individuals who are convicted of stalking.

5. *Gun surrender provision for permanent restraining orders (27).* States vary in terms of requiring individuals who are under DV-related restraining orders to surrender their firearms for the duration of the restraining order. While 27 states have adopted a law that requires firearm surrender, the circumstances of that surrender differ considerably depending upon the state. For example, a state may require a judge to mandate the surrender of firearms within a set time period, not immediately. Or a state may allow a judge to order the surrender of a firearm but not to mandate it. And even under a firearm surrender order, an individual may be allowed to give it to a third party who registers with the court as having possession of the firearm rather than turning it into law enforcement directly. The lack of uniformity in DV restraining order firearm surrender policies across states therefore produces uneven levels of safety for DV victims .

6. *Restriction for ex parte restraining orders (19).* States have enacted laws that give courts the power to issue a temporary restraining order and prohibit possession or ownership of firearms before a hearing occurs on the request for a temporary restraining order. This law can help protect women in emergency situations who are under direct threat of violence from a domestic partner. However, fewer than half of the states have this law in place.

7. *Prohibit stalking misdemeanants from buying or possessing firearms (26).* Just over half of the states prohibit stalking felons from purchasing or possessing a firearm, but more states are prohibiting stalking misdemeanants from doing so. To date, 26 states have some form of gun prohibitions on individuals who are convicted of misdemeanor stalking.

8. *Prohibit concealed carry permits for individuals with DV or stalking conviction or under a DVRO (40).* States have enacted laws that limit or prohibit such individuals or those who are under a DVRO from securing a concealed carry permit and/or carrying a concealed firearm. More than a majority of states have either or both of these restrictions on concealed carry of firearms in effect.

4.2 POLICY DIFFUSION AND FEDERALISM

Domestic violence is a significant policy issue that cuts across demographic, economic, and geographic lines. The majority of female homicides are by someone they know, and record keeping on DV typically underestimates the extent of familial or domestic connection that women have to their killers. More than 9,000 women were murdered due to DV between 2003 and 2017 and nearly 50 percent of the homicides that were reported were completed with a firearm (Centers for Disease Control and Prevention, 2021).

We argue that whether or not a state passes DVFLs is crucial to understanding women's equality in the United States because nearly half of all women who are murdered by DV abusers die by firearm. If a DV abuser can more easily obtain or keep a gun in one state, but not another, there is inequality in human security between the women who live in each state. In the former, a woman is rendered far less safe than in the latter. Many notable feminist and federalism scholars have shown that policies that pertain to women are typically handled at the state and local levels with varying laws and punishments for equivalent crimes (Resnik, 2002; Watts, 2005; Sawer and Vickers, 2016). If a DV perpetrator is required to relinquish his or her gun in one state under certain conditions but not in a neighboring state, we argue that women are necessarily rendered unequal in their personal safety across state lines. We also believe that DVFLs should be included in policy diffusion studies as a category by itself rather than being tangentially covered by broader harassment or stalking policies that are not necessarily intimate partner based.

In the earliest approaches to how policy spreads across states, scholars hypothesized that the adoption of policy fell along horizontal lines. The conclusions of scholarship on horizontal policy diffusion have been varied with some authors arguing that states do not learn from each other even when they are in same general region of the country or have similar political ideologies (Walker, 1969; Mooney, 2001; Shipan and Volden, 2008). Other work, such as that by Grossback, Nicholson-Crotty, and

Peterson (2004, p. 540), finds that learning can take place across state governments, but it is contingent not on regional location but on strong bonds of ideological perspectives. More recently, students of policy diffusion have departed more strongly from confidence in the idea of horizontal policy diffusion to one that encompasses networks of policy-makers and lawmakers in conjunction with ideology that forms the basis for innovation across policy issue spaces (Graham, Shipan, and Volden, 2013; Mallinson, 2019; LaCombe and Boehmke, 2020; Mooney, 2020).

In contrast, vertical policy diffusion is characterized by policy adoption at different levels of government from federal to state to local. The work of Berry and Berry (1990) argues that federal or state governments can "coerce" lower levels of government to adopt and implement a policy. Coercion most typically happens by granting or withholding financial assistance, and the potential for successful coercion can be a function of a state's fiscal capacity alone and relative to lower levels of government (Kim, McDonald, and Lee, 2018). Vertical policy diffusion does not happen in a vacuum; in particular, states may respond to federal policies by looking at whether other states have adopted or complied with them and how well they have fared in doing so. As Gilardi and Wasserfallen (2019) argue, states do not want to miss out on the advantages of federal funding that comes with federal policy change, but at the same time, they consider how other states that they view as similar to their own ideologically or econom-ically respond to federal action. In this chapter, we test the impact of both horizontal and vertical policy diffusion in the area of DV firearm policy.

Figure 4.1 provides the chronology of the enactments of DVFLs by state with notations for the passage of federal legislation. We know from the detailed federal DV policy analysis in Chapter 2 that Sen. Joe Biden (Democrat, Delaware) introduced VAWA twice prior to its 1994 passage. In 1990, the bill was introduced with wider punishments for sex offenders and created federal grants for DV law enforcement and prosecution but did not make it out of committee. In 1991, he introduced it again and increased the number of cosponsors from 26 to 56, including both Democrats and Republicans, but this version also failed to be reported out by the commit-tee. By the time he introduced his third version of the bill in January 1993, Sen. Biden had secured 67 cosponsors in the Senate from both sides of the political aisle, and the bill ultimately passed in 1994. Understanding this sequence of bills sponsorship by Biden on DV sheds light on the extent to which this issue was becoming more prominent on the national scene generally and at the state level during these years.

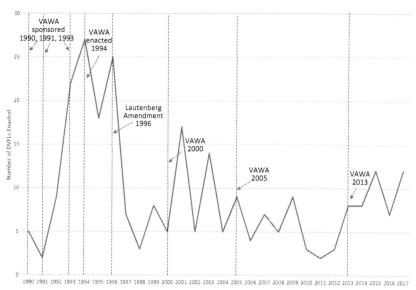

FIGURE 4.1 **Total number of DVFLs passed each year across the United States, 1990–2017**
This figure shows the relationship between state-passed DVFLs and Congressional legislation in the issue area of DV for the period stated.
Author constructed data set. This figure also appears in Schiller and Sidorsky (2022, p. 5).

The political environment in which Sen. Biden pressed for passage of VAWA was shifting toward increasing attention on the issue of the security of women from sexual harassment as well as sexual and physical violence. The combination of the Anita Hill Supreme Court hearings by the Senate Judiciary Committee, which Sen. Biden chaired, and the larger number of women who were elected to Congress in 1992 provided more support for enacting policies that addressed DV. As Karch (2012, p. 49) explains, getting issues on the policy agenda is a large part of the challenge to the policymaking process, and drawing public "visibility" to an issue is an essential first step in that process. The attention paid to VAWA at the federal level generated the type of visibility to which Karch refers, and it was sufficient to engage state level lawmakers in this issue space.

Figure 4.1 also presents the rate of DVFL adoption by states and highlights three key trends. First, DV was on the federal policy agenda in the years leading up to DVFL adoption at the state level, which may indicate that the federal government was signaling states that they too should address this issue. To that end, 22 states enacted DVFLs in the years prior to the initial enactment of VAWA, which suggests a more complex directional picture of DV policy evolution.[2] Second, it appears that there was much more legislative activity on DV firearm regulation in the 1990s as compared to the 2000s with a steep decline between 2005 and 2013. Third, most DVFL policymaking at the state level occurred in the years encompassing the passage of both VAWA and the Lautenberg Amendment: 22 laws in 1993, 27 laws in 1994, 18 laws in 1995, and 25 laws in 1996.

When we explore the types of DVFL laws that were enacted, we find that restraining order restrictions and firearm surrenders, ex parte laws, and the misdemeanor and felony stalking laws were adopted in the early part of the time period under study here. Restrictions on concealed carry permits related to DV had a more interrupted pattern of adoption, passing between 1994 to 1997 and then between 2004 to 2015. Table 4.2 shows the years, states, and number of DVFLs enacted from 1990 to 2017. States frequently enacted multiple DVFLs at one time; in 1994, for example, 11 states enacted 27 DVFLs; 6 of these states adopted multiple laws: Massachusetts adopted 5 and Virginia adopted 4. As Krutz (2001) argued in his work on omnibus legislating, enacting multiple laws in a single policy area can be helpful in weakening resistance to single laws considered independently.

The history of federal and state legislation in the area of DVFLs supports the assertion that vertical policy diffusion exists. However, there are varying levels of influence associated with VAWA; the descriptive data suggest that both VAWA's initial adoption and the passage of the Lautenberg Amendment appear to have had a strong impact on state policy adoption, but subsequent reauthorizations in 2000, 2005, and 2013 do not. It may be that the strength of vertical policy diffusion ebbs with bill reauthorizations. A second explanation from the qualitative analysis in Chapter 3 suggests that the increasingly polarizing nature of firearm laws decreased the chances for vertical policy diffusion for DVFLs at the state level, starting shortly after the adoption of the Lautenberg Amendment.

---

[2] New Jersey, California, and Colorado adopted DVFLs in 1990. The New Jersey and California legislatures were controlled by the Democratic Party while the Republican Party controlled Colorado's state legislature. New York and New Jersey were the only two states to adopt DVFLs in 1991 while a wider range of states (Illinois, Delaware, Minnesota, Iowa, Alabama, and Massachusetts) adopted some of these laws in 1992. Of the 10 states that passed the 22 DVFLs in 1993, the state legislatures of five were controlled by the Democratic Party. While Democratic-leaning states seemed more likely to pass DVFLs prior to VAWA in 1994, Republican states did so also.

TABLE 4.2. *Passage of DVFLs by year*

Year	Number of States that Enacted a DVFL	Number of States that Enacted Multiple DVFLs	Total Number of DVFLs Enacted
1990	3	1	5
1991	2	0	2
1992	6	3	9
1993	10	8	22
1994	11	6	27
1995	11	4	18
1996	11	8	25
1997	5	1	7
1998	2	1	3
1999	4	2	8
2000	4	1	5
2001	8	4	17
2002	3	1	5
2003	11	2	14
2004	5	1	6
2005	5	3	9
2006	2	2	4
2007	5	1	7
2008	3	2	5
2009	5	3	9
2010	1	1	3
2011	1	1	2
2012	2	1	3
2013	5	3	8
2014	3	2	8
2015	6	4	12
2016	4	3	7
2017	6	3	12
Total	144	72	262

This table presents the number of DVFLs passed by states, including the number of laws passed in the same year.
Source: Constructed from author database.

Although vertical policy diffusion comes with a type of forced coercion in terms of withholding of funds, for example, we have not found evidence of it in this policy issue area. Not only has the federal government not made use of mandates to force states to enact DVFLs but also it does not even use the tools at its disposal to provide incentives for states to do so. Our analysis of the Office of Violence Against Women grants discussed in Chapter 2 finds that the federal government neither requires nor encourages states to enact laws that comply with federal law as proscribed in the Lautenberg Amendment.[3] The 2000 reauthorization of VAWA has not included any coercive measures either. The 2005 VAWA linked Services, Training, Officers, and Prosecutors Formula Grant Program (STOP) to attempts by states to make sure that DV offenders know that they cannot own or possess a firearm but did not mandate that steps force them to surrender their guns (Sacco, 2019, pp. 27–28).

As we also showed in Chapter 2, states that have failed to pass any DVFL have still been given federal grant money, which sheds some doubt on the reliance on vertical policy diffusion as the main explanatory variable for the enactment of DVFLs at the state level. It can still be argued that federal policymaking draws sufficient attention to a policy issue and that it spurs states to action in that arena but in conjunction with other variables ranging from shifts in party policies as a result of advocacy activism and more general "normative" pressure to address women's security. (Weldon, 2002, 2006; Gilardi and Wasserfallen, 2019). At the same time, ideological and partisan shifts in attitudes toward related issue areas, such as gun control, can act to thwart vertical policy diffusion in the area of DVFL. Indeed, the reduction in the enactment of DVFLs after VAWA and the Lautenberg Amendment were enacted at the federal level is in line with intensifying political polarization on gun control policy and an increase in the number of state governments that are wholly controlled by conservative Republicans, which we discuss next.

4.3 POLITICAL POLARIZATION AND THE PASSAGE OF DOMESTIC VIOLENCE FIREARM LAWS

As we have discussed here, polarization centering on the issue of Second Amendment rights and firearm regulation has increased significantly since VAWA was enacted in 1994 with strong bipartisan support. Today, Republican opposition to the extension of protections from gun violence by dating partners in VAWA was so strong that it blocked attempts to reauthorize the legislation in 2021. According to the research report by Parker et al. (2017), which was funded by the Pew Foundation in 2000, 20 percent of Democrats versus 38 percent of Republicans felt it was

---

[3] The Office of Violence Against Women Office lists grant awards by state dating back to 2005. The list of awards can be found at www.justice.gov/ovw/awards.

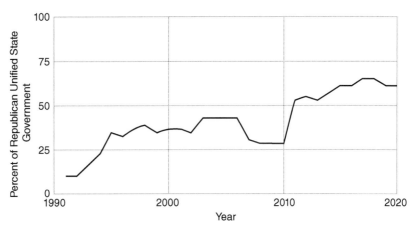

FIGURE 4.2 Percent of Republican unified state governments, 1990–2020
This author-generated graph depicts the rise in the number of state governments
that were under Republican unified party control from 1990 to 2020. This figure
also appears in Schiller and Sidorsky (2022, p. 8).

important to protect gun rights, but by 2017, 76 percent of Republicans
said it was important to protect gun rights whereas 22 percent of
Democrats agreed.[4]

The growing control of state governments by the Republican Party
over the past two decades has also been a factor in explaining the
adoption of DVFLs across states. Figure 4.2 shows the percentage of
Republican unified state governments from 1990 to 2020, demonstrating
a steady increase in Republican control of the legislative and executive
branches. Along with the shift toward Republican control of state governments, scholars have demonstrated that the party's ideology has
grown more extreme (Levendusky, 2009). Other research has shown that
the elite members of both major political parties perceive that there are
greater benefits from confronting each other than cooperating with each
other, which produces difficult conditions for enacting any gun control
laws including DVFLs.

---

[4] Goss (2015) notes that one of the few areas where gun control measures were enacted was
in the area of mental health. She finds that the presence of a focusing event (such as a mass
shooting) was the impetus for almost half of the laws that were passed regarding gun
control and mental health. We test for the effects of mass shootings in our analysis and it
was not statistically significant (see Model 9. Table 4.8).

Attitudes on gun control policy can be determined a range of factors. One study by Godwin and Schroedel (2000) found that firearm limitations adopted by local governments between 1994 and 1998 were a function of population density, educational levels, and Democratic Party affiliations; it was more likely that a locality enacted gun control with higher levels of these variables. Additionally, Godwin and Schroedel found that a firearm regulation characterized as a public health and safety concern was more acceptable, even though such policy faced significant obstacles from advocates who make arguments about preserving Second Amendment rights and oppose the costs of regulations. In his work, Lacombe (2019) shows how the National Rifle Association (NRA) has worked to build an entire "social identity" around gun possession and ownership, and Mason (2018) demonstrates how that social identity can subsequently support an ideology that informs views on public policies including but not limited to gun control. Another study (Joslyn et al., 2017) found interesting patterns of the impact of owning a gun versus not owning a gun on voting behavior; gun ownership was a stronger explanatory variable than other more typical variables such as education and had influence equal to that of race and party identification. All of these studies point to the resonant impact that attitudes on gun control and Second Amendment rights alone and interaction with partisanship have on American politics more broadly. We explore this impact on DV laws in the sections that follow.

These trends in ideology and partisanship can serve as the foundation for our exploration of the variables that explain and predict the adoption of DVFLs. Scholars have documented the interaction of partisanship, ideology, and attitudes on gun control (see Goss, 2015; Hetherington and Rudolph, 2015; Mason, 2015; Ryan et al., 2020), and we expect that states that are wholly controlled by Republicans or display conservative ideology will be less inclined to enact DVFLSs. Moreover, the divisions associated with gun control and polarization tend to be more pronounced during election years, which yields the expectation that state legislatures and governors will be less likely to support DVFLs in years when they are facing reelection.

Overall, the policy issue of DV and its associated injury and mortality, especially when firearms are present, is an understudied arena in which to study horizontal and vertical policy diffusion and the impact of ideology and partisanship on policy enactments. The remainder of this chapter presents the results of our quantitative analysis of these dynamics.

4.4 RESEARCH DESIGN AND METHODS

The following sections, including research design, methods, data analysis and results, are derived in part from an article published by Schiller and Sidorsky (2022). For our study, we created a dataset with DVFLs spanning eight categories, homicide data, and political control variables for all 50 states. The selection of DVFLs we used in this study built on the compilation by Zeoli et al. (2018) by supplementing it with data available from Everytownresearch.org.[5] It is our primary interest in this chapter to identify the factors that explain and predict which states might adopt DVFLs and in what years. We focus on explaining the variation around one dependent variable: whether a state enacted any of the eight DVFLs under study between 1990 and 2017.

We treat the dependent variable whether to adopt a DVFL or not. as a binary choice. Within the policy literature domain, event history analysis (EHA) has been the most commonly employed type of analysis to explain policy adoption at the state or local level. Numerous variants of EHA are used in policy adoption research (e.g., Berry and Berry, 1990; Godwin and Schroedel, 2000; Mooney, 2001; Shipan and Volden, 2008; Smith, 2019). Buckley and Westerland (2004) make the argument that the fundamental assumptions underlying event history models are frequently violated with state policy adoption models. One of the most significant assumptions is that policy adoptions are adopted independently of each other, which is unrealistic. Moreover, the method of dropping states from the analysis after they adopt a policy skews the distribution of the dependent variable toward 0 over time, which makes an accurate estimate of parameter effects more difficult.

Our data has both challenges. Our dependent variable, DVFL, is measured as 1 if the state enacted any one of the eight DVFLs in a given year and 0 if not; out of 1,400 observations of 50 states, there are 144

---

[5] Our data collection preceded the publication of the Zeoli et. al. (2018) research, but shortly after it was published the authors of that study graciously shared their compilation of laws and effective dates with us. We have confirmed the year of passage and extended the set of laws to include state legislation on concealed carry permits for firearms. There is considerable variation in the implementation of all these laws across states. For example, on the issue of surrendering firearms, some states will require that surrender within a set timeframe while other states will refrain from setting a specific time line. Some states will allow judges to require the surrender of the firearms while other states maintain that policy as law but do not give judges the power to require specific individuals to do so. Also, see Everytown for Gun Safety.

state-year combinations when states passed at least one of the DVFL across these eight categories. In our sample, as noted, many of the states adopt one or more of these laws or revisit an existing law to amend it. Buckley and Westerland (2004) offer several remedies to the errors produced by the violations of EHA assumptions; among them is the use of logistic regression with robust standard errors and/or clustering on states. We chose to employ logistic regression, clustering on states, to analyze DVFL adoption at the state level. We code our dependent variable as a binary variable as 1 if a state passed any law in a given year in the eight categories we delineate, and 0 if the state did not pass any law.

Our goal is to identify the factors that might explain when and why states choose to act in this policy domain on any level. As discussed earlier, federal and state policy diffusion may play a role in state policy adoption in the area of DV; based on existing research, we expect vertical policy diffusion to be a more powerful predictor of state policy adoption in this arena. To assess the extent of vertical policy diffusion, we created variables measuring the passage of VAWA and subsequent related amendments and reauthorizations. To measure horizontal policy diffusion, we included two variables: one measures whether a contiguous neighboring state enacts a DVFL, and the other variable measures the number of states within the same region that enact a DVFL.

When states initiate and consider new policy, they note where their neighboring states stand on that issue, both through bureaucratic learning and regarding examples of the policy's success (Smith, 2019). We expect that when a neighboring state or multiple states within the same region adopt a DVFL, other states may do so as well. We lagged our horizontal diffusion variables by one year to provide time for a state to assess the policy adoptions by their neighboring and regional states. We also included a variable named policy innovation index to measure the impact of policy innovation by states using the State Policy Innovation and Diffusion Database (Boehmke et al., 2018). This is a broad and inclusive database that includes a range of policy topics but does not include DV firearm policies specifically.[6]

---

[6] We also tested the impact of two other commonly used variables to explain state policy-making: state culture using Elazar's 1966 typology; (Leckrone, 2013), and a measure of state legislative professionalism constructed by the National Council of State Legislatures ([NCSL] 2017). Elazar's typology includes three categories: moralistic (community oriented), traditionalistic (elite security centered), and individualistic (limited government role). In the arena of DV policy, we might expect that as one moves across these categories,

Gun homicides as an indicator of overall violence should also prompt state legislators to take action to keep guns out of the hands of DV abusers. There are a number of ways to measure gun homicides using the FBI Uniform Crime Reporting Data that we have available. We chose to use the absolute number of gun homicides rather than a per capita or percentage measure because our expectation is that the political impact of gun deaths on constituents and legislators can be powerful with even just one egregious DV firearm murder. We present results of models that were run with a measure of gun homicides per 100,000 residents as well as measures of deaths of women at the hands of family members and mass shootings, the latter defined as three or more gun deaths, to assess whether an external event like these may systematically prompt states to take action in this issue domain.

At the same time, we recognize that partisan and ideological positions on gun rights may have an impact on the likelihood of adopting a restrictive gun law even when it is intended to save the lives of DV victims. As mentioned earlier, the Republican Party has long been actively associated with the NRA. In her 2019 work, Smucker demonstrated how legislators worked to dampen NRA opposition to passing DVFLs in order to garner Republican support for them. We expect states that are under unified Republican control will be less likely to pass DVFLs. We also construct an alternative model using the state ideology; conservative ideology is associated with support for Second Amendment rights to own guns with as few restrictions as possible. For citizen ideology, we use the data from Berry et al. (2010) and Fording (2018) who compute state ideology on a scale of 1–100 through a combination of interest group ratings of members of Congress on certain issue areas, the ideology score of the congressional incumbent and the person's challenger (estimated if necessary), and district election results (Fording, 2018). To measure support or opposition to firearm regulations, we collected data on the number of state residents who purchase hunting firearm licenses as Kivisto et al. (2019) used in their study of firearm ownership and homicide.

---

the state would be less inclined to enact DV laws, especially firearm laws. We use the NCSL measure of state legislative professionalism: full-time (i.e., sufficient salary by itself and large staff), hybrid (i.e., need outside income to supplement legislative salary and medium-size staffs), and part-time (i.e., salary insufficient to live on and small staffs). We might expect that with professionalism as one moves from part-time to full-time legislatures, states would be more likely to enact DV laws. Neither of these variables was statistically significant or changed any of the outcomes in our models and was dropped from the analysis.

To further understand the role that party and ideology play in the adoption or failure to adopt DVFLs, Wyoming and Mississippi, both of which failed to adopt any DVFLs over our time period, were the extreme examples. Wyoming has had strong Republican control across the governorship (17 years) and Republican legislature (30 years) for the majority of the years that DVFLs have been adopted. Its citizen ideology ranks among the lowest across all states with an average value of 29.1 over this time period (on a scale from 1 to 100). Mississippi looks to be the reverse in that its governor's mansion has been occupied by Republicans longer (24 years), but its state legislature has been under unified Republican control for only 8 years. Mississippi ranks only slightly higher in citizen ideology with an average value of 36.4. Additionally, the average percentage of women in the legislature in Mississippi was below the national average. We would expect Republican partisan control of state government and conservative ideology to make the passage and implementation of DVFLs difficult to achieve.

In terms of gender, we might expect that a higher number of female legislators would pay more attention to DV as Brown (2014) shows in her work on African American female state legislators in Maryland. But it is also equally plausible that that gender does not influence whether or not someone supports measures for DV. Whitesell (2019) did not find that women legislators were more likely to support more generous welfare policies for DV survivors, arguing that "even policy makers who are usually opposed to generous welfare policies may perceive this subgroup as deserving of aid" (pp. 515–516). The data on female members of state legislatures are available going back to 1990, but the racial breakdown of state legislators is more difficult to find for our time period. As such, we include a measure of the percentage of legislators who are female in our model. We also include a measure of whether it was a state legislative election year on the rationale that restricting access to guns is a controversial issue that could deter legislators from taking on the issue of gun control and DV.

Table 4.3 lists the variables and their coding for all the models.

4.5 RESULTS AND DISCUSSION

In Model 1 (represented in Figure 4.3 and Table 4.4), we report the results of predicting the probability of adopting a DVFL as a function of the number of gun homicides (lagged) interacted with (1) whether the state government was under unified Republican control, (2) whether a

TABLE 4.3. *Variable statistics and coding*

Variable	Range	Mean	Standard Deviation	Coding
Dependent variable DVFL	0,1	0.10	0.30	1=State passed any DVFL per year 0=State did not pass any DVFL per year
Independent variables				
Gun homicides	0–2,263	188	255	Number of gun homicides reported in the state per year
Gun homicides per 100k	0–56	3.00	2.68	Number of gun homicides reported in state per 100,000 residents per year
Female murders by family member by gun	0–98	10.39	13.42	Number of women killed by a family member with a gun
Number of mass shootings (3 or more deaths)	0–3	0.06	0.26	1=Mass shooting (3 or more deaths) 0=No mass shooting
Unified Republican state government	0,1	0.27	0.45	1=Unified Republican party control of state legislature and governorship, 0=Divided party control
Citizen ideology	8.4–97.0	50.10	15.30	Using Fording (2018) scale 1–100 conservative to liberal
Neighboring state DVFL	0,1	0.31	0.46	1=Contiguous state adopted DVFL , 0=No contiguous state adopted DVFL in a given year
Number regional DVFLs	0–6	0.95	1.15	Continuous variable for the number of states in the same region that adopted DVFLs in a given year
Per capita hunting firearm licenses	0.002–4.311	0.09	0.14	Number of hunting firearm licenses issued to residents of a state per capita and per year
VAWA 1994	0,1	0.04	0.19	1=Value for the year that the VAWA was first

Variable	Range	Mean	Standard Deviation	Coding
				authorized (1994) 0=All other years
1995 one year after VAWA enactment	0.1	0.04	0.19	1=Value for the year 1995 0=All other years
2000 VAWA reauthorization	0.1	0.04	0.19	1=Value for the year 2000 0=All other years
2005 VAWA reauthorization	0.1	0.04	0.19	1=Value for the year 2005 0=All other years
2013 VAWA reauthorization	0.1	0.04	0.19	1=Value for the year 2013 0=All other years
Lautenberg Amendment 1996	0.1	0.04	0.19	1=Value for the year that the Lautenberg Amendment was enacted (1996) 0=All other years
1997 one year after Lautenberg	0.1	0.04	0.19	1=Value for 1997, 0=All other years
Legislative election year	0,1	0.47	0.50	1=Value indicating that there were regular legislative elections held, 0=No legislative elections that year
Percent of female state legislators	0.02–0.42	0.22	0.07	Percentage of female state legislators
State policy innovativeness score	0.006–0.188	0.05	0.02	Boehmke et al. (2018) Policy Innovativeness Static Score for states from 1990 to 2017.

neighboring state adopted a DVFL (lagged), (3) the number of hunting firearm licenses per capita (lagged), (4) a binary variable for 1994, which was the year of the adoption of VAWA, (5) a binary variable for 1995, the year after VAWA was passed by Congress, (6) a binary variable for the Lautenberg Amendment in 1996, which addressed gun ownership and misdemeanor DV, (7) a binary variable for 1997, which was the year after the Lautenberg Amendment passed, (8) whether it was a state legislative election year, (9) the percent of women in the state legislature, and (10) the state's policy innovativeness score.

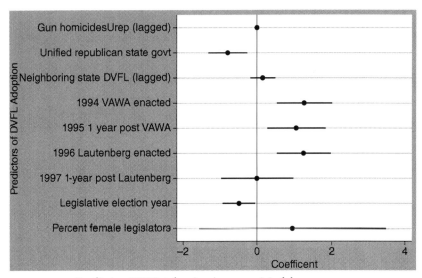

FIGURE 4.3 **Predicting DVFL adoption in states, Model 1**
This figure shows the relative impact of the independent variables included in the model on the passage of DVFLs. We find that Republican Party control of state governments decreases that likelihood as does election year, but original federal policy action increases that likelihood. Source: Author generated from original data analysis.

Unified Republican state government depresses the likelihood of adopting a DVFL by 5.6 percent (see Model 1, Table 4.4). We find that the number of gun homicides interacted with unified Republican state government has a very small but statistically significant and positive effect on the adoption of a DVFL; moving from the first quartile to the third quartile, the probability of enacting a DVFL goes up by 0.01 percent. Our additional measure of latent political support for gun rights, the per capita number of paid resident hunting firearm license holders, did not exert a statistically significant effect in this model.

States appeared to respond to the initial adoption of VAWA in 1994 and continue to adopt DVFLs in the year after its adoption. The 1994 VAWA legislation increased the likelihood of enacting a DVFL by 18 percent, and the year after its adoption, increased the likelihood of DVFL adoption by 14 percent. The Lautenberg Amendment in 1996 increased the likelihood of enacting a DVFL by about 18 percent, but there was no effect from it associated with the following year. Although there is evidence for federal vertical policy diffusion, there was no statistically significant impact on DVFL adoption by a neighboring state (measured as contiguous to a state's

TABLE 4.4. *Predicting DVFL adoption in states, Models 1 and 2*

Variable	Model 1	Impact	Model 2	Impact
Gun homicides$_{t-1}$			0.0006*	0.011
			(0.0002)	
Gun homicidesUrep$_{t-1}$	0.0015**	0.0001		
	(0.0006)			
Unified Republican state government	−0.793**	−0.056		
	(0.272)			
Citizen ideology$_{t-1}$			0.016*	0.026
			(0.006)	
Neighboring state DVFL$_{t-1}$	0.150			
	(0.173)			
Number regional DVFL$_{t-1}$			−0.041	
			(0.089)	
Per capita hunting firearm licenses$_{t-1}$	−2.421			
	(1.738)			
1994 VAWA enacted	1.280***	0.176	1.351***	0.191
	(0.380)		(0.368)	
1995 1 year post-VAWA	1.057**	0.137	1.172**	0.154
	(0.405)		(0.390)	
1996 Lautenberg enacted	1.259**	0.176	1.406***	0.200
	(0.370)		(0.389)	
1997 1 year post-Lautenberg	−0.005		0.193	
	(0.496)		(0.488)	
Legislative election year	−0.491*	−0.041	−0.498*	−0.042
	(0.232)		(0.234)	
Percent female legislators	0.949		0.775	
	(1.283)		0.0486	
Policy Innovation Index	−0.540		(7.157)	
	(8.342)		(1.371)	
Constant	−2.095***		−3.272***	
	(0.511)		(0.486)	
N	1,270		1,270	
Pseudo R²	0.047		0.043	
Prob > Chi²	0.0000		0.0000	

*p < 0.05, **p < 0.01, ***p < 0.001. Logistic regression with standard errors in parentheses, clustered on state, listed below the coefficient. The impact of statistically significant coefficients is generated through Clarify and is listed next to the coefficient. For binary independent variables, the impact reports the estimated change in the probability of adopting a DVFL as the value of the variable is changed from 0 to 1. For continuous variables, the impact reports the estimated change in probability of adopting a DVFL as the value of the variable is changed from its first quartile value to its third quartile value.

border). This follows other scholarship on policy diffusion that has not found support for horizontal policy diffusion (Walker, 1969; Mooney, 2001; Shipan and Volden, 2008). We found that states were about 4 percent less likely to adopt DVFLs in election years for the state legislature. We found no statistical significance associated with the percentage of female legislators or with the state's policy innovativeness score. This supports the findings by Whitesell (2019) that being a woman does not increase support for expanded welfare policies for DV survivors.

We also analyzed alternative specifications of our main model. When we replace gun homicides with gun homicides per 100,000 residents, the results hold (see Model 5 in Table 4.6). We also tested a variable that measures the number of women who were murdered by a family member by gun, and the results are similar (see Model 8 in Table 4.7). Lastly, we ran a model with mass shootings as a measure of firearm violence, but the parameter estimate was statistically insignificant (see Model 9 in Table 4.8). Our results on mass shootings and their lack of impact on the adoption of DVFLs is not necessarily surprising. As Goss (2015) and others have noted, over the past two decades, states have not generally responded to incidents of mass gun violence by restricting access to guns.

When we run comparable measures of Democratic state control interacted with gun homicides (see Model 4 in Table 4.5), the interactive term is statistically significant and negative, but the parameter estimate for unified Democratic state government is not statistically significant. In this model, we also find that paid hunting license holders is significant at the 0.05 level and reduces the likelihood of DVFL adoption by 2.6 percent (see Model 4 in Table 4.5). Part of what might be driving these conflicting results for each political party is the fact that over our time period (1990–2017), the state governments in the South switched their regional control from Democratic to Republican dominance. From our data, gun homicides tend to be higher in the South overall, so a state with high gun homicide numbers in the 1990s could have been controlled by Democrats but by 2017 had shifted to Republican control. For example, the legislative compositions of state legislatures in Alabama, Arkansas, Georgia, Kentucky, Louisiana, Mississippi, Oklahoma, and Tennessee were majority Democratic for that entire decade of 1990–2000 (National Council of State Legislatures). Subsequent reauthorizations in 2000, 2005, and 2013 do not exert a statistically significant impact (see Models 3 and 4 in Table 4.5). There are two potential reasons why the reauthorizations do not affect the passage of DVFLs at the state level. The first could be because no reauthorization

TABLE 4.5. *Predicting DVFL adoption in states, Models 3 and 4*

Variable	Model 3	Impact	Model 4	Impact
Gun homicides x Unified Republican Government$_{t-1}$	0.0015**	0.0001		
	(0.0006)			
Unified Republican state government	−0.782**	−0.054		
	(0.272)			
Gun homicides x Unified Democratic Government$_{t-1}$			−0.0017*	0.000
			(0.0009)	
Unified Democratic state government			−0.305	
			(−0.252)	
Neighboring state DVFL$_{t-1}$	−0.150		−0.151	
	(0.172)		(0.173)	
Per capita hunting firearm licenses$_{t-1}$	−2.426		−3.836*	−0.026
	(1.750)		(1.735)	
1994 VAWA enacted	1.299***	0.178	1.380***	0.191
	(0.371)		(0.364)	
1995 1 year post-VAWA enacted	1.036**	0.133	1.038**	0.154
	(0.403)		(0.404)	
2000 VAWA reauthorization	0.303		0.297	
	(0.549)		(0.558)	
2005 VAWA reauthorization	−0.049		−0.044	
	(0.519)		(0.519)	
2013 VAWA reauthorization	−0.489		−0.577	
	(0.615)		(0.614)	
1996 Lautenberg enacted	1.273**	0.170	1.279***	0.200
	(0.372)		(0.375)	
1997 1 year post-Lautenberg	0.017		−0.020	
	(0.495)		(0.484)	
Legislative election year	−0.537*	−0.043	−0.548*	−0.042
	(0.228)		(0.229)	
Percent female legislators	0.976		0.813	
	(1.276)		(1.093)	
Policy innovation index	−0.097		−1.586	
	(8.315)		(7.385)	
Constant	−2.098***		−1.987***	
	(0.516)		(0.509)	
N	1,270		1,270	
Pseudo R²	0.0490		0.0460	
Prob > Chi²	0.0000		0.0000	

*p < 0.05, **p < 0.01, ***p < 0.001. Logistic regression with standard errors in parentheses, clustered on state, listed below the coefficient. The impact of statistically significant coefficients is generated through Clarify and is listed next to the coefficient. For binary independent variables, the impact reports the estimated change in the probability of adopting a DVFL as the value of the variable is changed from 0 to 1. For continuous variables, the impact reports the estimated change in probability of adopting a DVFL as the value of the variable is changed from its first quartile value to its third quartile value.

TABLE 4.6. Predicting DVFL adoption in states, Models 5 and 6

Variable	Model 5	Impact	Model 6	Impact
Gunhomicidesper100k$_{t-1}$			0.0166	
			(0.0234)	
Gunhomicidesper100k x Unified Republican Government$_{t-1}$	0.220*	0.003		
	(0.112)			
Unified Republican state government	−1.136**	−0.077		
	(0.347)			
Citizen ideology$_{t-1}$			0.016*	0.027
			(0.006)	
Neighboring state DVFL$_{t-1}$	0.159			
	(0.173)			
Number regional DVFL$_{t-1}$			−0.042	
			(0.089)	
Per Capita Hunting Firearm Licenses$_{t-1}$	−2.374			
	(1.732)			
1994 VAWA enacted	1.280***	0.175	1.392***	0.199
	(0.380)		(0.362)	
1995 1 year post-VAWA	1.051**	0.132	1.221**	0.166
	(0.395)		(.391)	
1996 Lautenberg enacted	1.252***	0.170	1.428***	0.208
	(0.363)		(0.389)	
1997 1 year post-Lautenberg	0.002		0.214	
	(0.491)		(0.488)	
Legislative election year	−0.492*	−0.039	−0.490*	−0.040
	(0.232)		(0.233)	
Percent female legislators	1.084		0.513	
	(1.328)		(1.356)	
Policy innovation index	−.883		1.497	
	(8.494)		(6.682)	
Constant	−2.116***		−3.217***	
	(0.514)		(0.507)	
N	1,270		1,270	
Pseudo R^2	0.049		0.039	
Prob > Chi^2	0.0000		0.0000	

*p < 0.05, **p < 0.01, ***p < 0.001. Logistic Regression with standard errors in parentheses, clustered on state, listed below the coefficient. The impact of statistically significant coefficients is generated through Clarify and is listed next to the coefficient. For binary independent variables, the impact reports the estimated change in the probability of adopting a DVFL as the value of the variable is changed from 0 to 1. For continuous variables, the impact reports the estimated change in probability of adopting a DVFL as the value of the variable is changed from its first quartile value to its third quartile value.

TABLE 4.7. *Predicting DVFL adoption in states, Models 7 and 8*

Variable	Model 7	Impact	Model 8	Impact
Femalemurdersbyfamilybygun$_{t-1}$			0.0094*	0.009
			(0.004)	
Femalemurdersbyfamilybygun x Unified Republican Government$_{t-1}$	0.0148**	0.000		
	(0.0054)			
Unified Republican state government	−0.655**	−0.047		
	(0.284)			
Citizen ideology$_{t-1}$			0.017*	0.027
			(0.006)	
Neighboring state DVFL$_{t-1}$	0.149			
	(0.173)			
Number regional DVFL$_{t-1}$			−0.041	
			(0.088)	
Per capita hunting firearm licenses$_{t-1}$	−2.624			
	(1.762)			
1994 VAWA enacted	1.269***	0.172	1.369***	0.199
	(0.382)		(0.364)	
1995 1 year post-VAWA	1.058**	0.139	1.206**	0.166
	(0.404)		(0.391)	
1996 Lautenberg enacted	1.255***	0.172	1.426***	0.208
	(0.378)		(0.390)	
1997 1 year post-Lautenberg	0.007		0.207	
	(0.496)		(0.488)	
Legislative election year	−0.487*	−0.039	−0.496*	−0.040
	(0.232)		(0.234)	
Percent female legislators	0.854		0.673	
	(1.254)		(1.337)	
Policy innovation index	−0.391		0.803	
	(8.133)		(7.085)	
Constant	−2.066***		−3.303***	
	(0.500)		(0.469)	
N	1,270		1,270	
Pseudo R²	0.046		0.042	
Prob > Chi²	0.0000		0.0000	

*p < 0.05, **p < 0.01, ***p < 0.001. Logistic regression with standard errors in parentheses, clustered on state, listed below the coefficient. The impact of statistically significant coefficients is generated through Clarify and is listed next to the coefficient. For binary independent variables, the impact reports the estimated change in the probability of adopting a DVFL as the value of the variable is changed from 0 to 1. For continuous variables, the impact reports the estimated change in probability of adopting a DVFL as the value of the variable is changed from its first quartile value to its third quartile value.

concerns additional firearm regulation. Because both VAWA and Lautenberg include firearm restrictions in their legislation, this may be what was needed for emulation at the state level. A second reason why the reauthorizations did not impact the passage of DVFLs at the state level is

TABLE 4.8. *Predicting DVFL adoption in states, Model 9*

Variable	Model 9	Impact
Numbermassshootings$_{t-1}$	0.446	
	(0.312)	
Citizen ideology$_{t-1}$	0.016**	0.028
	(0.005)	
Number regional DVFL$_{t-1}$	−0.077	
	(0.090)	
1994 VAWA enacted	1.472**	0.212
	(0.352)	
1995 1 year post-VAWA enacted	1.142**	0.149
	(0.389)	
2000 VAWA reauthorization	0.137	
	(0.525)	
2005 VAWA reauthorization	−0.030	
	(0.511)	
2013 VAWA reauthorization	−0.181	
	(0.452)	
1996 Lautenberg enacted	1.555***	0.228
	(0.393)	
1997 1 year post-Lautenberg	0.167	
	(0.484)	
Legislative election year	−0.542*	−0.046
	(0.225)	
Percent female legislators	−0.699	
	(1.295)	
Policy innovation index	7.421	
	(6.033)	
Constant	−3.137***	
	(0.427)	
N	1,350	
Pseudo R^2	0.041	
Prob > Chi^2	0.0000	

*p < 0.05, **p < 0.01, ***p < 0.001. Logistic regression with standard errors in parentheses, clustered on state, listed below the coefficient. The impact of statistically significant coefficients is generated through Clarify and is listed next to the coefficient. For binary independent variables, the impact reports the estimated change in the probability of adopting a DVFL as the value of the variable is changed from 0 to 1. For continuous variables, the impact reports the estimated change in probability of adopting a DVFL as the value of the variable is changed from its first quartile value to its third quartile value.

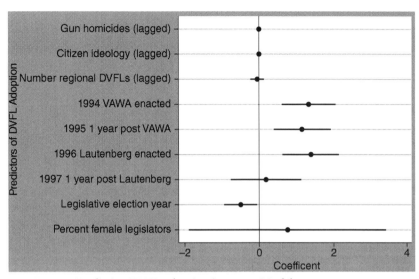

FIGURE 4.4 **Predicting DVFL adoption in states, Model 2**
Here we ran the model with citizen ideology instead of Republican Party control, and we found that the more liberal the citizen ideology in the state, the greater likelihood a state will adopt a DVFL.
Source: Author generated from original data analysis.

because of the increasing levels of polarization on gun control and Republican control of legislatures that hinder passage of DVFLs after 2000.

In Model 2 (represented in Tables 4.4 and 4.3), we sought to assess the impact of gun homicides (lagged) and citizen ideology (in lieu of party control of state government) and expanded our scope of horizontal policy diffusion by including the number of states within a shared region that adopted DVFLs. Gun homicides by themselves exert a statistically significant effect; as the value of gun homicides (lagged) moves from the first quartile to the third quartile, the likelihood of adopting a DFVL increases by 1.1 percent. Citizen ideology also exerts a positive and statistically significant impact; as the value of citizen ideology moves from the first quartile to the third quartile and thus becomes more liberal, the state is 2.6 percent more likely to adopt a DVFL. The results for the VAWA in the year it was enacted, the year after it was enacted (1995), the Lautenberg Amendment 1996 and state legislative elections remain robust. We did not find a statistically significant impact associated with regional adoption of DVFLs.

4.6 CONCLUSION

In this chapter, we show the disparity in legislative action on policies designed to address and prevent DV-related firearm homicides. We tested the impact of both vertical and horizontal policy diffusion and found that federal action in this area increased adoption of DVFLs for the initial passage of VAWA and the Lautenberg Amendment but that subsequent reauthorizations did not have a statistically significant effect on state policy adoption. Still, reauthorizations can present an opportunity to remedy shortcomings in previous law. Such was the case with the 2013 VAWA authorization, which created special domestic violence jurisdictions to allow the prosecution of DV assaults against Native American women by non-Native American men on tribal lands. In tribes that have adopted these courts, abusers who were formerly out of reach are now subject to prosecution.

Part of the waning influence of federal policy on state policy enactment may be the lack of coercive behavior in federal grant making in this policy arena. We found that the federal government does not use funding to coerce states to adopt their own laws that comply with federal laws and guidelines. Even when federal grants are competitive across states in the area of women and violence, states that enact as well as states that do not enact DVFLs are both likely to receive these grants. With respect to horizontal policy diffusion, when states adopted DVFLs, their neighboring states or states within their broader region did not always follow suit. In 2021, Secretary of the Interior Deb Haaland expanded on the efforts to improve protection against DV abuse among Native American women by forming a new unit to investigate the cases of murdered and missing women from indigenous communities.

Another factor particular to DV legislation in these intervening years is partisan control of Congress. In 2000, 2005, and 2013 when reauthorization for VAWA occurred, the House of Representatives was controlled by a Republican majority as was the Senate in 2000 and 2005. Given Republican Party resistance to gun control legislation more broadly, it is not surprising that these reauthorizations did not contain additional firearm-related measures, and therefore we would not see state DVFL enactments following the enactment of these bills. In fact, our analysis points to the negative impact that Republican control of state governments has on the adoption of DVFLs at the state level. Even before federal legislation was enacted in 2022, a number of states moved ahead with expanding DV gun restrictions for dating partners (closing the boyfriend loophole). Now that the federal government has expanded the protections of VAWA to dating partners, our expectation is that additional states may do so as well, contingent on the partisan control of their governments.

Our analysis revealed that gun homicides do have a direct impact on the adoption of DVFLs independently, but when they interacted with Republican control of state government, the chances for passing a DVFL declined. As we expected, legislators are less likely to adopt DVFLs in a state legislative election year. The percentage of women in the legislature did not exert an effect on DVFL adoption nor did the state's overall policy innovativeness score.

In this chapter, we argued that DV policy exists at the crossroads of federalism and public policy, and we explored which variables can explain what prompts states to take legislative action on the ownership and possession of firearms by DV abusers. We found that DVFL adoption appears to be most heavily influenced by action taken at the federal level as well as the partisan control of state government and state ideology. When DVFLs are depicted by politicians, advocacy groups, and media more generally as limitations on gun possession and ownership rather than public health and security measures to protect women and children, opposition is generated more frequently in conservative and Republican-dominated state legislatures. Based on the results presented in this chapter, we believe that new federal legislation or simply reauthorizing VAWA with additional provisions could exert pressure, even coerce, states to take far stronger steps in this issue domain. In Chapter 5, we will demonstrate that where and how a DV case is adjudicated has a significant impact on the outcome of a case and by definition, the safety of DV victims.

5

The View from the Courtroom

Inconsistent Implementation of Domestic Violence Policy at the Local Level

"There are large variations on how domestic violence crimes are treated by county within the state. My experience in a very difficult county is not likely representative of the entire state" according to one state public defender in response to the State Public Defender and District Attorney Survey 2017.[1]

On May 20, 2018, a York City, Pennsylvania, police officer was arrested for simple assault and harassment charges. The police had responded to a call at his home; his wife there had scratches to her neck and chest and injuries to her wrist. The couple had been having an argument when the wife hid her husband's cell phone down her shirt. The husband, Ritchie Paige Blymier, attacked his wife Brenda and "got on top of her, using his knee on her stomach and grabbing her wrists to hold her down. Brenda then advised that Ritchie placed his hands on her chest and throat while grabbing at her chest to get the phone" (Dornblaser, 2018). On October 25, 2018, Blymier pleaded guilty to harassment. As part of his plea agreement, his simple assault charge was dropped, and he was ordered to pay $300 within 90 days. Nowhere in this domestic violence (DV) incident is it reported that Blymier faced a DV charge despite the fact that his actions fit the law that defines domestic abuse as "attempting to cause or intentionally, knowingly or recklessly causing bodily injury."[2] Following her husband's arrest, Brenda obtained a temporary protection from abuse and stated that her husband was "very

---

[1] This quote also appears in Sidorsky and Schiller (2020).
[2] Penn. Cons. State Title 23 § 6102.

controlling... and has 8 cameras inside and outside of our home watching everything we do" (Dornblaser, 2018).

Five months before the Blymier DV case in Pennsylvania, Alwin Carter King III committed a DV offense in the neighboring state of Ohio. A former North Carolina resident on probation, King shot Amber Carrouzzo, mother of three, in the leg and was charged with DV, felonious assault, obstructing official business, tampering with evidence, and using weapons under disability (Breda, 2018). On May 11, 2018, King was sentenced to three years probation and anger management classes after pleading guilty to misdemeanor DV, felony tampering with evidence, and felony having weapons under disability. Although the assistant county prosecutor asked for a prison sentence given King's prior illegal activity including motor vehicle theft and a previous firearms conviction, the judge on the case felt King deserved the opportunity to make better choices in his life (Mahoney, 2018).

The King and Blymier incidents illustrate the power that law enforcement personnel exercise in determining the disposition of a DV incident. Blymier was never charged with a DV offense, and even his simple assault charge was dropped. This shows the power and discretion of prosecutors. At the end of the day, it is prosecutors who decide whom to charge and with what offenses. Since lead prosecutors are most often locally elected, who receives a DV charge could be decided by someone chosen at the polls – an inherently political process.

Both the Blymier and King cases also exemplify the power of plea bargains in either reducing a sentence or completely eliminating a charge. This brings in the legal acumen of public defenders (PDs) in cases when the accused needs access to legal resources. Finally, King's case shows the amount of discretion a judge has over how punitive the punishment is for a DV offense. In his case, despite committing a serious crime and having a prosecutor who wanted a stronger sentence, King was never incarcerated for this crime. While punitive punishment may not be the answer to all incidents of DV – as many legal feminists have noted – King's sentence does not seem appropriate if DV policy is designed to stop the cycle of abuse.

In this chapter, we argue that a law "on the books" is only as good as its implementation; DV laws need to be adopted and properly implemented so that women are safe in their homes and intimate relationships. In this chapter, we also turn our attention to how these laws are implemented at the local level from the point at which a DV case is initiated by law enforcement and prosecutors, to how the accused is defended, to how the case is ultimately resolved. Essentially, we seek to understand the effect specific DV laws have on the outcomes of cases that make it to the courtroom. Prosecutorial discretion, judicial discretion, capacity of the defense system, options for remediation and punishment, and existing state laws on DV are all factors that can influence the outcome of a single case and, in turn, whether a woman is protected from future assault by a current or former intimate partner. We focus on explaining the implementation side of the equation by demonstrating how these factors affect the outcomes of DV cases.

The chapter proceeds as follows. First, we provide a description of existing punishments for DV, including financial penalties, incarceration, and rehabilitation at the state and local levels. Second, we present the results from our survey of PDs and district attorneys (DAs) on what types of punishment they typically see for DV crimes and their perspective on the system they work in each and every day. Third, we present our analysis of the outcomes associated with the DV cases that PDs handled. We conclude with a discussion of the relative treatment of DV cases across states.

5.1 POLICY IMPLEMENTATION AND JUDICIAL TREATMENT OF DOMESTIC VIOLENCE CASES

In this chapter, we explore how DV cases are adjudicated in courts across different states from both the defense and prosecution perspectives. As part of this endeavor, we collected data on the punishments individuals face if they commit a DV crime. These data delineate how states punish violence against women in two categories: financial penalties and incarceration (see Table 5.1). We did not collect systematic data on rehabilitation as alternatives to punishment for DV, but this remains a viable additional option in the adjudication of these cases.

It is important to note that the punishments range widely. Some states may sentence a serial abuser to only one year in prison while another state may sentence that same abuser to five years. The same is true for financial punishments. A first offense could cost the abuser (and potentially the victim if they share finances) $500 in a low financial punishment case and in another state, that same offense could come with a $5,000 fine. In Table 5.1, we present the range of punishments across the survey sample of our states. It illustrates the examples of inconsistency of these punishments across the United States. Why should a DV abuser in one state receive a different outcome for a crime than another abuser receives in a different state for the same crime?

TABLE 5.1. *Punishments for DV crimes*[*]

	Financial Punishment	Incarceration Punishment
Very Low	First offense: Less than $500 Second offense: $500–$1,000 Third offense: $1,000–$3,000	First offense: Less than 6 months Second offense: 6 months–1 year Third offense: 1 year–3 years If it involves a counseling and/or community service program
Low	First offense: $500–$1,000 Second offense: $1000–$5,000 Third offense: $5,000–$10,000	First offense: 6 months–1 year Second offense: 1 year–5 years Third offense: 5 years–10 years
Medium	First offense: $1,000–$5,000 Second offense: $5,000–$10,000 Third offense: $10,000 or more	First offense: 1 year–5 years Second offense: 5 years–10 years Third offense: More than 10 years
High	First offense: $5,000–$10,000 Second offense: $10,000–$25,000 Third offense: More than $25,000	First offense: 5 years–10 years Second offense: More than 10 years

[*]To fall into one of these categories, a state does not have to fit the exact criteria of each subset; it must have to fulfill at least two of the criteria.
Source: Author generated.

Prosecutorial discretion affects the trajectory of DV cases. A defendant who is charged with a felony rather than a misdemeanor, for example, is potentially subject to strict penalties, including incarceration. When charged with a misdemeanor offense, a defendant is far less likely to be incarcerated and more likely to be referred to counseling and rehabilitation programs (Pinchevsky, 2017). Most DV cases are "charged down" in the course of plea bargaining to misdemeanor crimes, which has significant implications for the degree of punishment meted to abusers and the future safety of the victim because it could mean the accused is allowed to keep a firearm. In some cases, prosecutors pursue assault charges against an abuser rather than a DV charge because the evidence will support that charge more readily than a DV charge. Only in jurisdictions where there is a "no-drop" policy that prevents the complainant from dropping the charges after the case is started does every aspect of how a DV case is handled rely in part on prosecutorial discretion in that jurisdiction.

In addition, the availability and accessibility of adequate legal defense counsel for the accused is crucial. Pinchevsky (2017) found that having legal representation increased the likelihood of being asked to pay a fine but not being sentenced to a "batter intervention program," but it had no effect on receiving jail time rather than being sentenced to such a program. Earlier work by Belknap et al. (2000) concentrated more deeply on the attitudes of the participants in DV cases. They surveyed 30 PDs as part of a broader study of 62 judicial participants in DV cases in Cincinnati, Ohio, and focused on the techniques used to minimize punishment for their clients. PDs reported using a variety of techniques to discredit victim or witness testimony that could harm their client's case. Hartman and Belknap (2003) also found "that a prevalent theme among public defenders, in addition to their extreme hostility toward victim advocates, was a sense of the domestic violence laws as pandering to inconsequential feminist concerns" (p. 361). The PDs in their study felt the DV laws in their state were too expansive and too punitive. Two drawbacks of the Hartman and Belknap study are that it was limited to a single jurisdiction, which precluded any analysis of the variation of the impact of state laws on sentencing, and it focused only on misdemeanor cases.

We take two components of the adjudication process of DV – the roles of the PD and prosecutor – and seek to distinguish trends in how they perceive DV cases within the broader framework of both their localized judicial system and their overall caseload. The PD system is organized differently across states and counties. Twenty-eight states have state-run PD systems that are organized and funded at the state level; the remaining states have either partial state- and county-funded systems or county-based systems with referral to private attorneys. We created a database that includes the contact information and county for all PDs in a sample of 16 states. In state-run systems, the contact information is typically (but not always) available, but in county-run systems with referrals, it was nearly impossible to identify PDs in the same way. In some cases, the jurisdiction and city were listed for offices for PDs, so we used the statewide PD database to try to look up the specific individuals. But in other cases, it was not possible to obtain individual-level PD information without making a formal request for representation.

Finding contact information for DAs was also difficult. Although they complete the same tasks, each state has a different name for the prosecutors who handle cases for each county in the state. Furthermore, some states elect the main prosecutor while others appoint that person. For example, North Carolina's prosecutors are called DAs and are elected by each of the 39 prosecutorial districts. However, in three states (Alaska, Connecticut, and New Jersey), the chief prosecutor is appointed. In Connecticut, these prosecutors are known as state's attorneys while in New Jersey they are known as county prosecutors. We were able to find the contact information for the district and assistant DAs through the state's website or association of DA's roster or county or judicial district website.

Despite these obstacles, we were successful in constructing a sample database of 2,132 PDs from Alaska, Louisiana, Massachusetts, Minnesota, Mississippi, Missouri, Nevada, North Carolina, North Dakota, Ohio, Pennsylvania, Tennessee, Vermont, Washington, West Virginia, and Wisconsin. We chose a sample of 16 states for several reasons. First, we felt that as long as we chose a diverse group of states along population, ideological, and institutional variables, this would be sufficiently representative of PDs across the United States. Second, access to PD data is challenging in that states and counties can make it difficult to find who the PDs are let alone their contact information. We are therefore confident that we are properly representing PDs' methodologically by choosing these 16 states. Of these, Alaska, Massachusetts, Minnesota, Missouri, North Carolina, North Dakota, Tennessee, Vermont, and Wisconsin are primarily state-funded PD systems as part of which PD services are coordinated and provided by the state; West Virginia is state funded, but the services are provided by the counties; Louisiana, Mississippi, Nevada, Ohio, and Washington are primarily county funded with some cost sharing with the state, and services are provided by counties; Pennsylvania is entirely funded at the county level, and services are provided by counties (Stevens et al., 2010). We surveyed approximately 1,925 PDs and received 182 responses agreeing to participate in the survey and six responses declining to participate in the survey; 62 of the PDs were from the state of Minnesota alone.[3]

---

[3] Overall Minnesota PDs comprised about 26.7 percent of the total survey universe. We found no specific patterns among the respondents from Minnesota that differed systematically from the rest of the sample or that would suggest a consistent reason for the high response rate. The number of respondents answering each survey question ranged from 124 to 183; we provide the average responses in each table. See Appendix A5.1 for a full description of the survey and the survey instrument itself.

We compiled a database of 1,309 DAs and assistant DAs across the states of Alaska, Louisiana, Massachusetts, North Dakota, Minnesota, Vermont, Ohio, and North Carolina. From these states, 104 DAs responded to the survey, although not all of them answered every question. Finding the names and contact information of prosecutors in these eight states was even more challenging than finding the PDs. Although it is beyond the scope of this project, we feel it is important to note how difficult it is to find this information, which is particularly concerning given the limited resources and time many women who are victims of DV have in seeking legal aid.

5.2 RESULTS FROM THE STATE PUBLIC DEFENDER AND DISTRICT ATTORNEY SURVEY

This section is derived in part from an article published in the *Journal of Women, Politics & Policy* (Sidorsky and Schiller, 2020). In Table 5.2, we provide profile information from the state PD and DA surveys. On average, the typical state PD in our sample is male, white, and 43 years old. This is very similar to the average DA who is only one year younger than the PDs. Slightly more DAs identified as female, and similar numbers of both identified as non-white. More than half of the PDs graduated from a private law school, and a majority of them self-identify as liberals. While just as likely to have graduated from a private law school, DAs were not as likely to consider themselves liberal.

It is unclear what role ideology may play in how DAs prosecute their cases. DAs who are more conservative may be more likely to stick to the letter of the law. As we have shown numerous times throughout this book, a wide degree of latitude is given to law enforcement, judges, and prosecutors when it comes to DV. This means that law enforcement can choose to take away a firearm in some states, judges can choose to prohibit firearm possession, and prosecutors can choose to drop DV charges, making these offenders invisible to DV firearm laws. More conservative prosecutors may be less willing to drop chargers, or they may be more invested in a harsher punishment, which could mean applying a different charge where available.

In Table 5.3, we present a typology of the types of cases these defenders and prosecutor's handle. Not surprisingly, the average caseload for PDs and state prosecutors is high at over 150 cases for each. About 25 percent of these cases are DV cases with 80 percent of them including a female victim for both prosecutors and PDs. These responses further underscore

TABLE 5.2. *Profile of PAs and DAs*

	PDs	DAs
Average age (years)	43.49	42.30
Gender (female)	47.29%	54.32%
Race (non-white)	8.90%	9.88%%
Private law school	59.73%	56.80%
Ideology (strongly/ weakly liberal)	75.68%	41.25%
Ideology (strongly/ weakly conservative)	11.49%	33.75%
Family income	$75,001–$100,000	$75,001–$100,000
N	152	80

TABLE 5.3. *Typology of cases (means)*

	PDs	DAs
Average number of years of practice	10.50	10.18
Average number of cases	151 cases	154 cases
Percent DV cases	24.75%	26.96%
Percent DV cases that were felonies	42.09%	64.75%
Percent DV cases that had female victim	80.83%	89.06%
Percent DV cases that had child victim	13.09%	42.65%
Percent DV cases that had repeat offender	43.07%	58.23%
Number of investigators	2.54	1.40
Specialized DV court	16.89%	8.54%
Received specialized training	37.41%	84.15%
Defended/Prosecuted IPV cases	96.85%	98.79%
Percentage of DV cases with vertical prosecution in a majority or all cases	40.33%	58.21%
N	151	79

the gendered nature of DV offenses. If we apply the average of our results to each of the PDs and DAs in our sample, each would be handling about 38 DV cases a year. We have 262 PDs and DA survey respondents, which means they collectively handle almost 10,000 DV cases a year across only 16 of the 50 states we included in the survey. Any one of these cases could involve access to a firearm.

About 42 percent of PDs' cases are felonies, and 43 percent involve a repeat offender; 65 percent of DAs' cases were felonies, and 58 percent of their cases involved a repeat offender. The high levels of repeat offenders are further evidence of a broken system. If states properly handled DV offenders and properly protected DV victims, the frequency of repeat offense would be much lower. DAs were also more likely to handle cases that involved children; this fit as many of them noted that they typically handle felony cases. Violence against children is more likely to be classified as a felony. Unfortunately, only one-third of PDs received specialized training to handle DV cases. On a more positive note, the vast majority of DAs received such training.

In the cases in which these PDs participated, DV cases are more likely to end with a financial penalty of up to $1,000 followed by rehabilitation of 30 days to six months and then by jail time of 30 days to six months. Less than one-fifth of the cases are charge down bargained (i.e., the defendant tries to plea to a different charge instead of an assault or DV crime). Plea bargain can also include sentence or fact bargaining. PDs report that half of their DV cases are plea bargained down to a lesser offense (see Table 5.4).

TABLE 5.4. *Profile of DV sentencing (means)*

	PDs	DAs
Percent of DV Cases that resulted in jail time	40.23%	50.06%
Average jail sentence	30 days–6 months	30 days–6 months
DV cases that resulted in financial penalty	66.95%	49.88%
Average financial penalty	Under $500–$1,000	Under $500–$,1000
DV Cases that resulted in rehabilitation	50.63%	61.63%
Average time for rehabilitation	30 days–6 months	6 months–1 year
DV Cases with combination of jail, fine, & rehabilitation	64.03%	72.12%
DV cases charge bargained	16.66%	30.49%
DV cases plea bargained	47.32%	54.87%
N	140	61

We further explored how gender may play a role in how cases are plea or charge bargained for the cases handled by PDs. Overall, female PDs were less likely to have plea deals associated with their DV cases; 43 percent of female PDs reported 25 percent or less of their DV cases were pled down to a lesser charge or punishment compared to 26 percent of male PDs ($p<0.10$). This holds true for the more specific charge bargain; 85 percent of female PDs compared to 68 percent of male PDs stated that less than 25 percent of their DV cases were charge bargained to a lesser offense ($p<0.10$). This is an interesting phenomenon for a few reasons. First, it is possible that women may be less likely to accept plea deals for gender-based crimes although we unfortunately cannot confirm this with the data we have collected. Second, female PDs are more likely to identify as liberal when compared to the male PDs, and it is not clear how PDs' ideology may influence their willingness to seek a plea deal or the likelihood that they will accept one. There does not seem to be a pattern in our data of the percentage of liberal versus conservative PDs whose DV cases have plea or charge bargains.

On the other side of the courtroom, state and county prosecutors reported higher levels of DV cases that resulted in jail time. There is a noticeable gap, however, between the cases that resulted in financial penalty or rehabilitation. Prosecutors reported fewer cases resulting in financial penalties but more cases that resulted in rehabilitation. Furthermore, prosecutors reported longer rehabilitation sentences than PDs. Prosecutors also reported higher levels of charge bargaining and plea bargaining. Charge and/or plea bargains may especially place DV victims in greater levels of danger because they may negate the effects of DV firearm legislation that specifically limits firearm possession or ownership for DV convictions.

Finally, Table 5.5 presents the descriptive statistics on what constitutes a DV crime according to each PD and DA. The most common type of crime that constitutes DV is assault. After this, more than 70 percent of PDs and DAs said that battery, threatening, sexual violence, and stalking all constituted DV crimes. Half or fewer than PDs and DAs said that burglary, criminal mischief, and terrorist threats constituted a DV crime; however, such crimes are not always categorized as DV. Consequently, women who are victims of burglary or criminal mischief from an intimate partner may not always appear in statistics counting the total number of DV incidents.

Even if the law does not classify certain crimes as DVs, we know from the Power and Control Wheel in Chapter 1 that they are DV crimes.

TABLE 5.5. *Profile of DV crimes*

	PDs (%)	DAs (%)
Assault a DV crime	92.36	98.7
Battery a DV crime	78.47	69.62
Burglary a DV crime	22.22	35.44
Criminal mischief a DV crime	9.03	13.92
Threatening a DV crime	77.78	75.95
Terrorist threats a DV crime	47.92	40.51
Sexual violence a DV crime	71.53	72.15
Stalking a DV crime	84.03	72.15
Statutory definition of DV followed closely	87.69	91.67
N	142	72

Many of the controlling behaviors that lead up to physical violence – including firearm violence – encompass manipulation, coercion, financial control, and the use of threats. In many ways, abusers groom their victims, cutting them off from family and friends and limiting their access to resources that could help them. Abusers know how to control their victims by threatening their physical well-being and that of their children, and even the safety or lives of their pets. Making terroristic threats and threatening a DV crime are as close to these types of abuse as states typically get, and yet less than half of the PDs and DAs say they "count" as a DV crime. This is yet another way abusers slip through the cracks of the scope of definition and interpretation of what constitutes DV crimes. We discuss this further in Chapter 6.

It is essential to go beyond the quantitative evidence presented here to see what the PDs and DAs said about the laws they encounter on a daily basis. In particular, gaps may be present between what the PDs and DAs say constitutes DV compared to what their statute says. As a follow up to the specific crimes we asked about in the survey listed in Table 5.5, we also asked the respondents to provide the statutory definition of DV in their state. It is notable that many of the respondents did not cite the specific statute and that many of them provided overly broad definitions despite the specific statutes that are present in their states that we reviewed in Chapter 2.

For example, one Massachusetts PD stated that DV was defined as "any criminal act of abuse committed by one family or household member against another, including placing another in fear of imminent serious physical harm"; a second PD from the same state broadly defined

DV as "abuse between a household member or person in a relationship or prior relationship."

Similarly, a Minnesota PD stated DV in that state was "any of the following against a household member: physical harm; fear of imminent physical harm; interference with a 911 call; threats of violence; or unlawful sexual contact," yet another Minnesota PD said that DV in that state was the "kitchen sink." A third Minnesota PD stated there was no statutory definition of DV, but "it is any enumerated crime of violence (from the preceding list [included in the survey question]) committed on a household or family member." A prosecutor from Minnesota said the statutory definition of DV was when a person "(1) commits an act with intent to cause fear in another of immediate bodily harm or death or (2) intentionally inflicts or attempts to inflict bodily harm upon another." The actual Minnesota definition of DV states that domestic abuse "means the following, if committed against a family or household member by a family or household member: a) physical harm, bodily injury, or assault; b) the infliction of fear of imminent physical harm, bodily injury, or assault; or c) terroristic threats, criminal sexual conduct, or interference with an emergency call."[4]

Three prosecutors in Ohio provided another example of the different perspectives on what constitutes DV as well as how the understanding of what constitutes DV is different from what the actual statute says. We list the following three responses and then compare each to the actual definition from the Ohio code of laws:

- "Knowingly cause physical harm to a family or household member."
- "Cause or attempt to cause physical harm to a family or household member."
- "Cause, attempt to cause, or threaten to cause physical harm to a family or household member."

Ohio Statute § 3113.31 states that DV is the occurrence of one or more of the following acts against a family or household member:

1) Attempting to cause or recklessly causing bodily injury;
2) Placing another person by the threat of force in fear of imminent serious physical harm or committing a violation of section 2903.211 (stalking) or 2911.211 (aggravated trespass) of the Revised Code;
3) Committing any act with respect to a child that would result in the children being an abused child, as defined in section 2151.021 of the Revised Code;
4) Committing a sexually oriented offence.

---

[4] Minn. Stat. § 518B.01.

According to the first prosecutor, only actual physical harm would constitute DV. The second prosecutor claims actually causing or attempting to cause physical harm would count toward DV, while the description of the third prosecutor is closest to the actual definition including threats. These gaps in the understanding of DV statutes raises questions of how well they are being prosecuted and defended in American courtrooms. Given the large workload of these prosecutors, it is entirely possible that they did not have the time to fully explain the law on the survey and simply provided an overview.

More generally, PDs and DAs had important insights about DV in the judicial system itself. A Massachusetts PD had the following to say about the DV law in that state: "Domestic Violence is too broadly defined and sweeps too wide. It is harshly prosecuted with a mandated, expensive treatment program that likely does not address all the issues that bring a person into the system. It needs reform." One prosecutor from Ohio stated, "DV cases are extremely important and should be treated with the utmost care." Two Minnesota PDs called for reform in their states as well. One said, "How domestic assault is treated and viewed is widely different by county across the state. Certain judges and prosecutors refuse to work with the defense on the case. I very strongly believe that we are doing everybody a disservice by the way we treat domestic assault."

The other Minnesota PD stated,

I think probation sets my clients up to fail. While I understand the purpose of probation is to rehabilitate and provide classes to help clients learn/better themselves, there are too many rules that clients have to abide that. In addition, the chemical evaluations, treatment, anger classes, domestic violence courses all cost money and most of my clients are obviously indigent and cannot afford to pay for these classes. They get violated for not abiding probation rules, then we see them back in court again. Often times they are ordered to be sanctioned/punished to serve some jail time for the violation. Other times, [the] Court will order them to execute the entire jail or prison sentence. While I understand these violations are the fault of my clients for failing to complete courses, not staying in contact with probation or failing to meet with probation, however, I feel there are very limited resources to accommodate my client's living situation, their access to financial support, their access to transportation, etc.

Finally, one Vermont prosecutor provided insight into how federal grants are important for on the ground implementation of DV laws, explaining:

We have a federal grant that pays for 1 full-time prosecutor that is assigned to all intimate partner violence. Our office has to adhere to federal definitions contained within the grant as to what can be assigned to that prosecutor, and I'm not that person. DV that falls outside of that definition, such as parent on child violence or violence between siblings, those are the cases I am assigned. Also, while there is some interpretation as to how to assign cases, we strictly adhere to the grant requirements so we don't lose that funding.

In general, the words of PDs and DAs show that the system fails victims as well as those who commit DV crimes. The system is disorganized, unequal, and at times is not flexible enough to help victims where they need it the most. Although we often focus on the state-by-state variation in the system, these PDs are also showing us the variation in the application of the law within a state itself. Our analysis illuminates the gaps between statute and practice that also does a disservice to women in each state.

The State Public Defender and District Attorney Survey provides an understanding of who is defending and prosecuting these cases, what kinds of crimes constitute DV, who the victims of these crimes are, and the punishments associated with DV. This chapter is also concerned with understanding women's equality through the lens of DV. An indispensable element of this equality is the implementation of specific policies that make women safer and appropriately punish individuals who commit DV crimes. In the next part of our analysis, we predict the percentage of DV cases that result in jail time versus a financial penalty or rehabilitation as reported by the PDs versus DAs.

5.3 EFFECTS OF DOMESTIC VIOLENCE STATUTES ON CASE OUTCOMES FOR PUBLIC DEFENDERS

We focus on the sample size of PDs for this analysis; unfortunately, the survey of DAs sample lacked sufficient response rates to several key survey questions. We constructed a model with 11 independent variables that we hypothesize might have an effect on the outcome of cases to predict jail time, financial punishments, and rehabilitation. Overall, our goal is to demonstrate that there are different outcomes for DV offenses depending on the state where they occurred and the laws that have been passed there. We exemplified this in the beginning of this chapter by comparing the two DV incidences in Pennsylvania and Ohio. This analysis will show that DV laws at the state level have a direct impact on women's safety, equality, and access to justice. Each of the variables we discuss in this section speaks to three overarching areas: a state's passage of specific laws concerning DV, characteristics of the PDs who handle these cases, and the capacity of a state to properly handle these cases. Each of these areas has a direct bearing on the outcomes of DV cases.

For state-level variables, we include two statutes that have been adopted by states that can affect the outcomes of DV crimes. The first is a composite variable accounting for gun laws regarding DV based on our dataset used in the Chapter 4 analysis. These statutes ranged from whether or not there was a prohibition on gun possession for individuals convicted of misdemeanor DV crimes to whether or not there is required removal of certain firearms by law enforcement for DV incidents (Hess et al., 2015). In this analysis, we code this variable differently and use it as an independent variable rather than a dependent variable. We assign a value between 0 and 8 to each state depending on how many of these statutes were enacted at the time they responded to the survey; each statute translated into one point in the cumulative tally for each state. We expect that a higher score on DV gun laws signals a greater commitment by a state to prosecute DV crimes, which will result in higher penalties for DV crimes. We also incorporated a variable that measures whether the state has a mandatory arrest policy for DV incidents; we expected that in states with such a law, there would be a similar increase in the number of DV crimes receiving punishment.

We analyzed four variables that measure the judicial treatment of DV cases: county-funded PD, percent of felonies, percent plea bargained, and whether there was vertical prosecution. As described earlier, states generally have different types of PD structures: state-level funded, county-level funded, and state- and county-funded. Primus (2017) argues that PDs are generally at a disadvantage when facing prosecutors because they tend to have higher caseloads, fewer investigators, and lower pay. More specifically, county-level public defense systems are even more strained because their funding streams are not always constant and counties frequently rely on a combination of staff PDs and contracted private attorneys who serve as PDs. For urban counties, the difficulties intensify under the weight of very large caseloads. Under these circumstances, we hypothesize that DV cases handled by county-funded PDs will result in harsher punitive outcomes.

The model also has a variable that measures the percent of DV cases that were felonies because felonies may have harsher penalties; it also has a variable that is the percent of cases that were plea bargained because plea bargaining may reduce or substantially change the punishment. Vertical prosecution is in the model as well. In vertical prosecution, one prosecutor is assigned to a case from start to finish whereas in horizontal prosecution, a prosecutor is assigned to a case at different points of the process (charging, hearing, sentencing, and appeal). Vertical prosecution has the potential of affecting how cases are handled because it usually means that the prosecutor assigned to the case has developed expertise in DV crime (Abadinsky, 1988; Soler, 1987; Spohn and Holleran, 2001).

At the individual PD level, we assess the effects of five variables that are associated with the PDs themselves; ideology, sex, years as a PD, race, and the number of cases they handled in the year that preceded the survey. We measure ideology on a 1 to 7 scale with 1 representing very liberal and 7 representing very conservative; we hypothesize that a more conservative PD may not believe that DV crimes warrant criminal punishment and may fight harder to make sure the client avoids jail than a more liberal PD. We believe that because DV is a gendered crime in that the vast majority of the victims are women and/or children, it is reasonable to explore whether a female PD brings a different perspective to cases and may handle them differently than a male PD. This is the same reason that we included the race of the PD because many non-white communities (Native American and African American in particular) have high levels of DV.

We also analyze the number of years as a PD to see whether patterns emerge that differentiate younger PDs from older PDs in terms of career experience, and we include the race of the PD to see if there are differences in case outcomes between white and non-white PDs. The model also has the total number of cases the PD handled in a year to see whether a higher total caseload has an effect on the outcome of individual cases. Our dependent variables are percent of DV cases resulting in jail time, financial penalty, and rehabilitation; they are continuous variables. We used ordinary least squares regression clustered on state identity to predict each of the punishments respectively. See Table 5.6 for the descriptive statistics for each variable.

Table 5.7 presents the results of our model that explain the variation in the percentage of PDs' DV cases that resulted in jail time, financial penalties, and rehabilitation. When we predict cases that result in jail time, 5 of our 11 explanatory variables are significant: PD ideology, the percentage of DV cases that were felonies, the scale of DV gun laws, whether or not the state had mandatory arrest, and the number of cases the PD handled. The more ideologically conservative PDs become, the less likely their DV cases will result in jail time. When larger portions of PDs' DV cases are felonies, this results in a higher portion of their cases resulting in jail time (see Table 5.7).

Similarly, the more DV gun laws a state has, the higher the share of a PD's DV cases will result in jail punishment. Additionally, the presence of mandatory arrest for DV in a state also results in a higher portion of PD cases receiving jail punishments. Finally, the more cases a PD handles in a year, the more likely it is that jail punishment will be a case outcome,

TABLE 5.6. *Description of variables and coding to predict punishments in DV cases*

Variable	Range	Mean	Standard Deviation	Coding
Percent of DV cases resulting in jail time	0–100	40.23	34.69	Responses from PDs of their DV cases
Percent of DV cases resulting in financial punishment	0–100	66.95	40.51	Responses from PDs of their DV cases
Percent of DV cases resulting in rehabilitation	0–100	50.63	36.40	Responses from PDs of their DV cases
PD ideology	1–7	2.37	1.56	1 = Strongly liberal, 2 = Liberal, 3 = Weakly liberal, 4 = Moderate, 5 = Weakly conservative, 6 = Conservative, 7 = Strongly conservative
PD sex	0, 1	0.473	0.50	0 = Male 1 = Female
Years as PD	1–25	10.50	8.07	Responses from PDs
Non-White PD	0, 1	0.09	0.29	Responses from PDs
County-Provided PD services	0,1	0.21	0.41	0 = State does not have county-provided PDs 1 = State has county-provided PDs
Percent of DV cases that were felonies	0–100	42.09	34.71	Responses from PDs of their DV cases
Percentage of cases that were plea bargained	0–100	47.43	31.15	Responses from PDs of their DV cases

Variable	Range	Mean	Standard Deviation	Coding
Vertical prosecution	1–5	2.73	1.54	1 = None of the cases, 2 = Rarely, 3 = About half of the cases, 4 = Most of the cases, 5 = Every single case
DV gun laws	0–8	3.69	2.27	Each state is awarded 1 for every gun law it has associated with DV. Up to 8 laws.
Mandatory arrest	0,1	0.32	0.47	0 = State does not have mandatory arrest for DV crimes 1 = State has mandatory arrest for DV crimes
Number of cases 2016	0–280	150.73	57.94	Responses from PDs on their total number of cases

which may indicate that an overworked PD may not have the time and resources to represent a person accused of a DV offense as well as a PD who takes on fewer cases.

The variables that affect financial punishment of PD cases are slightly different. Non-white PDs' cases have a lower percent of cases that receive financial penalty. Neither PD ideology nor the percentage of cases that were felonies is significantly related to financial punishments. More DV gun laws and the presence of a mandatory arrest policy increase the percentage of cases that incur financial punishment, just as it did for jail punishment. A higher caseload also leads to a higher percentage of cases that receive financial penalties.

When we predict rehabilitation sentencing, we see different results. Here, county-funded PD services and vertical prosecution are strongly statistically significant while they were statistically insignificant when predicting punitive punishments. For county-provided PDs, there is a lower percentage of PDs' DV cases resulting in rehabilitation. When instances of vertical prosecution increase, however, a higher percentage

TABLE 5.7. *Predicting punishments in DV cases*

	Percent of DV Cases Resulting in Jail Time	Percent of DV Cases Resulting in Financial Penalty	Percent of DV Cases Resulting in Rehabilitation
Ideology	−4.267[+] (2.080)	1.082 (2.078)	−3.851[*] (1.514)
Sex 1 = Female	−8.035 (6.545)	6.085 (4.334)	−2.132 (7.019)
Years as PD	−0.133 (0.276)	0.239 (0.310)	0.106 (0.233)
Non-White PD 1 = Non-White	3.836 (10.975)	−9.038[+] (5.470)	8.499 (13.810)
County-provided PD 1 = County-provided PD	−5.777 (9.296)	−2.299 (9.890)	−20.018[*] (7.530)
Percent felonies	0.356[**] (0.083)	−0.198 (0.167)	−0.092 (0.085)
Percent plea bargained	−0.207 (0.123)	−0.009 (0.728)	0.175 (0.125)
Vertical prosecution	−1.010 (1.836)	2.831 (2.833)	5.033[**] (1.678)
DV gun laws	6.914[*] (2.555)	7.566[**] (1.888)	2.085 (2.017)
Mandatory arrest 1 = Mandatory arrest	23.889[+] (12.607)	32.606[**] (9.977)	−5.694 (8.913)
Number of cases in 2016	0.085[*] (0.039)	0.153[*] (0.067)	−0.003 (0.040)
Constant	8.868 (20.462)	−1.416 (15.085)	37.726[+] (18.480)
N	110	110	110
R^2	0.330	0.227	0.232
Prob > F	0.000	0.000	0.000

Standard errors in parentheses [+] $p < 0.10$, [*] $p < 0.05$, [**] $p < 0.01$. Using ordinary least squares regression analysis clustered on state.

of PDs' DV cases result in rehabilitation, which is the opposite effect from county-provided services. PD ideology is significant when predicting rehabilitation; the more conservative PDs, the smaller the percentage of their DV cases resulted in rehabilitation.

Our analysis has several results of note. First, there is a difference in what predicts punitive punishment (jail or financial penalty) versus rehabilitation for DV cases. There is a stronger link between the DV laws passed in the legislature and the outcome of PD cases regarding punitive punishment; these results reinforce the consequences of differing laws on gendered violence. For each additional DV gun law a state has on its books, both the percentage of cases receiving jail time and financial penalties on an index of 1–8 increase by 7 percent and 8 percent, respectively. In states with mandatory arrest, the percentage of cases receiving jail time and financial penalties increases by 24 percent and 33 percent, respectively, although the coefficient for jail time is statistically significant at the 0.10 level. For every percent increase in cases that were charged as felonies, there was a 0.40 percent increase in cases receiving jail time.

Both the type of funding for PDs and whether one prosecutor follows a case from beginning to end affect the percentage of PD cases that receive rehabilitation but in opposite directions. When a PD is funded by the county as opposed to the state, there is a statistically significant drop in the percentage of that PD's cases (20 percent) receiving rehabilitation.[5] County-funded PDs may be full-time public employees, or they can be private attorneys who take cases on a low fee for service basis. Caseloads in general have a statistically significant impact on both jail time and financial penalties; for every additional 11 cases that a PD handles, cases receiving jail time increase by 1 percent and cases receiving financial penalties increase by 1.6 percent. Taken together, these results indicate that overworked PDs or private attorneys who take on the occasional DV case are not likely to try to find a nonpunitive solution for a defendant who is accused of DV.

At first it may be surprising that vertical prosecution leads to more rehabilitation instead of punitive punishments; where there is vertical prosecution, there is a 5 percent increase in the percentage of cases receiving rehabilitation. We believe it makes sense because in jurisdictions

---

[5] The directions of the parameter estimates for the impact of a county-funded PD on cases receiving jail time and financial punishment are also negative, but they fall so far below standard levels of statistical significance that they cannot be considered in the same way as the coefficient for the percentage of cases receiving rehabilitation.

where vertical prosecution is common, there is usually a specific number of prosecutors who handle all DV cases and become experts in this area of the law. With that experience may come the knowledge that jail time or financial penalties may not actually help victims, especially in lower income communities. These prosecutors may be more willing to offer PD clients a plea bargain that includes rehabilitation to try to fix the problem instead of punish the consequence.

In our quantitative results, the variable capturing gender never achieved standard levels of statistical significance. This may be due to the interactive effect occurring between gender and ideology. On the whole, PDs are more liberal, but this is especially true for female PDs, 86 percent of whom identified on the liberal side of the spectrum as opposed to 66 percent of male PDs. Other PD characteristics, such as their ideology and whether they were non-white, did become significant when predicting the outcome of their DV cases, although their effects varied across the type of punishment. For non-white PDs, there was a 9 percent decrease in cases receiving financial penalties; the coefficient was not significant for jail time or rehabilitation. Further research into the types of clients that PDs represent by gender, race, ethnicity, and income could yield more insights into this result.

In terms of PD ideology, for every increase on the 7-point scale for ideology, with 1 being most liberal, the percentage of cases receiving jail time dropped by 4 percent and receiving rehabilitation also dropped by about 4 percent, although the coefficient for jail time is statistically significant at the 0.10 level. The findings for financial penalties were not statistically significant. The results for ideology were particularly interesting as more conservative PDs had fewer DV cases that resulted in jail time and rehabilitation. It may be that more conservative PDs have stronger beliefs that punishments of any kind for certain DV offenses are not merited and they are less likely to accept a plea bargain on behalf of their client to settle a case.

5.4 CONCLUSION

The State Public Defender and District Attorney Survey is an important part of the larger journey in trying to understand women's equality through the lens of personal safety statutes at the county and state level. Although our survey captures only one small part of a much more complicated process, we were able to show the varied outcomes of DV cases including the punishments for these crimes and how they are handled by individual PDs and DAs. Each respondent, even from the same state at times, had different levels of DV cases and varied levels of access to training or specialized DV courts. One can argue that varying caseloads and levels of training contributes to inequality among women within the same jurisdiction. Victims who have a prosecutor with a reasonable caseload and some training in DV cases may receive more protection and a more secure outcome for them and their family.

It is clear from this research that the women who make it to the courtroom as victims of DV are seeing their perpetrators receive varying punishments for similar crimes. When governmental bodies pass laws that disadvantage DV victims, they prevent victims from living full, private lives. It is not difficult to think of the consequences that varied sentencing for DV crimes across states can have on women's personal safety. One has to wonder how the incidence of DV would change if the federal courts had decided that Congress could apply the Commerce Clause to the civil remedies for DV crimes. Federal responsibility for these crimes means more resources, attention, and equitable application of the law for victims and defendant alike.

Earlier chapters of this book have shown the varying degrees to which states define DV and protect DV victims from firearms. The responses from the DAs and PDs presented here on what constitutes a DV crime further underscore how poorly local, state, and federal governments in the United States handle violence against women. For many of these women, there is not even a law on the books to hold their assailants accountable for the abuse they endure.

This variation in the implementation of the law raises larger questions of federalism, equality, and the meaning of justice for the thousands of women who suffer from DV across the United States. In our concluding Chapter 7, we discuss where we believe federal and state action could be taken to remedy these inequality-generating differences in the adjudication of DV cases. But first, in Chapter 6, we delve more deeply into the ways we believe women are disadvantaged politically and personally by DV.

6

The Costs of Inequality in Domestic Violence Policies

Many of the specific incidences of domestic violence (DV) that we have depicted throughout this book make their personal costs clear, especially when many of the women victims have been killed by an abuser. Even so, there are other, less deadly consequences that women face in their personal lives ranging from forced custody agreements with abusive former partners, to loss of income due to controlling spouses, and to limited access to resources to help them either get out of an abusive relationship or recover from one. The parallel side of the personal costs of DV policy is the political cost. It can be difficult for women to exercise their right to vote when their domestic partner controls where they go. Or women may fear going to vote because their address may become publicly available. Even more concerning, women might be treated as offenders instead of as victims, convicted of a crime, and subsequently be disenfranchised because of the color of her skin.

The chapter proceeds as follows. We begin by discussing the difficulties that victims face when trying to participate politically while in or removed from an abusive relationship. We then focus on the treatment of women of color in DV cases and how they are often convicted of DV despite being victims of abuse; this discrimination of DV victims who are women of color is one of the most direct political costs of DV policy we can study. We also discuss the relationship between being the victim of DV and incarceration, which also results in disempowering women politically and economically. We conclude the chapter by discussing how these DV costs were exacerbated during the COVID-19 pandemic and how stay-at-home orders limited access to resources that help women in abusive relationships. These lockdowns left women isolated and without any help to escape their abusers. Many states also implemented court restrictions, potentially limiting or delaying protection and justice for many DV victims. The personal costs for these women – from injuries, to loss of income, to psychological abuse – can be staggering.

6.1 POLITICAL COSTS OF UNEQUAL DOMESTIC VIOLENCE POLICIES: BARRIERS TO POLITICAL PARTICIPATION

As we discussed in Chapter 1, DV can include physical abuse, psychological abuse, and isolation. Very few people think about the additional direct political costs that women pay when they are victims of DV. We have spent the majority of this book demonstrating that DV policy has failed its victims at both the federal and state levels because of different applicable laws in each state, varying levels of implementation of DV law, and the lack of a uniform federal response to violence against women. Women pay the price when the government fails to protect them from domestic abuse in terms of their physical safety, financial well-being, and opportunity to participate fully in political life.

In 2018, the Center for American Progress released a report about the obstacles to voting for victims of intimate partner violence. The report acknowledged that few studies specifically included limitation of political participation as a form of abuse because both abuse and voting are typically private acts (Root, 2018). Table 6.1 provides an overview of the types of voter suppression tactics that abusers use.

Victims of DV explain how a common form of political suppression is to attack their self-esteem to the point that they do not perceive their vote as mattering. As survivor Ferial Nijem stated, "When I was in an abusive relationship, I was told all the time that my voice didn't matter. But it does. My voice matters. That's why I vote [now]" (Root, 2018). Ruth Glenn, director of the National Coalition Against Domestic Violence

TABLE 6.1. *DV and voter suppression tactics*

- Preventing victim from voting.
- Coercing victim to vote for specific candidates.
- Controlling whom victim votes for, including filling out their absentee ballot.
- Withholding information about the election, candidates, or registration.
- Utilizing publicly available voter registration information including addresses and phone numbers to stalk, intimidate, or physically harm victims.

Source: Author compiled.

(NCADV), shared how this type of emotional abuse can have the greatest impact on victims: "I've heard from victims that emotional abuse can be the most impactful, because it can last so long. When you tell someone how worthless they are or they don't have an opinion, that can disempower them for a long time" (Cheung, 2020). Survivor Tawni Maisonneuve supported this claim; she stopped voting during her abusive first marriage because her husband "made her feel as if [she wasn't] even intelligent enough to vote" (De La Cretaz, 2020). Maisonneuve also described another form of political suppression: preventing a DV victim from voting or voting for the candidate the person prefers. When she would go to vote, her husband would go with her and tell poll workers she was "slow" and could not vote by herself (De La Cretaz, 2020).

Political canvassers who knock on citizen's doors during elections have had a unique glimpse into the lives of many women, some of which may be in abusive relationships. In her reporting on this subject, Solnit (2018) described Annabel Park, a progressive organizer in Dallas, Texas, and her experience knocking on the door of an apartment in a low-income housing complex:

After I knocked a couple of times, she answered the door with her husband just behind her. She looked petrified and her husband looked menacing behind her. When I made my pitch about Senate candidate Beto O'Rourke, her husband yelled, "We're not interested." She looked at me and silently mouthed, "I support Beto." Before I could respond, she quickly closed the door (Solnit, 2018).

Solnit documented another example when a husband "jokingly" threatened to beat his wife into political submission "'if she needs to know how to vote, I'll just take her in the back and beat her.' He was sort of joking but sort of not" (Solnit, 2018).

Other canvassers relayed how common it was for husbands to refuse to let their wife speak to canvassers, to shout over her, or not to know what party she was actually registered to; women told canvassers they were not "allowed" to vote for a certain candidate Solnit (2018). Unfortunately, the steps taken by states to expand absentee voting or voting by mail due to the pandemic may have made it easier for abusers to politically control their victims. They could simply throw out their victims' ballots or monitor for whom they voted.

It was common for abusers to actively prevent their victims from accessing the information they need to register to vote or know where to vote. This can be particularly easy for abusers who speak English but who have partners that do not. As the Center for American Progress report noted, voting is an act of power and something an abuser may seek to stifle or influence through violence or intimidation. This is particularly true in intimate partner relationships that adhere to strict patriarchal standards, where a wife or female partner's desire to vote for different candidates or policies than her male partner may be seen as a rebellion against patriarchal norms and a challenge to an individual's maleness (Root, 2018).

Controlling victims' access to the Internet or social media also means that victims may miss information about the election, including whom to vote for, when to vote, and how to vote. Such control was again made easier during lockdowns where victims were forced to stay in their homes with their abusers.

Even when survivors of DV are able to leave their abusers, voting can be a dangerous gamble. This is because voter registration information is often publicly accessible, meaning that abusers can easily track down where their victims live. As one survivor recounted, "DV victims can have their safety jeopardized if their location is made public, because it allows offenders to easily find them. All the steps I had painfully taken to protect my safety could be jeopardized by one vote" (Root, 2018). Midori Davidson, a victim of DV who had been held at gunpoint and strangled, was terrified to register to vote after fleeing Charlotte, North Carolina, in the middle of the night. She recounted: "What if he finds me online? I was scared, paranoid and anxious, and I felt alone. Because for the first time I had the freedom to do something and I'm supposed to do, but I didn't want that freedom to be snatched" (Bose, 2020).

Gabrielle Perry is a victim whose information from public voter registration rolls was used to abuse her. After one date, Perry's abuser began texting her details about her life that she had never shared with him; he then threatened to kill her and her mother (Andrew, 2020). Many states are aware of the dangers victims face when their registration information is publicly available, and many have implemented an Address Confidentiality Program (ACP) to assist with this (Farris, 2022). Figure 6.1 is a map that shows the states that have ACPs and whether or not they require a restraining order (or protective order) in order to qualify or some kind of documentation to prove they were abused.

ACPs create a substitute or fake address for participants so that abusers cannot easily find them. Programs typically last three to four years with the option for renewal, but each state differs as to what is included in the confidentiality. California's Safe at Home program includes confidential voter registration (which would be of greatest help to victims like Gabrielle Perry) and suppression of Department of Motor Vehicle records along with rerouting a participant's mail. The majority of

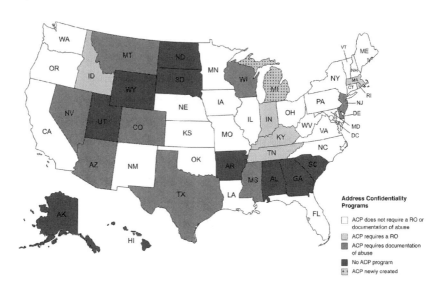

Created with mapchart.net

FIGURE 6.1 **Presence and eligibility requirements of ACPs**
Idaho and Kentucky require either a protective order or documentation of abuse
from an attorney; Texas requires either documentation or meeting with a DV
advocate. We utilized the National Network to End Domestic Violence (NNEDV)
listing of state address confidentiality programs and confirmed the eligibility
requirements using each state's website for its program or the statute that created
the program. See https://nnedv.org/wp-content/uploads/2019/07/Library_Safety_
Net_ACP_Chart_April_2020.pdf.

states require applicants to contact a local domestic or sexual violence
shelter or organization and work with an applicant assistant, which are
often listed on the program's website. While ACPs are an important
component of any survivor's safety plan, some of them do not go far
enough to protect women. The ACPs of New York and North Carolina
do not cover voter registration. In North Carolina, participants must go
through the extra step of submitting an application to conceal their voter
registration information with the county board of elections.

New York does not require any proof of violence or a restraining order
to qualify for its ACP. But if victims want to prevent their registration
information from being released, they have to obtain a

court order in the county where they are registered to vote... this law also allows
survivors who fear for their safety to be excused from going in person to their
polling place, if they are worried their abuser might be waiting for them there. In

order to apply for the exception, however, requires a court order to be acquired and brought to the Board of Elections (De La Cretaz, 2020).

Overall, ACPs are viewed to be effective in enabling victims of DV to register to vote, but in many states, they are underutilized. This failure of reach is due to several factors, the most important of which is that many victims do not know they exist. The National Association of Confidential Address Programs, a group of 29 member states, reported in summer 2021 that 4,000 participants and 1,500 households had taken part in Arizona's ACP over its 10-year history (Root, 2018). In 2020, the organization was able to get 21 states to report the number participants enrolled in their programs: the total was 31,765 with an average of 1,513 per state. This per state average was slightly higher than in 2019 when each state had about 1,398 active participants in its ACP program (National Association of Confidential Address Programs, 2021). While every person being served is important in her or his own right, these numbers show that there are many people who are abused and could benefit from an ACP program but either do not know about it, do not have a restraining order or proof of abuse, or find the process too arduous to complete. As we stated at the start of this book, the NCADV estimates that more than 10 million women and men will be abused every single year in the United States; state ACPs have much more work to do to reach those victims (National Coalition Against Domestic Violence, 2021).

6.2 DISPROPORTIONATE IMPACT OF DOMESTIC VIOLENCE ON WOMEN OF COLOR, IMMIGRANT WOMEN, AND NATIVE AMERICAN WOMEN

For women of color, the negative effects and costs of DV are especially acute because of the combination of greater economic hardships, lack of trust in law enforcement, greater inclination in the judicial system to prosecute and incarcerate them, and more general voter suppression efforts aimed at reducing turnout among voters of color. Crenshaw (1991, pp. 1252–1253) found that combatting DV in minority communities was compromised by efforts to reduce racial stereotypes held about black men and communities of color more generally. She also argues that because of the negative interactions between the black community and law enforcement, black women are "often reluctant to call the police" (Crenshaw. 1991, p. 1257). Few (2005) finds this disparity true for rural communities as well; white women there are more likely than non-white

TABLE 6.2. *Victimization according to race, ethnicity, sex, and DV (%)*

	All Women	White	Black	Native American	Hispanic	Asian/ Pacific Islander
Lifetime psychological aggression	47.1	47.2	53.8	63.8	43.9	29.8
Lifetime physical violence	31.5	30.5	41.2	51.7	29.7	15.3
Percent Intimate partner violence (IPV)-related homicides 2003–2013	55.3	56.8	51.3	55.4	61.0	57.8
Number of IPV-related homicides 2003–2013	4,442	2,446	1,360	112	406	118

Sources: Statistics on percent of lifetime psychological and physical abuse compiled from the Status of Women; see https://statusofwomendata.org/explore-the-data/violence-safety/ violence-and-safety-full-section/#Intimate%20Partner%20Violence%20by%20Race% 20and%20Ethnicity. The Status of Women reported that 61.1 percent of women of two or more races suffered psychological aggression and 51.3 percent suffered physical violence. Statistics on homicide by race compiled from the Centers for Disease Control and Prevention; see www.cdc.gov/mmwr/volumes/66/wr/mm6628a1.htm.

women to call the police for DV incidents and more likely to receive help from them. Table 6.2 presents statistics on the differences of DV victimization by race and ethnicity among women.

This perception of who is a "legitimate victim" of DV crime influences law enforcement in decisions about whether to arrest both the abuser and the abused when there is a conflict in which the abused is defending herself. These perceptions extend to influence prosecutors as to whether to prosecute abusers and how juries will respond to victims from black versus white communities or male versus female victims. Condon (2010) argues that the higher likelihood of dual arrests among minorities involved in DV is a negative by-product of police intervention. Removing and imprisoning the abuser can create economic hardship for many women – especially if they are arrested as well as their abusers. Therefore, she explains, women may be more physically safe but in more dire economic circumstances.

A set of studies on incarcerated women also shows the impact of DV. In her survey of research on incarcerated women, Dichter (2015) describes research findings that anywhere from 55 percent to 70 percent of women who are incarcerated experienced intimate partner violence in their life-time. These studies also often find that women are convicted of crimes of violence against their DV perpetrators, or they are coerced into taking part in crimes by their abusers. Other studies find that even beginning in childhood, women who are victims of DV are statistically more likely to engage in "property crimes, drug offenses, and commercial sex work" (DeHart, 2008; DeHart et al., 2014). Drug addiction can be common among these women and lead to repeated periods of incarceration as a result. Women subsequently face all of the barriers that come with criminal convictions and serving jail time in terms of economic stability; as con-victed criminals, they lose their right to vote while serving their sentence and on parole. Although the rate of difference is declining, women of color are still more likely to be incarcerated in state prisons than white women (Mauer, 2013). According to The Sentencing Project, 5.17 million people could not vote in the 2020 election due to a felony conviction; this was proportionately higher for African Americans; more than 1.2 million of those disenfranchised are women. Maine and Vermont are the only two states that have no restrictions on who can vote whether they are in prison, on parole/probation, or have been convicted of a felony (Uggen et al., 2020).

Bailey builds on Crenshaw's work and argues that DV-related policies such as mandatory arrest, victimless prosecutions (statements about an incident can be substituted for in-person testimony), and no-drop pros-ecution (which means the complainant cannot drop the charges after the case is started) remove "decisional privacy" from women, and dispropor-tionately so for poor women and women and color (Bailey 2009, 2011, pp. 151–152). Because these women are typically the subject of more state monitoring and interference regarding child safety that results in having their communities depleted through mass incarceration, she argues that the remedy may be worse than the harm.

Bailey also writes that policies that do not require a woman's partici-pation in the criminal proceedings from pressing charges to testifying "encourage the legal silence of women" (Bailey, 2009, p. 33), and women are "disempowered from participating in a legal system that is supposed to help them" (Bailey, 2009, p. 37). Rather than advocating for more intervention and consistent practices, Bailey argues that a woman should be heard in the legal proceedings regarding what solutions would work best for her safety, which may mean relying less on punishment. She advocates for providing services related to economic support to enable women to remove themselves and their children from their homes and to make programs available to the abuser to prevent that person's future violence in the household. Condon (2010) echoes this point albeit more forcefully by recommending the use of "restorative justice" methods that remove DV from the purview of the prosecutorial state and place it in the community where it occurs. She argues that encouraging a community approach that works to maintain family units while deterring future abuse within the household would be a more productive and better solution, especially for women of color. These multiple streams of research emphasize the long-lasting cycle of disempowerment that is associated with DV and the sheer failure of current policies to prevent it.

For immigrant women who are either permanent legal or undocumented residents, the negative impact of DV is intensified because seeking remedies for DV may be even more difficult than for citizens. In their study of DV among immigrant women, Ammar et al. (2012) conducted interviews with Latina immigrants from Mexico and Central and South America in the Washington, D.C., area. Less than 30 percent of the women in their sample (N = 230) reported calling the police to report a DV incident; the primary factors identified to explain whether they called the police for help were immigration status (legal or undocumented) and whether their children were exposed to the violence. But these authors also noted that when the police were called and responded, the majority of the conversation was conducted in English, which put the women with limited English proficiency at a significant disadvantage. Their study also revealed that only 28.6 percent of cases produced arrests of the accused domestic abuser and that these arrests were typically made when a restraining order was already in place.

Messing et al. (2015) built on this work in their study using a subset of Latina women who participated in surveys conducted by the Pew Hispanic Center in 2008. They collected demographic data including immigration status on the women in the sample and asked them questions about their fear of deportation, their perceptions of the use of excessive violence against Latinos and how fairly the police treat Latinos, and how fairly they believe the courts treat Latinos. The authors found that perceptions of how Latinos are treated by law enforcement had a strong effect on whether they reported DV incidents; the more confident they were that they would be treated fairly and that the police would not use excessive force on the alleged abuser, the more likely they were to report the DV incident. Of particular interest is that running the Messing et al. model with just the variable measuring fear of deportation for themselves or family members exerted a depressive effect on survey participants' likelihood of reporting a DV incidence; once the perceptions of police and the courts were added to the model, the effect of fear of deportation was no longer statistically significant. This result about immigrant women dovetails with the arguments cited previously about black women's interaction with law enforcement and how it can depress the likelihood of reporting DV incidents (Bailey, 2009; Crenshaw, 1991; Few, 2005).

Immigrant women also face the intersection of multiple forces that run counter to each other in creating an environment that discourages these women to report and seek protection from DV (Condon, Filindra, and Wichowsky, 2016; Sokoloff, 2005; Sokoloff and Dupont, 2005; Sokoloff and Pratt, 2005). Women who come from patriarchal cultures, for example, may feel more constrained in challenging male dominance in any way, including the commission of violence. At the same time, active stereotypes that pervade the judicial system may discount DV in immigrant communities by attributing it to "culture" and deemphasizing it as a crime. In this circumstance, immigrant women may face obstacles to obtaining protection and prosecution for DV crimes against them because of obstacles in and outside their communities. These women are also potentially more vulnerable to threats from their abusers because they may have limited English proficiency, may depend economically on their abusers, and may fear being deported or losing their legal immigration status if it is tied to their abuser (Sokoloff, 2008, pp. 238–240). As did Condon (2010), Sokoloff raises the possibility that a government-centered judicial solution to DV may be an unrealistic option for immigrant women for the reasons stated previously and because community-based solutions that work to discourage DV and maintain household stability may be more effective.

Native American women also face increased risks of DV. According to a 2016 report issued by the US Department of Justice (Office of Justice Programs, 2016), over 80 percent of Native American adults had been a victim of violence. Native American men and women have similar levels of physical and psychological violence although women experience significantly higher levels of sexual violence and stalking (Office of Justice Programs, 2016). Native American DV is unique because it occurs with high amounts of substance abuse in places that are poor, rural, expansive, and isolated (Jones, 2008). A considerable amount of violence against Native American women is committed by non-Native men who are on tribal lands (National Congress of American Indians, 2018).

The 2022 bipartisan Violence Against Women Act (VAWA) reauthorization created new programs specifically for Native American communities. Sen. Lisa Murkowski (Republican, Alaska), who was vice chairman of the Senate Committee on Indian Affairs, cosponsored the bill and specifically worked on the Tribal Title section with Sen. Brian Schatz (Democrat, Hawaii), chairman of the Senate Committee on Indian Affairs. As we discussed in Chapter 2, the last reauthorization of VAWA in 2013 created special domestic violence criminal jurisdictions (SDVCJ) that allowed tribal governments to prosecute non-Native American offenders for DV against Native Americans on their reservation. In Alaska, however, only one tribe, the Metlakatla, has a reservation; other tribes function as villages and therefore are not considered as a reservation or Indian country. Put simply, the creation of the SDVCJs excluded Alaska, which is the state where the highest number of Native Americans live (Granitz, 2013).

The Tribal Title of the 2022 reauthorization bill aimed to correct this. The provision "allow[ed] a limited number of Tribes in Alaska, on a pilot basis, to exercise special tribal criminal jurisdiction. This special tribal criminal jurisdiction will be exercised on a concurrent basis with the State" (United States Senator for Alaska Lisa Murkowski, 2022). The reauthorization increases funding to support tribes who want to adopt an SDVCJ but limits the number of tribes that could exercise a Special Tribal Criminal Jurisdiction to 30 with the US attorney general in consultation with the secretary of interior choosing up to five tribes each year.[1] While this is a good start to expanding tribal sovereignty to cases of DV with non-Native American offenders, only a small number of the 574 federally recognized tribes have adopted SDVCJs since 2013, suggesting much more work needs to be done to ensure justice for Native American victims of DV.

Compounding all these formidable barriers to full political engagement are more widespread efforts to suppress the votes of people of color and low-income individuals at the state level. According to the Brennan Center for Justice (2021), in 2021, "19 states enacted 33 laws that make it harder for Americans to vote." Included in these restrictive laws are measures that would allow states to delete voters from the election rolls; this has become a more common tool in recent years directed at reducing

---

[1] United States Senator for Alaska Lisa Murkowski. 2022. "Schatz, Murkowski Applaud Senate Passage of Historic Provisions in Violence Against Women Act Reauthorization." United States Senate. March 11, 2022. www.murkowski.senate.gov/press/release/schatz-murkowski-applaud-senate-passage-of-historic-tribal-provisions-in-violence-against-women-act-reauthorization.

the number of minority voters in some states. Other states have increased the specifications associated with voter ID laws that have already been shown to discourage or make it more difficult for low-income and minority individuals to vote. The states of Georgia and Florida literally made it a crime to bring food and water to people waiting in line to vote (Brennan Center for Justice, 2021).

Although it may seem that voter suppression and DV are worlds apart, they intersect in their capacity to disempower women. We know that women comprise the majority of victims of DV; we know that abuse is not limited to physical violence and extends to coercive financial and even political control; we know that women who are incarcerated have typically been abused by an intimate partner, and we know that the criminal justice system does not treat women of color as it does their white counterparts when considering whether to make arrests in DV incidents. The failure to address and prevent DV therefore produces a systemic ripple effect of disempowerment among women in American society that can literally last their entire lives.

6.3 PERSONAL COSTS OF UNEQUAL DOMESTIC VIOLENCE POLICIES: THE EFFECTS OF THE COVID-19 PANDEMIC

Public health crises such as the COVID-19 pandemic refocused our lens on the danger that many women live in every day. It is important to understand what policies that can assist women in violent situations during a public health crisis are in place; the COVID-19 pandemic has underscored how broken the system is across the entire United States. The policy decisions to impose lockdowns and close courts due to the pandemic perfectly illustrate the unintended consequences of public health policies and the lack of voice that abused women had in these policy decisions. Not until DV cases rose and/or the type of abuse worsened did many government officials recognize the negative impact their policies were having on abused women. Too often we have seen a late policy response instead of considering this vulnerable population from the onset. This chapter is designed to showcase the need to consider the collateral impacts of policies on the personal safety of women even when the core policy problem is not directly connected to DV.

The bottom line is this: women were still being abused during lockdown, and states and cities provided different levels of response for essentially the same public safety problem. All of the systematic factors that produce DV were still present during the COVID-19 pandemic, but they were more intense. However, rather than increasing the number of calls for help during periods of lockdown, COVID-19 produced a "hidden epidemic" characterized by drops in calls to law enforcement (Selvaratnam, 2020). Most experts recognized that the drop was not a good sign: "The problem we think people are having is how to notify us," said Melinda Katz, Queens, NY district attorney, about her own district's plummet of almost 40 percent in DV arrests during the quarantine (Selvaratnam, 2020). Whereas DV hotlines all over the country were at first experiencing spikes in calls, they were experiencing a concerning drop off in calls as sheltering in place dragged on: "Experts have viewed the decline in calls for help with alarm, as it suggests survivors might not be able to get away from abusers long enough to reach out" (Kelley, 2020).

Immediately following strict lockdown enforcements, the volume of calls in Maine dropped "steeply, in a way that was scary," described Regina Rooney, communications director for the Maine Coalition to End Domestic Violence (Lundy, 2021). It was also reported that contact with survivors in Maine during May 2020 was down 39 percent from the previous month of April; shelter requests declined by 55 percent, and helpline calls decreased by 15 percent (Lundy). This decrease in calls was not an indication of decreased violence. Rather, the pandemic "has made intimate partner violence more common—and often more severe" reported *Time Magazine* (Kluger, 2021). According to a statement released by Human Rights Watch (2020), "crises and lockdowns can trigger a greater incidence of domestic violence for many reasons," citing increased stress, cramped and difficult living conditions, and breakdowns in community support mechanisms. A study done at Brigham and Women's Hospital in Boston reported that radiology scans and superficial wounds consistent with domestic abuse from March 11 to May 3, 2020, the nine-week period following Governor Baker's lockdown order, exceeded the totals for the same period in 2018 and 2019 combined (Mozes, 2020). Mardi Chadwick Balcom, a coauthor of that report, stated that the data confirmed their suspicion: "[B]eing confined to home for a period of time would increase the possibility for violence between intimate partners" (Mozes, 2020). Hema Sarang-Sieminski, policy director at Jane Doe Inc., the Massachusetts Coalition Against Sexual Assault and Domestic Violence, experienced this overall trend as well, expressing "the reports from programs are that there was an initial dip in calls, and then it escalated" (Vigna, 2021).

A hotline operator in Austin, Texas, described the calls that did come in as heightened in intensity and urgency, going from zero to 60 in an instant (Vigna, 2021). The *Los Angeles Times* reported on a study that revealed not only an increase in DV cases during the pandemic but also an increase in and escalation of the physical injuries that abusers had been inflicting on their victims (Healy, 2020).

A study of DV crime in Atlanta during the first seven months of the year in 2018, 2019, and 2020 by Evans, Hawk, and Ripkey found that during the period of lockdown, DV crimes there increased and then decreased after the lockdown was lifted (2021, p. 142). Moreover, even as other types of crime decreased during lockdown, DV crime increased. Davis, Gilbar, and Padilla-Medina (2021) conducted a survey of respondents during the COVID-19 pandemic to assess its impact on the likelihood of either being a victim of DV or committing an act of DV. These authors found that testing positive for COVID-19 and/or experiencing symptoms increased the likelihood of being the victim of DV while losing a job increased the likelihood of committing an act of DV. It is apparent that the tangible effects of the pandemic and lockdown on DV in the United States produced worrying trends in both higher levels of actionable cases and more extreme physical violence.

Figure 6.2 provides the timeline of each region's lockdowns. We chose to show the percentage of states in each region instead of the number to better compare the length of lockdown between each region. Figure 6.3 and Table 6.3 provide the exact start and end dates of the lockdowns; keep in mind that just because a state is represented as being in lockdown for a specific period does not mean it was in lockdown for that entire time. States had varying beginning and end dates for lockdowns; therefore, we counted a state as being in lockdown during a month even if it was only for one day. April was the most common month for lockdowns in all regions across the country, suggesting that it would have been an especially dangerous month for DV victims. It is also important to note that northern states were in lockdown over two months while southern states were typically in lockdown for only one month if at all.

In February 2021, the National Commission on COVID-19 and Criminal Justice released a study that conducted a meta-analysis of data on DV during the pandemic. The authors analyzed data from 12 US-based studies and 6 international studies; primary source data varied across these studies and included "police crime/incident reports, police calls for service, DV hotline registries, and health records" (Piquero et al. 2021). Using the US-based studies alone, the authors found that the incidence of DV increased an average of 8.1 percent during the pandemic. It is a reasonable assumption that this is an undercount of DV incidents

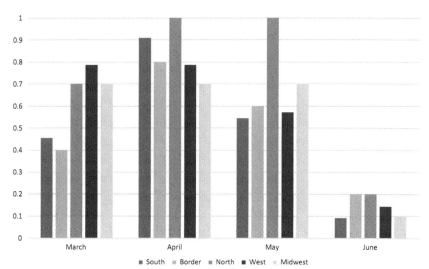

South: Alabama, Arkansas, Florida, Georgia, Louisiana, Maryland, Mississippi, North Carolina, South Carolina, Texas, Virginia
Border: Kentucky, Missouri, Oklahoma, Tennessee, West Virginia
North: Connecticut, Delaware, Maine, Massachusetts, New Hampshire, New Jersey, New York, Pennsylvania, Rhode Island,
    Vermont
West: Alaska, Arizona, California, Colorado, Hawaii, Idaho, Montana, Nevada, New Mexico, North Dakota, Oregon, Utah,
    Washington, Wyoming
Midwest: Illinois, Indiana, Iowa, Kansas, Minnesota, Nebraska, Ohio, Wisconsin

FIGURE 6.2 **Percentage of states in each region with COVID-19 stay-at-home orders by month, March–June 2020**
Sources: Information in this chart was compiled from the following sources: https://ballotpedia.org/State_court_closures_in_response_to_the_coronavirus_(COVID-19)_pandemic_between_March_and_November,_2020#cite_note-May11-10; www.usatoday.com/storytelling/coronavirus-reopening-america-map/.

given that a phone call made from home in close proximity with one's abuser could put the victim in greater danger (Gupta and Stahl, 2020).

To the extent that they could, organizations were prepared to receive fewer calls and pivot toward text and online chat services: "Text messages to the hotline have also skyrocketed, suggesting that victims have little physical distance from their abusers and find texting is safer than calling" (Bosman, 2020). For example, in Baltimore, Maryland, DV services provided by organizations such as TurnAround also received fewer calls than normal but believed that this did not mean the need for their services had decreased: "Baltimore-area service providers believe that's because survivors are confined with their abusers and can't reach out. They also say confusion about what services are available during this period may be contributing to fewer people coming forward" (Anderson, 2020).

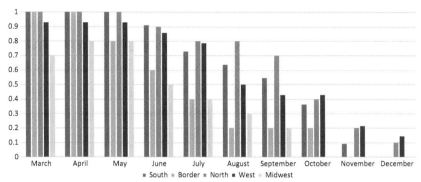

South: Alabama, Arkansas, Florida, Georgia, Louisiana, Maryland, Mississippi, North Carolina, South Carolina, Texas, Virginia
Border: Kentucky, Missouri, Oklahoma, Tennessee, West Virginia
North: Connecticut, Delaware, Maine, Massachusetts, New Hampshire, New Jersey, New York, Pennsylvania, Rhode Island, Vermont
West: Alaska, Arizona, California, Colorado, Hawaii, Idaho, Montana, Nevada, New Mexico, North Dakota, Oregon, Utah, Washington, Wyoming
Midwest: Illinois, Indiana, Iowa, Kansas, Minnesota, Nebraska, Ohio, Wisconsin

FIGURE 6.3 **Percentage of states in each region with COVID-19 court restrictions by month, March–December 2020**
Sources: Information in this figure was compiled from the following sources: https://ballotpedia.org/State_court_closures_in_response_to_the_coronavirus_(COVID-19)_pandemic_between_March_and_November,_2020#cite_note-May11-10; www.usatoday.com/storytelling/coronavirus-reopening-america-map/

However, this phenomenon does not seem to have been universal. In the cities of Sandy Springs and John's Creek, located near Atlanta, Georgia, the respective sheriff's department reported an increase in DV calls of 26 and 43 percent when the stay-at-home mandate was enforced (Murchison, 2020). The Atlanta Police Department reported a staggering 58 percent increase in DV in its jurisdiction between early March and late April 2020; it reported a 79 percent increase in DV filings during March 2020 compared to March 2019 (Burns, 2020). Governor Brian Kemp reminded his constituents of the state's DV hotline number as an Atlanta hospital experienced a 15 percent increase in the DV cases at its facilities (Kueppers, 2020).

COVID-19 also created a situation in which victims had limited access to shelters and other institutional services they relied on prepandemic. Nonprofit DV organizations in Baltimore, however, urged their constituents to continue to access the available resources through online services, reaching out to trusted friends, and making use of the still – albeit slow – operating courts, which continued offering emergency protection orders (Anderson, 2020). The Sexual Assault/Spouse Abuse Resource Center located in Harford County (Baltimore) operated its 24-hour

TABLE 6.3. *COVID-19 stay-at-home orders and court restrictions by state*

State	Period of Stay-at-Home Orders	Period of Court Restrictions (suspension of in-person proceedings and/or jury trials)
Alabama	4/4–4/30/2020	3/14–9/14/20
Alaska	3/11–4/21/2020	3/16–11/2020
Arizona	3/30–5/15/2020	3/16–6/15/2020
Arkansas	Never issued	3/17–7/1/2020
California	3/19/2020	3/24/20–10/9/2020
Colorado	3/26–5/8/2020	3/16–8/3/2020
Connecticut	3/23–5/20/2020	3/12–5/13/2020
Delaware	3/24–5/15/2020	3/15–10/5/2020
Florida	3/20–4/30/2020	3/16–7/17/2020
Georgia	4/3–4/30/2020	3/14 11/9/2020
Hawaii	3/25–5/31/2020	3/17–10/2/2020
Idaho	3/25–4/30/2020	3/16–12/6/2020
Illinois	3/21–5/30/2020	4/3–8/3/2020
Indiana	3/25–5/1/2020	3/16–7/1/2020
Iowa	Never issued	3/14–9/14/2020
Kansas	3/30–5/3/2020	3/16–5/1/2020
Kentucky*	3/26–6/29/2020	3/16–8/1/2020
Louisiana	3/23–5/14/2020	3/16–6/30/2020
Maine	4/2–5/31/2020	3/16–9/7/2020
Maryland	3/30–5/15/2020	3/16–8/31/2020
Massachusetts	4/24–5/18/2020	3/15–11/9/2020
Michigan	3/24–6/5/2020	3/16–9/25/2020
Minnesota	3/27–5/4/2020	3/14–6/1/2020
Mississippi†*	4/3–5/11/2020	3/16–5/15/2020
Missouri	4/6–5/3/2020	3/16–5/1/2020
Montana	3/26–4/24/2020	3/13–5/4/2020
Nebraska	None	None
Nevada†	3/31–5/15/2020	None
New Hampshire	3/27–6/15/2020	3/16–8/25/2020
New Jersey	3/21–6/9/2020	3/16–9/21/2020
New Mexico	3/24–5/15/2020	3/24–7/15/2020
New York	3/22–5/15/2020	3/16–9/9/2020
North Carolina	3/30–5/8/2020	3/16–10/15/2020
North Dakota	Never issued	3/16–7/1/2020
Ohio†	3/23–5/30/2020	Limited
Oklahoma	Never issued	3/16–4/16/2020
Oregon	3/23–6/19/2020	3/12–7/1/2020
Pennsylvania	4/1–5/8/2020	3/20–6/1/2020
Rhode Island	3/28–5/8/2020	3/16–9/7/2020
South Carolina	4/7–5/12/2020	3/16–9/21/2020
South Dakota	Never issued	Limited

State	Period of Stay-at-Home Orders	Period of Court Restrictions (suspension of in-person proceedings and/or jury trials)
Tennessee	4/2–4/30/2020	3/14–7/3/2020
Texas	4/2–4/30/2020	3/13–10/1/2020
Utah	Never issued	3/13– Unspecified date
Vermont	3/24–5/15/2020	3/17–1/1/21
Virginia	3/30–6/10/2020	3/16–10/11/20
Washington	3/23–5/4/2020	3/13–7/6/20
West Virginia	3/24–5/4/2020	3/12–6/29/2020
Wisconsin	3/25–5/26/2020	3/23–5/22/2020
Wyoming	Never issued	3/23–10/5/2020

*Partial reopening of Kentucky began 5/11/2020; full reopening was on 6/29/2020. Criminal procedures resumed 8/1/2020, and civil trials resumed 10/1/2020.
†The Mississippi Supreme Court let individual judges decide whether to postpone trials; Carson City and Las Vegas courthouses limited public access; state courts in Ohio remained open, but local courts suspended or delayed trials, and on May 19, 2020, the Ohio Trial Advisory Group published recommendations on resuming jury trials.
Sources: https://ballotpedia.org/State_court_closures_in_response_to_the_coronavirus_(COVID-19)_pandemic_between_March_and_November,_2020#cite_note-May11-10; www.usatoday.com/storytelling/coronavirus-reopening-america-map/.

hotline emergency shelter with the necessary precautions and its online chat option (Anderson, 2020). The Connecticut Coalition Against Domestic Violence experienced a similar trend, according to President Karen Jarmoc. She stated in a virtual call hosted in December 2020, "Shelters are at 150% capacity... 100% of the shelters are full and then 50% of that overload is being housed in hotels for their safety" (Gendreau and Fuller, 2020). According to Vigna (2021), individuals in Massachusetts seeking shelter were also put in hotels as Deborah Hall of the YWCA of Central Massachusetts explained, "[S]helters were already full and some had to be depopulated to maintain the health of survivors."

In the Northeast, the *Boston Globe* reported a decrease in calls made to the Boston police related to intimate-partner violence in March and April 2020 compared to the level of calls during the same time period in 2019, citing concerns that the reason for this trend was that victims feared to report abuse while they were stuck at home with their abusers and noting that cases were actually going unreported (Ebbert, 2020; Rosen, 2020). Suffolk County District Attorney Rachel Rollins said, "With the fact that we're all in our homes, this is a ticking time bomb, essentially, for victims of domestic violence, [and] children who are abused and neglected" (Ebbert, 2020). Similarly, the *Pittsburgh-Post Gazette* reported a sharp decrease in calls to DV hotlines during Pennsylvania's peak lockdown period, which quickly transitioned to a rapid increase in calls to shelters and police departments once the state transitioned into a less restrictive lockdown phase (Lauer, 2020).

When Pennsylvania started to loosen its lockdown, Hilary O'Toole, the assistant director at Crisis Center North, said, "Our counseling department is expecting an onslaught of calls in the next couple of weeks" (Lauer, 2020). *The Washington Post* similarly reported a drastic increase in calls during the pandemic to the non-profit D.C. Safe, a group that coordinates emergency victim services in response to federal and local agencies (Lang, 2020). Natalia Ortero, the organization's executive director, said, "Once people start spending more and more time together and you start having multiple incidents of violence at home, our call volume is just going to continue to increase" (Lang, 2020). Ultimately, the important takeaways are that the COVID-19 pandemic made it challenging for victims of DV to seek help due to the facts that they were in lockdown with their abusers and that the pandemic itself most likely contributed to an increase in abuse.

Regarding prosecution of abusers, the *Houston Chronicle* reported in August 2020 an increase in cases of DV reported to the sheriff's office which resulted in an increased number of arrests. Emilee Dawn Whitehurst, president and CEO of the Houston Area Women's Center, said, "Victims are becoming increasingly more vulnerable to tactics of their abusers. COVID-19 has been weaponized by abusers. They are using it as a way to further intimidate victims and coerce them to stay in situations that are truly untenable" (Dellinger, 2020). On the other side, legal aid attorneys were more swamped after the pandemic began than ever by requests for assistance in DV cases. Jo-Ann Wallace, president of the National Legal Aid & Defender Association, said, "[A]s the economic impacts really begin to hit – more people are going to be eligible for legal aid at a time when resources will be much scarcer" (Ayres-Brown, 2020).

The economic fallout of the COVID-19 pandemic is another variable increasing the number of women in danger. As Evans, Lindauer, and Farrell (2020, pp. 2302–2304) wrote:

Economic independence is a critical factor in violence prevention. For many people who experience [intimate partner violence], the financial entanglement with an abusive partner is too convoluted to sever without an alternative source of economic support. The pandemic has exacerbated financial entanglement by causing increased job loss and unemployment, particularly among women of color, immigrants, and workers without a college education.

Many of the reports on women's employment and the pandemic focus exclusively on how this affected women's earnings and job prospects, but very few of them considered the importance of access to money in order to escape an abuser or to support children while divorcing a violent spouse. Economist Anna Aizer (2010) showed that policies that narrow the male–female wage gap reduce violence against women, demonstrating the ways financial inequalities fuel inequalities in other parts of women's lives. Aizer's framework also overlooks how a male partner losing his job or wages may incite further stress and violence in the home.

The Women's Resource Center, an organization working to end DV in Rhode Island, reported on responding to new types of abuse. Executive Director Jessica Walsh explained how people often think of DV as just physical violence, but "it can also include financial, emotional or psychological abuse" (Ayres-Brown, 2021). Walsh noted that there had been cases of abusers invoking COVID-19 as a reason to monitor their partner's every move. Additionally, she explained how "financial abuse is one of the big reasons why folks who are experiencing DV either stay or return to an unhealthy situation" (Ayres-Brown, 2021). Deborah Hall, director of DV services at YWCA Central Massachusetts, expressed similar concerns due to the great difficulty of being financially independent amid the additional psychological, physical, and financial abuse exacerbated by the pandemic Vigna (2021). According to a study of intimate partner violence published in the *New England Journal of Medicine*, the pandemic did in fact exacerbate financial entanglement (Evans, Lindauer, and Farrell, 2020). The study explained how survivors' dependence on their partner's economic support had risen due to the pandemic, which caused increased job loss and unemployment.

Figure 6.3 provides the percentage of states in each region whose supreme court implemented restrictions. These included anything from suspending in-person proceedings, to suspending jury trials, to leaving it to the discretion of each judge to decide whether to delay trials. Most states opted to resume normal court operations using a phased approach. Therefore, the end dates from Figure 6.3 refer to the end of all restrictions, some of which may have been lifted at an earlier date. For example, California allowed some criminal trials without juries to resume in September 2020 but did not lift all restrictions until October 9 of that year. It is important to note that court restrictions lasted much longer than stay-at-home orders and were adopted much more widely. This means that even when women could escape their abusers after lockdown, they might not have had easy access to the courts. The earlier analysis in this chapter demonstrated the consequences of stay-at-home orders on DV victims, but these orders provide only half of the picture; court restriction dates also presented challenges for victims of DV during the pandemic.

In a March 2020 Center for Court Innovation podcast, Robyn Mazur, director of Gender Justice Initiatives, noted that even before COVID-19, it had been difficult for courts from different states and communities to work and learn from one another because "every community is unique and they're bringing their individual laws that they have and different resources" (Wolf, 2020). In this podcast, Kelly Greenough, chief judge of the Family Division in Tulsa, Oklahoma, and Carroll Kelly, administrative judge of the Domestic Violence Division of the Eleventh Judicial Circuit in Miami-Dade County, Florida shared their experiences during COVID-19. Judge Greenough described how her court continued issuing emergency protective orders as well as utilizing the local newspaper and social media to make sure residents understood the judicial process and resources available to them. Judge Greenough also discussed how her court was able to utilize a 1982 state law that said emergency protective orders could be handled remotely when the court building was closed (Wolf, 2020).

Judge Kelly described a different process in her court where victims could still physically go to the courthouse with as much social distancing as possible. She explained the challenging circumstances:

So, we're struggling. It's difficult. There's no doubt about it. There's people that are having their cases reset, they're feeling they're not getting access to the court. And we understand all of that. So, we're trying to constantly balance the rights of individuals and access to justice and due process versus the rights of individuals to stay healthy. And it's causing stress throughout our court system for sure. People don't want to go to court, the workers don't want to go to court. Our administrative order from our court is mandating that we do not go to court. And so, there's tension because some people are going to court based on the mandates of what cases must be continued to be heard (Wolf, 2020).

Judge Kelly went onto explain that requests for protective orders were down in Miami, which was concerning to her. She said:

Who really wants to have to go out in public, perhaps take public transportation and expose themselves and their children to come to a courthouse where again, they'd have to expose themselves and their children? And then, even if they receive a restraining order and it would be a spouse or a family member to have that person basically be thrown out of the house when there was effectively no place for people to go, when they're thrown out of the house. The system itself and the circumstances right now I think are particularly challenging for victims who are experiencing domestic violence from both a personal safety standpoint regarding COVID-19 for themselves, for their children, and for their spouses and loved ones that may be the individuals that are perpetuating the domestic violence (Wolf, 2020).

Offenders under existing orders of protection prior to COVID-19 had their orders extended in Oklahoma where courthouses were closed; in Florida, many batterer intervention programs moved to a virtual environment for offenders. Put together, the stay-at-home orders with the physical closure of courts made it difficult for women to escape their abusers, access resources, and seek justice for the abuse they endured. However, the Judges Greenough and Kelly described some of the innovations their courts had adopted, such as moving to virtual hearings and creating listservs with individuals and organizations invested in DV policy. These practices, such as holding DV emergency order hearings virtually, meant that women still had access to the judicial system even when the courts were closed; still that accommodation also fell short in instances where women did not have access to technology (Neumann, 2020). Overall, the pandemic has exacerbated the obstacles to protection from DV although some of these new practices may produce innovations in ways the judicial system could become safer and more easily accessible for victims.

While some states were reluctant to implement certain policies, such as lockdowns, they were more likely to restrict access to the courts. These restrictions on court access put victims at risk even after they could leave their homes because they might not have been able to secure the kinds of protective orders they needed. Because every state has their own judicial system with varying abilities to work virtually, women had varying levels of access to the justice system based on where they lived. The pandemic both intensified and revealed many public policy challenges at the local, state, and federal levels. For DV victims, the pandemic exacerbated a decades-long public safety problem for women in the United States.

6.4 CONCLUSION

In this chapter, we described the ways in which women are personally and politically disempowered by DV with specifically more severe impacts felt by women of color. Much of the attention that is paid by society to DV centers on injury and death, but there are day-to-day obstacles preventing women in participating in the economy and political life due to restrictions placed on them by their abusers. These obstacles are hard to see but no less real. We have presented qualitative evidence here that strongly suggests that political oppression is an active component of DV.

We also discussed the clearly disproportionately negative impact that DV has on women of color from the failure of enforcement by police, to dual arrests of black women who make DV complaints and their abusers, to higher rates of incarceration for minority and low-income women who have been victims of DV. When coupled with current efforts to suppress the votes of minority and low-income voters, it becomes readily apparent that the failure of policy in this area at both the federal and state levels is felt more acutely by women of color.

Lastly, we dealt with the effects of COVID-19 in this chapter to highlight how the regular channels of protection for women failed even more during lockdowns during the pandemic, especially in terms of limited access to the courts. One of the victims of this rise in DV was Louvenia Penwright who was fatally shot in the neck by her boyfriend Willie Shropshire Jr. in front of law enforcement in a suburb of New Orleans. Sheriff Joe Lopinto explained that "the couple began arguing at their home... just before 7:30 pm. A neighbor called 911 to report hearing gunshots as Shropshire attacked Penwright. Deputies arrived to find the couple arguing in the yard. The man grabbed the woman, held a revolver to her neck and pulled the trigger. Three deputies then shot him" (Hunter, 2020). Penwright's murder was one of many DV-related homicides that occurred during the pandemic. Many of these victims' stories will never be known, and the consequences of their murders will live with their family, friends, and communities long after the pandemic ends. In our final chapter, we present suggestions for reforms in federal and state approaches to DV to ensure greater levels of human security for women.

7

Pathways for Improving Human Security for Women

In the beginning of this book, we argued two points:

Existing federalist response to a widespread national problem does not successfully protect women, resulting in varying levels of inequality between men and women and among women across state lines. Decreased personal safety prevents women from living full private and public lives.

Women cannot be equal to men or to each other if they are victims of violence and if the law does not justly protect them. If women are unsafe in their personal security, they are not being treated equally under the law, which affects their civic and noncivic lives.

In this concluding chapter, we reflect on what we have learned about the policymaking process of domestic violence (DV) in the United States and how this has revealed that women are treated unequally under the law.

7.1 THE BIGGER PICTURE: DOMESTIC VIOLENCE POLICY IN A FEDERAL SYSTEM

In Chapter 1, we provided our theoretical framework for understanding DV policy in the United States. Our argument about federalism creating inequality under the law for DV victims – who are primarily women – rests on both ground-breaking scholarship that first uncovered the fact that federalism plays a role in creating gender inequality in the United States (Mettler, 1998; Skocpol, 1995) as well as our theory that this gender inequality is nuanced. Because practice related to DV is primarily in the hands of state governments, women are subject to varying levels of protection from their abusers based on where they live; this reinforces our first two levels of gender inequality in DV policy whereby women are unequal to men in human security and unequal to women across state lines and within legal jurisdictions. Utilizing the Power and Control Wheel used by DV advocates and experts, we discussed the disconnect between the federal definition of DV with that of numerous states and of scholarship. We also reviewed the levels of DV in the United States, paying particular attention to female DV homicides over the period of this study, from 1990 to 2017. We concluded our analysis in Chapter 1 by examining the various factors that have affected DV policy, including federal policy adoption, the rise of social conservatism, race and ethnicity, and the role of the gun lobby. Overall, Chapter 1 discussed the problem of DV in this country, provided a theoretical framework for how political science should study it, and suggested variables that will be studied in the remainder of the book.

Chapter 2 provided a detailed policy history of the federal government's minimal response to DV, setting the stage for a state-by-state approach to address violence against women that results in treating women unequally in the eyes of the law. We analyzed how three separate institutions – Congress, the executive branch, and the Supreme Court – have addressed DV policy. We illustrated how increasing polarization has undermined Congressional capacity to enact federal DV laws. Congress was able to enact and with presidential approval pass the 1994 Violence Against Women Act (VAWA) and reauthorize it three times after that in 2000, 2005, and 2013 with relatively little disagreement between the parties. Yet an expansion of DV policy to gun control exacerbated party differences on support for VAWA. This intersection of DV and gun control policies has been so divisive that it delayed the reauthorization of an otherwise publicly popular piece of legislation for nine years. It took a mass shooting in an elementary school in Texas for Congress to finally close the "boyfriend loophole" in a separate piece of legislation enacted in June 2022 after VAWA had been reauthorized earlier that year. We also presented a summary of funding patterns from the Office on Violence Against Women and showed how the federal government has failed to use these funds to coerce or incentivize states to align their policies with the provisions of the Lautenberg Amendment. Instead, the federal program designed to combat DV continues to fund states that ignore federal law. This is despite the fact that the Supreme Court has supported DV-related federal firearm provisions on numerous occasions. Overall, a poorly implemented federal DV policy has contributed to all four levels of gender inequality that we presented in Chapter 1.

Chapter 3 began our analysis of the state-level responses to DV, describing the policy feedback process and the evolution of DV policies at the state level. That chapter delved more deeply into the inequality among women across jurisdictions. We presented six case studies that demonstrate how each of three key factors – conservative ideology particularly around Second Amendment rights, DV levels, and vertical policy diffusion – plays a role in the adoption of, or failure to adopt, DV policies. Our case studies show just how conservative legislators, in particular Republican ones, depend on the approval or tacit acceptance by the National Rifle Association (NRA) of restrictions on gun access for DV abusers. These cases underscore how women who live very close to one another geographically but in different states are subject to substantially different laws in regard to their personal safety.

Chapter 4 provided more insight into the path by which states address gun-related DV through a quantitative analysis that predicted the adoption of domestic violence firearm laws (DVFLs). Our examination of this pathway emphasized how the levels of gun homicides, Republican control of state government, citizen ideology, reelection, and vertical pressure from federal policy influenced the adoption of state-level DVFLs. More conservative states measured in both unified Republican state government and citizen ideology are less likely to pass these laws, although the passage of the 1994 VAWA and the Lautenberg Amendment in 1996 led to an increase in state-level DV gun laws. State legislators are less likely to pass DVFLs during state legislative election years. When the federal government has taken significant action, states have responded to it, at least initially. However, our analyses in Chapter 4 show that a combination of hyperpolarized politics around gun control coupled with increasingly conservative ideology among Republicans has presented significant obstacles to creating a more uniform and consistent DV policy across states.

In Chapter 5, we analyzed the implementation of DV policies in local judicial systems that create inequality among women within a jurisdiction. We have argued in this book that having a law is not sufficient to protect women from DV if it is not enforced. We conducted a set of surveys of public defenders (PDs) and district attorneys (DAs) across 16 states to gauge how these cases are handled at the local level and to assess which factors might predict the type of response domestic abusers receive in the courts. The survey responses from these attorneys revealed a broken system within their states, underscoring the inequalities present for the personal safety of women at an even deeper level than we had considered before. The DVFLs on the books in states, as well as mandatory arrest laws, affect the outcomes of DV cases. The presence of these laws led to an increase in jail and financial penalties for DV offenders. Structural components of the judicial system also mattered; having vertical prosecution of these cases increases the likelihood of receiving rehabilitation services and having a county-provided PD who had high caseloads increased the likelihood of jail time and financial penalties for DV offenders. Criminalizing DV can be a controversial solution (Condon, 2010; Goodmark, 2018), and we are not promoting more or less punitive punishments for these crimes. Rather, we seek to draw attention to how these laws are passed and implemented and how effective they are in ensuring human security for women.

In Chapter 6, we examined the social and political costs of DV, both in general and under extraordinary circumstances such as the COVID-19 pandemic. We were able to trace the many ways abusers might politically suppress their victims; these range from preventing them from voting to withholding important election information from them. We also brought specific attention to the plight of women of color, immigrant women, and Native American women, noting the unique dangers they face in their households. Women of color are often arrested or receive disproportionate responses to violence committed by an intimate partner. Immigrant women, specifically those who are undocumented, have the added burden of deportation. Although it may be for different reasons, women of color and immigrant women both fear the police and distrust the legal system. This portion of the chapter explored the fourth level of inequality created by DV policy that involves the race and ethnicity of the victim. Chapter 6 ended with a discussion of the effects of the COVID-19 pandemic, specifically analyzing the role that lockdowns and court closures played on women's access to resources and justice.

7.2 ENHANCING FEDERAL LEVERAGE TO PROMPT STATE POLICY CHANGE

VAWA was an important start to providing necessary protections for women, but it was so narrowly tailored that it captured only a small percentage of DV crimes that crossed state borders. Congress successfully reauthorized VAWA in 2022, but did so without including an expansion of federal firearm prohibitions to dating partners, thereby failing to close the boyfriend loophole due to Republican opposition in the Senate. Congress finally closed the boyfriend loophole in federal law in June 2022 through the Bipartisan Safer Communities Act but limited federal firearm restrictions for dating partners to five years, contingent on having no additional convictions for DV (Treisman, 2022). That bill passed with 16 GOP senators voting for it; the external shock event of the Uvalde, Texas, school mass shooting proved to be an important catalyst for the turnaround among some Republican senators who had just a few months earlier rejected the provision to close the boyfriend loophole in the 2022 VAWA authorization.

Expanding federal firearm prohibitions is a tall order. We have shown throughout this book that increased partisanship and polarization surrounding gun control will make any bill that extends the Lautenberg Amendment difficult to pass. This is despite the fact that there are congressional members who are victims of DV themselves. Cori Bush made history when the State of Missouri elected her, its first African American woman to Congress on November 4, 2020. Bush is a victim of DV, and uses her platform to help victims: "I've allowed myself to be vulnerable about it,... because I feel like if we don't normalize the conversation – people are still being hurt, especially right now, with COVID, and the lockdown,... Every time we see that someone died at the hands of their partners,... that's something we could've stopped, as a society" (Ryzik and Benner, 2021).

Bush comes from a state that has real DV problems: it and Alaska are the top two states for per capita rates of men killing women. Missouri has failed to enact any significant legislation on DV and firearms during the period of this study. The absence of such laws led one local newspaper to run an editorial in 2018 literally pleading with state legislators in both Missouri and its neighbor Kansas to take action:

Both states are considering bills that would align with federal law, which already prohibits people convicted of domestic violence misdemeanors and those who are subject to certain protective orders from purchasing or possessing guns. More than two dozen states see the wisdom of such laws, which are an important tool for police as they try to prevent someone who has already been physically violent with a spouse or loved one from escalating the abuse to murder.... In both Kansas and Missouri, the legislation would apply only to certain protective orders, including those where a hearing has been held and the person has received actual notice and had the opportunity to participate.

Despite the constant pushback from those who believe in virtually no limits on the Second Amendment, there should be broad agreement across the political spectrum that convicted domestic abusers should not have access to guns. Yes, people kill people, not guns. But lax gun laws make it that much more likely that the violence will occur. And American women are 16 times more likely to be shot and killed than women in other developed countries. We know why. The links between domestic violence and guns are clear. But are our legislators willing to do something about it? (*Kansas City Star*, 2018)

Missouri did not take action on the bill, HB 2276, sponsored by state house member Donna Lichtenegger (Republican, Cape Girardeau), which sought to modify the "offense of an unlawful possession of a firearm" to bring state law more in line in with federal law regarding misdemeanor DV convictions (Missouri House of Representatives, 2018). In 2021, Missouri adopted a law making it a "Second Amendment sanctuary" state that "imposes a $50,000 fine on any state or local official who enforces a federal gun law that's not also a Missouri law" (Martin, 2021). Considering that Missouri has not enacted its own conforming law to the Lautenberg Amendment or any other DV firearm limitation, a literal reading of this law would make it difficult to keep guns out of the hands of misdemeanant DV abusers (Martin, 2021). Missouri is the latest example of just how difficult it is to have a consistent and effective human security policy for women across all 50 states in the US federal system.

Much attention is frequently paid to enacted federal laws that contain grant money for states and cities to implement the laws' policy provisions. However, the impact of federal laws on women's lives is conditional on states' willingness to implement these laws. Our work shows that federal or vertical policy diffusion competes with the strong forces of partisanship and ideology in state governments and that in the policy domain of DV, federal law loses more than it wins. The fact that we found that subsequent reauthorizations to VAWA did not produce more state policy activity on DV indicates that vertical diffusion may have significant limitations although we cannot say for sure whether the phenomenon we have uncovered is unique to DV legislation or is a broader pattern in policy adoption.

Subsequent reauthorizations of VAWA have not had as large an impact as its initial passage because they have excluded firearm provisions just as the 2022 reauthorization did. But in combination with the Bipartisan Safer Communities Act, which extended federal firearm restrictions to dating partners, federal action in this arena may produce long-awaited and necessary policy change at the state level. Or, at the very least, it may stem the tide of rollback in protections that has occurred in the past two decades in some states such as Wyoming. In 2003, State Sen. Cale Case, a Republican, who was consistently endorsed and highly rated by the NRA, sponsored a bill that would allow individuals convicted of certain misdemeanor DV offenses to regain their firearm rights. According to the bill, the state board of parole would review an application from the convicted individual and could restore the person's firearm rights if the individual had completed his or her sentence and probation and if the board determined that the individual would not be a danger to himself or herself or others.[1]

Sen. Case's bill never became law, but it laid the groundwork for HB 0106, which did become law. State Rep. Thomas E. Lubnau II, a Republican, also endorsed by the NRA, sponsored HB 0106, which expunged misdemeanor DV offenses in order to restore firearm rights. The law required five years to have passed after the sentence, including probation or mandated programs, expired. With 58 ayes and 1 nay, it passed the Wyoming House in February 2009, and with unanimous support, it passed in the Senate one week later. It was signed into law by the governor by the end of that month.[2]

Two years later, Sen. Case cosponsored SF 0088 with Rep. Lubnau and several others that provided a similar process to expunge nonviolent felony convictions in order to restore firearm rights.[3] Although this bill had extensive debate, it passed both chambers and was signed into law in 2011. This law completely ignores the tendency of violent abusers to repeat their behavior, even if it occurs years later. Additionally, many DV offenses may be dropped by the prosecution (or effectively charge bargained by the defense) in lieu of other nonviolent offenses such as drug charges. Dropping or lowering charges in this way gives DV abusers convicted of a nonviolent felony who subsequently commit a violent DV crime the right to possess or own a gun. No bills attempting to restrict firearm access of domestic abusers have been sponsored in either chamber since 2001, which is the first year of available data on Wyoming's legislature's website.

In light of the 2022 federal action on DV, it is important to point out that gaps in protections remain, especially regarding the specific needs of women of color, immigrant women, and Native Americans because of poor police response to DV in their communities. These needs include specific training for law enforcement, social workers, PDs, DAs, and judges on DV in communities of color. Such needs also include funding for

---

[1] www.wyoleg.gov/Legilsation/2003/SF0042.
[2] www.wyoleg.gov/Legislation/2009/HB0106.
[3] www.wyoleg.gov/Legislation/2011/SF0088.

comprehensive studies of each DV incidence, its severity, and its precipitating factors in these communities by federal and state agencies that do not now have the resources necessary to conduct such an investigation.

Of the hundreds of millions of dollars that the Office of Violence Against Women awards in grants each year, little of this money is for programs that are specifically tailored for communities of color. From 2010 to 2020, the percentage of grant money that went to programs specifically for these communities ranged from a low of 10 percent in 2011 to a high of 17 percent in 2014. These grants went to many programs aimed specifically for tribes, programs to improve culturally specific services, and outreach and services to underserved populations. While other general grants may also help communities of color, DV programs geared specifically for these populations needs to be expanded (Office of Violence Against Women, 2020).

There are two potentially effective pathways for the federal government to pressure states to increase DV firearm law adoption. The federal action taken in 2022 to extend domestic violence firearm restrictions to dating partners, and enhance tribal nations' capacities to address DV, may yield new policies at the state level. The second pathway is through a more systematic effort to enforce federal laws that already exist. At a time when states are clamoring for federal aid in a wide range of policy areas, invoking the threat of withholding or denying that aid is a powerful tool that could be used to create more consistent DV policies across all states.

7.3 PROPOSED DOMESTIC VIOLENCE POLICY REFORMS

In addition to conforming with the Lautenberg Amendment in all 50 states, including dating partners in the scope of DV laws and expanding firearm restrictions on gun possession and ownership for DV abusers, three additional reforms at the state level are needed: expanding firearm laws to address the use of ghost guns, expanding the definition and scope of DV to include coercive control, and considering the use of lethality assessments within and across states.

7.3.1 Extending State Firearm Laws: Ghost Guns

In addition to the original eight laws that we have discussed in this book, an even newer firearm law has the potential to save many victims' lives. Ghost guns are firearms that do not have a serial number because they are assembled from kits. They came under scrutiny in the Biden Administration in April 2021 when the president stated that he "wanted to see these kits treated as firearms control under the Gun Control Act" (Karni, 2021). Such guns are dangerous because a person does not need a background check to buy their parts and the guns are invisible to law enforcement, meaning they would not be readily visible in a search for weapons and not be confiscated. They are easy to assemble inexpensive, and create the perfect opportunity for an abuser to retain, or gain access to a firearm. Because they are very difficult to trace, it is unclear just how many ghost guns there are although a *New York Times* article reported that the Bureau of Alcohol, Tobacco, Firearms and Explosives (ATF) recovered about 10,000 ghost guns in 2019 alone (Karni, 2021). The numbers for 2020 would surely have increased.

The states and federal government have not addressed the impact of ghost guns on DV injuries because their popularity is relatively new. On October 8, 2021, Gov. Gavin Newson of California became one of the first governors to enact a law regulating ghost guns specifically for DV offenses. California Assembly Bill (AB) 1057 extended DV restraining orders to allow law enforcement to seize ghost guns. Prior to AB 1057, only a handful of states had regulated ghost guns at all; regulations that did exist most often prohibited assisting someone prohibited from owning firearms to obtain or assemble a ghost gun (Office of Governor, 2021). States need to consider the role that ghost guns play in DV offenses and prohibit their possession by DV misdemeanants. In 2021, California enacted another DV-related bill (AB 887) that allows DV survivors to file restraining orders online, make remote appearances, and file documents electronically in DV cases.

7.3.2 Expanding the Definition and Scope of Domestic Violence Laws to Include Coercive Control

States also need to extend the definitions of DV itself. As we discussed in Chapters 3 and 6, DV goes beyond physical abuse. In fact, much of the abuse begins with emotional, mental, or financial abuse long before the first punch is ever thrown. This type of abuse, called *coercive control*, includes "acts like creeping isolation, entrapment, denigration, financial restrictions, and threats of emotional and physical harm, including to pets or children, that are used to strip victims of power" (Ryzik and Benner, 2021). All of these actions can be found on the Power and Control Wheel;

those who specialize in DV recognize them as forms of abuse. Political suppression is a form of coercive control, and as we detailed in Chapter 6, is an often overlooked and underestimated form of abuse. Coercive control laws are important to accurately portraying and handling DV. These laws

> Recognize an evolution in thought and research about domestic abuse, once normalized and minimized as an unfortunate outgrowth of bad relationships. Experts say research has increasingly shown the insufficiency of law enforcement approaches that treat domestic assaults as isolated incidents, akin to being punched by a stranger in a bar fight, and ignore the experiences of those for whom the abuse was often broader in scope and not always marked by violence, but debilitating, repetitive and no less damaging. (Ryzik and Benner, 2021)

Several states have started to broaden their definitions of DV to include coercive control. On September 15, 2020, Hawaii was the first state to enact anticoercive control legislation based on the results of a similar policy enacted in Scotland that had shown to decrease DV (America's Conference to End Coercive Control, 2020). California followed shortly thereafter and enacted a law that allowed coercive control to be introduced as evidence of DV in court. Connecticut has also added coercive control to its definition of DV (Queram, 2021). There is a long way to go for states to pass these laws, and the passage of such a law at the federal level would be a good way to apply pressure to states considering such laws themselves.

7.3.3 Increased Use of Lethality Assessments

First introduced in 2019 by Reps. Janine Boyd (Democrat) and Sara Carruthers (Republican), Aisha's Law – House Bill 3 – passed in the Ohio House of Representatives by a 94 to 0 vote in 2020 but did not receive a vote in the Senate before the end of the legislative session. Boyd and Carruthers reintroduced the bill in 2021.[4]

Aisha's Law is named after Aisha Fraser Mason, a Shaker Heights resident and local school teacher who was brutally murdered in 2018 in front of her children by her ex-husband, Lance Mason, a former judge. Notably, he had a previous DV conviction after attacking her in 2014 in front of their children (Donatelli and Assad, 2019). On November 17, 2018, Aisha Mason was dropping off her children, ages 8 and 11, at her

---

[4] We thank Isabel Culver for her research assistance in drafting this section on the use of lethality assessments in Ohio.

sister-in-law's house for visitation with their father. Mr. Mason was waiting for her, and while she and the children were getting out of the car, he stabbed Mrs. Mason 59 times, killing her. He then fled the scene, hitting an officer responding to the situation with his vehicle (Hlavaty and Bash, 2018; Donatelli and Assad, 2019). In August 2019, Mason pleaded guilty to the murder of his ex-wife, and he was sentenced to life in prison with the possibility of parole in 35 years.

In Mrs. Mason's memory, Aisha's Law, which passed the Ohio House but not the Ohio Senate, seeks to modernize DV laws in Ohio to prevent similarly egregious murders. It proposes to change both DV sentencing and the way that law enforcement officers handle DV related calls. The law would classify intimate partner homicide in which the offender had a previous felony conviction for DV as aggravated murder, would codify strangulation of a household member as a form of DV, and would stipulate that prosecutors do not have to prove that offenders had any intent to hurt or kill victims in DV cases in order to bring felony charges.

Moreover, Aisha's Law would also require statewide use of lethality assessments by police officers when responding to DV calls. Several versions of lethality assessment programs are used by law enforcement around the country. A dominant version of it is the Lethality Assessment Program Maryland Model developed by the Maryland Network Against Domestic Violence (MNADV), which engages in training for police departments and social service agencies around the country.[5] The lethality assessment comprises 11 questions asked of victims of DV to assess the risk of their being murdered by their abuser. Answering yes to a certain number of the 11 questions indicates that the victim is at risk for homicide. See Figure 7.1 for an example of a lethality assessment.

Conducting the assessment frequently during a case means that law enforcement officers can capture changes in an abuser's actions, especially when certain parts of the legal process may trigger more violent behavior. Messing et al. (2014) conducted a quasi-experiment on the effectiveness of lethality assessments across rural, urban, and suburban communities in Oklahoma. They found that the act of taking the lethality assessment can make victims more alert to patterns of behavior that might result in lethal action taken by their abusers (Messing et al., 2014). The lethality

---

[5] For more information, see the Maryland Network Against Domestic Violence (2021), *Domestic Violence Lethality Screen for Law Enforcement.* Lethality Assessment Program – Maryland Model. www.lethalityassessmentprogram.org.

**DOMESTIC VIOLENCE LETHALITY
SCREEN FOR LAW ENFORCEMENT**

Lethality Assessment Program
A Project of the Maryland Network Against Domestic Violence

Officer:		Date:		Time:	am/pm
Badge #:		Department/Precinct:			

☐ Check here if victim declined to be screened
☐ Check here if the officer could not administer the screen

A "Yes" response to any of Questions #1-3 is an automatic High-Danger assessment

1. Have they ever used a weapon against you or threatened you with a weapon?	☐ Yes	☐ No	☐ Not Ans/Unk
2. Have they ever tried to choke/strangle (cut off breathing) you?	☐ Yes	☐ No	☐ Not Ans/Unk
3. Do you think they might try to kill you?	☐ Yes	☐ No	☐ Not Ans/Unk

"Yes" responses to at least four of Questions #4-11 is an automatic High-Danger Assessment

4. Do they have a gun or can they easily get one?	☐ Yes	☐ No	☐ Not Ans/Unk
5. Have they threatened to kill you or your children?	☐ Yes	☐ No	☐ Not Ans/Unk
6. Are they violently or constantly jealous or do they control most of your daily activities?	☐ Yes	☐ No	☐ Not Ans/Unk
7. Have you left them or separated after living together or being married?	☐ Yes	☐ No	☐ Not Ans/Unk
8. Are they unemployed?	☐ Yes	☐ No	☐ Not Ans/Unk
9. Have they ever tried to kill themselves?	☐ Yes	☐ No	☐ Not Ans/Unk
10. Do you have a child that they know is not theirs?	☐ Yes	☐ No	☐ Not Ans/Unk
11. Do they follow or spy on you or leave threatening messages?	☐ Yes	☐ No	☐ Not Ans/Unk

Is there anything else that worries you about your safety? (If "yes") What worries you?

An officer may make a High-Danger Assessment if the officer believes the victim is in a potentially lethal situation.

Check one:	☐ Victim is High-Danger based on score		
	☐ Victim is High-Danger based on officer belief		
	☐ Victim is not assessed as High-Danger		
If victim is High-Danger, did officer make a call to the hotline?		☐ Yes	☐ No
Did the victim speak with the hotline advocate?		☐ Yes	☐ No

FOR ADVOCATE USE ONLY

Victim:	Offender:
Victim consents to receive follow-up call: ☐ Yes ☐ No	Victim Alternative Phone:

Note: The questions above and the criteria for determining the level of risk a person faces is based on the best available research on factors associated with lethal violence by a current or former intimate partner. However, each situation may present unique factors that influence risk for lethal violence that are not captured by this screen. Although most victims who are assessed as "High-Danger" would not be expected to be killed, these victims face much higher risk than that of other victims of intimate partner violence. All domestic violence is serious. This Screen should not be used to determine whether someone is a victim or is at risk of re-assault. This project was supported by Grant No. 2011-TA-AX-K111 awarded by the Office on Violence Against Women, U.S. Department of Justice. The opinions, findings, conclusions, and recommendations expressed in this publication are those of the authors and do not necessarily reflect the views of the Department of Justice, Office on Violence Against Women.

© Lethality Assessment Program, a project of the Maryland Network Against Domestic Violence (MNADV). Use of the Lethality Screen without training approved by MNADV is prohibited.

January 2021

FIGURE 7.1 Lethality assessment
Note: This is an example of a lethality assessment used by law enforcement to question victims about their domestic violence experience and to assess probablity of future deadly violence.
Source: Maryland Network Against Domestic Violence (2021), *Domestic Violence Lethality Screen for Law Enforcement*. Lethality Assessment Program – Maryland Model. Maryland Network Against Domestic Violence. www .lethalityassessmentprogram.org.

assessment program works to make victims aware that they are in danger of being killed by their abusers. When finding the potential for lethal violence from the assessment, law enforcement personnel must connect the victim to support services at the time of the incident to get the full impact of reducing deaths from DV. Aisha Fraser Mason's uncle, George Fraser, believes that she could have answered "yes" to at least six of the questions on the lethality test (MacDonald, 2018). Aisha's Law would require law enforcement to conduct these assessments at the time of each DV incident, even if they respond to repeated incidents involving the same set of actors, and to connect victims to social services at the time they respond to the incident.

In her comprehensive study of the history of lethality assessments, Weisberg found that the 2013 reauthorization of VAWA "encouraged all VAWA-funded programs to undertake training… in evidence-based lethality indicators and homicide prevention" (Weisberg, 2019, p. 220) and thereby encouraged its adoption in states. According to the Maryland Police Training and Standards Commission (2016), lethality assessments had been implemented as of 2016 by 33 states. The Maryland Network Against Domestic Violence (www.mnadv.org/lethality-assessment-pro gram/lap-program-overview/) reports that 39 states had used lethality assessments tools in responding to domestic violence by 2021.[6] However, the usage of this kind of assessment differs in states; most states including Ohio do not mandate its use. This variation is an example of the unequal application of tools across states that are designed to prevent lethal DV.

There is opposition to the use of lethality assessments by critics who assert that their results should not be used in sentencing and bail hearings as mandated under law. During a public hearing about Aisha's Law, Ohio Chief Public Defender Cullen Sweeny argued that related data are collected at an "emotionally charged time" and victims have an incentive to either overstate or understate their risk.[7] At the same hearing, proponents of the proposed law who represented various local DV agencies and DV prosecutors cited a rise in the number of DV homicides and a general stigma surrounding strangulation as evidence that DV victims need more protection under the law and officers need to better understand risks for

---

[6] www.mnadv.org/lethality-assessment-program/lap-program-overview/.
[7] Statement of Cullen Sweeney, chief public defender, Cuyahoga County, Ohio to the Criminal Justice Committee Ohio House of Representatives in Opposition to H.B. 3, 2021st Gen. Assem., 134th Sess. (Ohio May 20, 2021)(www.ohiohouse.gov/).

repeat violence, and the matter is urgent.[8] If Aisha Fraser Mason had lived just six miles northwest where the police used the lethality assessment, she might not have become a DV murder victim. Returning to Weisberg's definitive review of the efficacy of lethality assessments, she writes, "For thirty years, experts in the field of intimate partner violence have been advocating for greater use of lethality assessments in the various stages of the legal process. It is time to heed that clarion call for reform before our failure to do so sounds the death knell for more victims" (2019). We agree.

7.4 AVENUES FOR FUTURE RESEARCH

As with all research endeavors, we have left a number of unanswered questions in our attempt to draw attention to the variation in state adoption and implementation of DV laws, as well as the impact of partisanship and ideology on the political climate in this issue domain. We present several new areas for future exploration prompted by our work.

7.4.1 Judicial Decision Making

In Chapter 5, we discussed the way that DV cases are adjudicated from the perspectives of PDs and DAs, but we did not survey judges who preside over these cases. Chapter 6 included a discussion of several judges' insight into how the courts were handling COVID-19 and court closures, suggesting new and innovative ways the courts could reach DV victims even beyond the pandemic. The work from both of these chapters suggests that judges have much discretion in adjudicating DV cases.

Many firearm laws have been passed that allow the judges to choose whether or not a DV offender should have access to a weapon or whether or not an offender who has access to a gun should be let out of jail on bail. This is especially problematic in states that elect their judges in partisan elections, the by-product of which often allows offenders to keep their firearm because it is a Second Amendment right issue instead of a personal

---

[8] *Proponent Testimony: Hearings on H.B. 3 Before the Criminal Justice Committee*, 2021st Gen. Assem., 134th Sess. (Ohio, May 20, 2021) (statement of Louis Tobin); *Testimony in Support of HB3: Hearings Before the Criminal Justice Committee*, 2021st Gen. Assem., 134th Sess. (Ohio, May 20, 2021) (statement of Melody Briand); *Testimony of Mary O'Doherty, executive director of the Ohio Domestic Violence Network, in Support of HB 3 to House Criminal Justice Committee*, 2021st Gen. Assem., 134th Sess. (Ohio May 20, 2021).

safety issue for victims. If a history of violence exists and offenders pose a danger to their partner or family, there should be no discretion as to whether or not they can access a firearm; this should not be a partisan issue. In future work, we intend to delve more deeply into the distortions in human security for women that come from judicial discretion in DV cases. We believe that one way to address this, at least from the judicial side, is to write more specific laws that leave less room for the role of judicial discretion in mandating the surrender of firearms by DV abusers.

7.4.2 Domestic Violence and Native American Women

Although the federal government has made a concerted effort to address violence against Native American women, many of the states where they live have not passed DV firearm laws. The National Congress of American Indians lists Alaska, Oklahoma, New Mexico, South Dakota, and Montana as the states with the largest Native American and Alaskan native populations.[9]

Additionally, the tribes themselves can pass their own laws removing firearms from DV offenders. Some examples of these laws can be found in the Oglala Sioux (South Dakota), the Makah (Washington State), and the Cherokee Nation (Oklahoma). The Oglala Sioux do not allow those who have an order of protection to "possess, own, buy, sell, trade, or have immediate access to any firearm or ammunition."[10] The Makah allow law enforcement to confiscate firearms after an incident of DV and the court to require the surrender of a firearm for a restraining order.[11] Finally, the Cherokee Nation as of 2005 allows protective orders to include the surrender of any firearm.[12] A more systematic analysis of tribal response to DV through the passage of firearm laws can reveal which tribes pass these laws and under what circumstances as part of a larger study of how tribal governments and state governments interact to address DV. To do so, we propose to study tribal adoption of a Special

---

[9] The National Congress of American Indians. 2021. "Demographics". www.ncai.org/about-tribes/demographics.
[10] Oglala Sioux Domestic Violence Code. Section 302. www.ncai.org/tribal-vawa/resources/code-development/TLPI_Domestic_Violence_Code_Resource_2012.pdf.
[11] Makah Domestic Violence Code. §11.8.01.
[12] The Cherokee Nation. 2005. "LA-33-05: Civil Protective Order Act." www.cherokee.legistar.com.

Domestic Violence Criminal Jurisdictional Courts (SDVCJC) and analyze whether adopting it reduces the incidence of DV injury and murder in indigenous communities.

7.4.3 Comparative Subnational Case Studies of Domestic Violence during the COVID-19 Pandemic

We hope to build on the work by Htun and Weldon (2018) and Htun and Jensenius (2020) that include country-specific case studies where the "federal" nature of the political system varies and to analyze the scope and implementation of DV laws in those systems and how the COVID-19 pandemic has affected them. We plan to collect our own data and incorporate the statistical work amassed by the womanstats.org project led by Rose McDermott and Valerie M. Hudson on rates of violence against women during this time and to use comparative case studies of political regimes that vary across Brazil, Egypt, Mexico, Peru, the Philippines, and the United States.

7.4.4 Making the Commitment to Human Security for Women

Domestic violence harms not only those who are directly abused but all those in their orbit as well. Remember these names: Aisha Fraser Mason, Louvenia Penwright, and Leah and Morgan Rogers; each died from DV. Also remember the hundreds of women severely injured or killed each year in DV situations. These people left behind children and families who pay the price every day for a poor state response to protecting the personal safety of women. Domestic violence is a political problem as much as it is a public health, sociological, and societal problem. In *Politics: Who Gets What, When, and How*, Lasswell stated that "the influential are those who get the most of what there is to get. Available values may be classified as deference, income, safety. Those who get the most are elite; the rest are mass" (1936, p. 1). Studying DV shows us that women are treated unequally under the law. Women cannot achieve fully equal participation in society compared to men until DV achieves its rightful place as a core political and public policy issue. It is our hope that this book will spur future research to accomplish that goal.

Appendices

State	
Alabama	1990–1998, 2000–2010
Alaska	1990–2016
Arizona	1990–2016
Arkansas	1990–2016
California	1990–2016
Colorado	1990–2016
Connecticut	1990–2016
Delaware	1990–1993, 1996–2016
Florida	1992–1995
Georgia	1990–2016
Hawaii	1990–2016
Idaho	1990–2016
Illinois	1990–2016
Indiana	1990–2016
Iowa	1990, 1992–2016
Kansas	1990–1992, 2001–2016
Kentucky	1990–1993, 1995–1998, 2004–2016
Louisiana	1990, 1992–2016
Maine	1990, 1994–2016
Maryland	1990–2016
Massachusetts	1990–2016
Michigan	1990–2016
Minnesota	1990–2016
Mississippi	1990–2016
Missouri	1990–2016
Montana	1991–1992, 1995, 2000, 2003–2016
Nebraska	1990–1992, 2004, 2009–2016
Nevada	1990–2016
New Hampshire	1990–1996, 1998–2016
New Jersey	1990–2016

(*continued*)

APPENDIX A1.1. (*continued*)

State	
New Mexico	1990–2016
New York	1990–2016
North Carolina	1990–2016
North Dakota	1990, 1992–2011, 2013–2016
Ohio	1990–2016
Oklahoma	1990–2016
Oregon	1990–2016
Pennsylvania	1990–2016
Rhode Island	1990–2016
South Carolina	1990–2016
South Dakota	1990–2016
Tennessee	1990–2016
Texas	1990–2016
Utah	1990–2016
Vermont	1990–2016
Virginia	1990–2016
Washington	1990–2016
West Virginia	1990–2016
Wisconsin	1990–2016
Wyoming	1990–2016

This table summarizes the availability of data on female murders between the years of 1990 and 2016 in the FBI Uniform Crime Reporting database, EZASHR.

Appendix A5.1 Public Defender and District Attorney Survey

1. Part I. We would like to begin by asking you a few questions regarding your current position. How many years have you worked as a public defender in your state?
2. What year did you graduate from law school?
3. Approximately how many cases did you handle last year (2016) as a public defender?
4. How satisfied are you with your work as a public defender in your state?
5. Below is a list of variables that could affect your satisfaction with your work as a public defender. For each one choose whether you are satisfied or dissatisfied.

	Very Dissatisfied	Dissatisfied	Neither Satisfied or Dissatisfied	Satisfied	Very Satisfied
Level of Responsibility	o	o	o	o	o
Number of Cases	o	o	o	o	o
Chances for Advancement	o	o	o	o	o
Policies and Administration	o	o	o	o	o
Salary	o	o	o	o	o
Access to Specialized Training	o	o	o	o	o

6. How many investigators does your office have?

7. Part II. This next series of questions concerns domestic violence cases you have handled as a public defender. Thinking back to the total number of cases you handled last year (2016) as a public defender, what percentage of these cases dealt with domestic violence?

8. What percentage of the domestic violence cases that you handled as a public defender last year resulted in jail time for the accused?

9. What would you estimate is the average amount of time the accused was sentenced to prison for the domestic violence cases you handled last year?
   a. 30 days
   b. 6 months
   c. 1 year
   d. More than 1 year

10. What percentage of the domestic violence cases that you handled as a public defender last year resulted in a financial penalty for the accused?

11. What would you estimate was the average financial penalty for an act of domestic violence for the cases you handled last year as a public defender?
    a. Less than $500
    b. $500–$1000
    c. $1001–$2000
    d. $2001–$3000
    e. More than $3000

12. What percentage of the domestic violence cases that you handled as a public defender last year resulted in a rehabilitation program for those accused?

13. What you would you estimate is the average amount of time those accused of domestic violence needed to spend in a rehabilitative program?
    a. 30 days
    b. 6 months
    c. 1 year
    d. More than 1 year

14. What percentage of the domestic violence cases last year resulted in some combination of jail time, a fine, or a rehabilitation program for the accused?

15. What percentage of the domestic violence cases you handled last year involved an individual accused of repeated domestic violence offenses?

16. What percentage of the domestic violence cases you handled as a public defender last year involved a female victim?

17. What percentage of the domestic violence cases you handled last year involved a child victim?

18. What percentage of the domestic violence cases you handled last year were felonies?

19. What percentage of all domestic violence cases that you handled last year were plea-bargained down to a lesser offense?

20. What percentage of the domestic violence cases that you handled last year were charge-bargained down to a lesser offense?

21. In cases of domestic violence, how often is vertical prosecution utilized?
    a. None of the cases
    b. Rarely
    c. About half of the cases
    d. Most of the cases
    e. Every single case

22. Which forms of domestic violence have you defended? Check all that apply.
    a. Intimate Partner Violence
    b. Elder Abuse
    c. Child Abuse
    d. Violence between other relatives
    e. Violence between roommates
    f. Other types

23. Part III. We would now like to ask you about the judicial system in your county. What crimes constitute a domestic violence crime in your county: Check all that apply.
    a. Battery
    b. Assault
    c. Stalking
    d. Threatening
    e. Terrorist Threats
    f. Criminal Mischief
    g. Burglary
    h. Sexual Violence

24. Is there a specialized court in your county for domestic violence crimes?
    a. No
    b. Yes
25. Have you received any specialized training on domestic violence crimes?
    a. No, there is no training available
    b. No, training is available but I have not taken it
    c. Yes
26. What is the statutory definition of domestic violence in your state?
27. Is this definition followed closely, or is it open to interpretation on cases you handle?
    a. No, this definition is not followed closely
    b. Yes this definition is followed closely
28. Finally, we would like to end by asking you a few questions about your background. Would you describe yourself as ideological? If so, how so?
    a. Strongly Liberal
    b. Liberal
    c. Weakly Liberal
    d. Moderate
    e. Weakly Conservative
    f. Conservative
    g. Strongly Conservative
29. Have you, a family member, or close friend ever been a victim of domestic violence?
    a. No
    b. Yes
    c. Choose not to answer
30. What is your sex?
    a. Male
    b. Female
31. What is your age?
32. What is the best description of the kind of university you received your law degree from?
    a. Private University
    b. Public University
33. In what category does your family income fall?
    a. Under $50,000
    b. $50,001–$75,000

    c. $75,001–$100,000
    d. $100,001–$200,000
    e. Over $200,000

34. What is your race/ethnicity?
    a. White
    b. Black or African American
    c. American Indian or Alaska Native
    d. Asian
    e. Native Hawaiian or Pacific Islander
    f. Other

35. Is there anything else you would like to share about your political history or experiences as a public defender in your state?

References

Abadinsky, H. 1988. *Law and Justice.* Chicago: Nelson-Hall.

Aizer, Anna. 2010, September. "The Gender Wage Gap and Domestic Violence." *American Economic Review*, 100: 1847–1859.

America's Conference to End Coercive Control. November 13. "Hawaii and California Lead the Way Signing the First Coercive Control Bills in the Americas." www .theacecc.com/post/hawaii-and-california-lead-the-way-signing-the-first-coercive-control-bills-in-the-americas.

Ammar, Nawal H., Leslye E. Orloff, Mary Ann Dutton, and Giselle A. Haas. 2012. "Battered Immigrant Women in the United States and Protection Orders: An Exploratory Research." *Criminal Justice Review*, 37(3): 337–359.

Anderson, Jessica. 2020, March 29. "A Side Effect of Coronavirus: More Domestic Violence and Fewer Victims Seeking Help, Maryland Experts Warn." *Baltimore Sun.* www.baltimoresun.com/coronavirus/bs-md-domes tic-violence-coronavirus.

Andrew, Scottie. 2020, October 27. "For Abuse Victims, Registering to Vote Brings a Dangerous Tradeoff." CNN. www.cnn.com/2020/10/27/us/domes tic-violence-voting-election-privacy-trnd/index.html.

Associated Press. 1996a, September 16. "Gingrich Backs Domestic-Abuser Gun Ban." *Chicago Tribune.*

  1996, September 16b. "Gingrich: No guns for domestic abuser." *Boston Globe.*

  2018, March 2. "Minnesota Not Enforcing Domestic Abuse Gun Law, Report Says."

Ayres-Brown, Antonia. 2020, May 12. "Legal Aid Attorneys Strained by Increase in Virus-Related Cases: Including Domestic Violence and Jobless Claims." *Chicago Tribune.* www.chicagotribune.com/coronavirus/ct-coronavirus-legal-aid-volunteer-lawyers-20200511-gvfzuhvzova6jlna7vf5vudmle-story .html.

  2021, May 14. "Domestic Violence Advocates Describe Increased Demand for Support Services during Pandemic." WBUR. www.wbur.org/news/2021/05/ 14/domestic-violence-coronavirus-isolation-newport

Bailey, Kimberly D. 2009. "The Aftermath of Crawford and Davis: Deconstructing the Sound of Silence." *Brigham Young University Law Review*, 1: 1–56.

2011. "Response to Beth Richie's Black Feminism, Gender Violence and the Build-Up of a Prison Nation." *Washington University Journal of Law & Policy*, 37: 149–152.

Ballotpedia. 2022. "Georgia." https://ballotpedia.org/Georgia.

Bassett, Laura and Christina Wilkie. 2014, April 23. "The NRA Quietly Backs Down on Domestic Violence." HuffingtonPost.com. www.huffingtonpost .com/2014/04/22/nra-domestic-violence_n_5191555.html.

Batlan, Felice. 2015. *Women and Justice for the Poor: A History of Legal Aid, 1863–1945*. New York: Cambridge University Press.

Bech, Erin. 2014, July 30. "Hearing Links Guns, Domestic Violence." *Charleston Gazette*, A 1.

Beland, Daniel, Philip Rocco, and Alex Waddan. 2016. *Obamacare Wars: Federalism, State Politics, and the Affordable Care Act*. Lawrence: The University Press of Kansas.

Belknap, Joanne, Dee L. R. Graham, Jennifer Hartman, and P. Gail Allen. 2000. *Factors Related to Domestic Violence Court Dispositions in a Large Urban Area: The Role of Victim/Witness Reluctance and Other Variables*. Washington, DC: National Institute of Justice.

Bendery, Jennifer. 2022, February 9. "Senators Unveil Bipartisan Bill to Renew the Violence Against Women Act." *Yahoo! News*. https://news.yahoo.com/ senators-unveil-bipartisan-bill-renew-011257332.html.

Bergen, Raquel K., Jeffrey L. Edleson, and Claire M. Renzetti. 2011. *Sourcebook on Violence Against Women*. Los Angeles: Sage.

Berry, Frances Stokes and William D. Berry. 1990. "State Lottery Adoptions as Policy Innovations: An Event History Analysis." *American Political Science Review*, 84(2): 395–415.

1994. "The Politics of Tax Increases in the States." *American Journal of Political Science*, 38(3): 855–859.

Berry, William D., Richard C. Fording, Evan J. Ringquist, Russell L. Hanson, and Carl Klarner. 2010. "Measuring Citizen and Government Ideology in the American States: A Re-appraisal." *State Politics and Policy Quarterly*, 10: 117–135.

2019. "SPID: A New Database for Inferring Public Policy Innovativeness and Diffusion Networks." *Policy Studies Journal*, 48(2): 517–545.

Bose, Devna. 2020, October 9. "Don't Let Them Take Your Voice Away: Domestic Violence Survivors Face Voting Challenges." *Charlotte Observer*. www.charlotteobserver.com/news/politics-government/election/ article246265510.html.

Bosman, Julie. 2020, August 7. "Domestic Violence Calls Mount as Restrictions Linger: 'No One Can Leave.'" *New York Times*. www.nytimes.com/2020/ 05/15/us/domestic-violence-coronavirus.

Brautigan, Bailey. 2021, August 23. "Mink Shoals Deaths Being Investigated as Double Murder-Suicide." www.wowktv.com/news/local/developing-kana wha-county-deputies-investigate-two-bodies-found-on-elkdale-drive/.

Breda, Cindy. 2018, January 8. "Man Arrested at Westlake Motel Friday Faces Domestic Violence, Weapons Charges." *Chronicle.* www.chroniclet.com/cops-and-courts/2018/01/08/Man-arrested-at-Westlake-hotel-Friday-faces-multiple-domestic-violence-weapons-charges.html.

Brennan Center for Justice. 2021. "Voting Laws Roundup: October 2021. www.brennancenter.org/our-work/research-reports/voting-laws-roundup-october-2021.

Brieding, Matthew J., Sharon G. Smith, and Kathleen C. Basile. 2015. "Prevalence and Characteristics of Sexual Violence, Stalking, and Intimate Partner Violence Victimization: National Intimate Partner and Sexual Violence Survey, United States, 2011." *MMWR Morbidity and Mortality Weekly Report*, 53(8). www.cdc.gov/mmwr/pdf/ss/ss6308.pdf.

Brown, Nadia. 2014. *Sisters in the Statehouse: Black Women and Legislative Decision Making.* New York: Oxford University Press.

Browne, Angela and Kirk R. Williams. 1989. "Exploring the Effect of Resource Availability and the Likelihood of Female-Perpetrated Homicides." *Law & Society Review*, 23(1): 75–94.

Brownlee, Chip. 2022, February 18. "Bipartisan Deal over Violence Against Women Act Targets People Who Lie on Gun Background Checks." The Trace. www.thetrace.org/2022/02/violence-against-women-act-reauthorization-background-checks/.

Buckley, Jack and Chad Westerland. 2004. "Duration Dependence, Functional Form, and Corrected Standard Errors: Improving EHA Models of State Policy Diffusion." *State Politics & Policy Quarterly*, 4(1): 94–113.

Bureau of Justice Statistics. 2017. "National Crime Victimization Survey." US Department of Justice. https://bjs.ojp.gov/content/pub/pdf/cv17.pdf.

Burling, Stacey. 2005, June 17. "Domestic Violence Is Down, but Problem Remains Huge," *Philadelphia Inquirer*, A19.

Burns, Asia Simone. 2020, April 28. "Stay-at-Home Order Poses New Problems for Family Violence Victims, Shelters," *Atlanta Journal-Constitution.* www.ajc.com/news/breaking-news/stay-home-order-poses-new-problems-for-family-violence-victims-shelters.

Campbell, Jacquelyn C., Nancy Glass, Phyllis W. Sharps, Kathryn Laughon, and Tina Bloom. 2007. "Intimate Partner Homicide: Review and Implications of Research and Policy." *Trauma, Violence, & Abuse*, 8(3): 246–269.

Campbell, Jacquelyn. C., Daniel Webster, Jane Koziol-McLain, et al. 2003. "Risk Factors for Femicide in Abusive Relationships: Results from a Multisite Case Control Study." *American Journal of Public Health*, 93(7): 1089–1097. https://doi.org/10.2105/ajph.93.7.1089.

Campbell, Sean, Alex Yablon, and Jennifer Mascia. 2021, February 22. "Red Flag Laws: Where the Bills Stand in Each State." *The Trace.* www.thetrace.org/2018/03/red-flag-laws-pending-bills-tracker-nra/.

Carlson, Jennifer. 2020. *Policing the Second Amendment: Guns, Law Enforcement, and the Politics of Race.* Princeton, NJ: Princeton University Press.

Centers for Disease Control and Prevention. 2021a. "The National Violence Death Reporting System." https://wisqars.cdc.gov:8443/nvdrs/nvdrsDisplay.jsp.

2021b. "Preventing Intimate Partner Violence." www.cdc.gov/violencepreven
tion/intimatepartnerviolence/fastfact.html.

Charleston Gazette. 1998, December 5. "Domestic Violence by the Numbers."
2002, August 27. "Hideous: Domestic Violence Horror," A6.
2006, February 21. "Tragedy: Domestic Violence Rate," A4.

Cheung, Kylie. 2020, September 8. "How Domestic Violence Is Also a Form of
Voter Suppression." *Supermajority News.* https://supermajority.com/2020/
09/how-domestic-violence-is-also-a-form-of-voter-suppression/.

Clark, Paul O. 2010. "Mandatory Arrest for Misdemeanor Domestic Violence: Is
Alaska's Arrest Statute Constitutional?" *Alaska Law Review*, 27(2): 151–194.
https://scholarship.law.duke.edu/cgi/viewcontent.cgi?article=1031&context=alr.

Condon, Meghan. 2010. "Bruise of a Different Color: The Possibilities of
Restorative Justice for Minority Victims of Domestic Violence."
Georgetown Journal on Poverty Law & Policy, 17(3): 487–506.

Condon, Meghan, Alexandra Filindra, and Amber Wichowsky. 2016.
"Immigrant Inclusion in the Safety Net: A Framework for Analysis and
Effects on Educational Attainment." *Policy Studies Journal.* 44(4): 424–448.

Congressional Record, 1994, June 21–June 28. Volume 140, Part 20., 13658.
www.congress.gov.

Congressional Record, US Senate. 1996. "Lautenberg Amendments Nos. 5241–5243."
www.congress.gov/104/crec/1996/09/11/CREC-1996-09-11-pt1-PgS10329.pdf.

Cook, Lindsey. 2014, September 25. "Domestic Violence Is as American as Apple
Pie." *U.S. News and World Report.*

Cook, Mike. 2014a, March 25. "Domestic Abusers Could Be Prohibited from
Having a Gun." St. Paul, MN: Minnesota House of Representatives.
2014b, April 30. "Domestic Abusers, Stalkers Could Be Prohibited from
Having a Firearm." Minnesota House of Representatives.

Cook, Philip J. and Kristin A. Goss. 2020. *The Gun Debate: What Everyone
Needs to Know.* New York: Oxford University Press.

Cook, Rhona. 2016, September 4. "Judges Often Reluctant to Confiscate Guns in
Domestic Violence Cases." *Atlanta Journal-Constitution.* www.ajc.com/
news/local/judges-often-reluctant-confiscate-guns-domestic-violence-cases/
DjU7a74MsbPsxkroZmlvDI.

Costa, J. 2018, April 23. *Pennsylvania Senate Legislative Journal*, pp. 347–348.
http://www.legis.state.pa.us/WU01/LI/SJ/2018/0/Sj20180423.pdf#page=13.

Crenshaw, W. Kimberlé. 1991. "Mapping the Margins: Intersectionality, Identity
Politics, and Violence against Women of Color." *Stanford Law Review*, 43
(6): 1241–1299.

Davis, Maxine Ohad Gilbar and Diana M. Padilla-Medina. 2021. "Intimate
Partner Violence Victimization and Perpetration among U.S. Adults during
the Earliest Stage of the COVID-19 Pandemic." *Violence and Victims*, 36(5):
583–603.

Davis, Susan. 2021, March 17. "House Renews Violence Against Women Act,
But Senate Hurdles Remain." NPR. www.npr.org/2021/03/17/977842441/
house-renews-violence-against-women-act-but-senate-hurdles-remain.

DeHart, Dana D. 2008. "Pathways to Prison: Impact of Victimization in the Lives
of Incarcerated Women." *Violence Against Women*, 14: 1362–1381.

DeHart, Dana D., S. Lynch, J. Belknap, P. Dass-Brailsford, and B. Green. 2014. "Life History Models of Female Offending: The Roles of Serious Mental Illness and Trauma in Women's Pathways to Jail." *Psychology of Women Quarterly*, 38: 138–151.

De La Cretaz, Britni. 2020, October 27. "Domestic Violence Is about Power & Control – It's Also a Tool of Voter Suppression." Refinery29. www .refinery29.com/en-us/2020/10/10099003/domestic-violence-voter-suppres sion-2020-election.

Dellinger, Hannah. 2020, August 11. "Domestic Violence Cases Continue to Rise during Pandemic, Data Shows." *Houston Chronicle*. www.houstonchronicle .com/news/houston-texas/houston/article/domestic-violence-continue-to-rise-pandemic-covid-15475751.php.

Dewar, Helen. 1996, July 22. "Domestic Abuse Bill Hits Snag Gun Control Issue Could Kill Measure." *Denver Post*.

Dichter, Melissa E. 2015. "Women's Experiences of Abuse as a Risk Factor for Incarceration: A Research Update." VAWnet.org. www.researchgate.net/ profile/Melissa-Dichter/publication.

Díez, Carolina, Rachel P. Kurland, Emily F. Rothman, et al. 2018. "State Intimate Partner Violence-Related Firearm Laws and Intimate Partner Homicide Rates in the United States, 1991 to 2015." *Annals of Internal Medicine*, 167(8): 536–543. https://annals.org/aim/fullarticle/2654047/state-intimate-partner-violence-related-firearm-laws-intimate-partner-homicide.

Domestic Abuse Intervention Programs. 2022. Duluth, MN: Domestic Abuse Intervention Programs. www.theduluthmodel.org.

Donatelli, Joe and Samah Assad. 2019, September 10. "What We Know about the Death of Aisha Fraser and the Arrest of Ex-Judge Lance Mason." News 5 Cleveland. www.news5cleveland.com/news/local-news/cleveland-metro/ everything-we-know-so-far-about-death-of-aish-fraser-and-arrest-of-ex-judge-lance-mason.

Dornblaser, Christopher. 2018, October 25. "Ex-York City Cop to Pay Fine in Domestic Assault Case." *York Dispatch*. www.yorkdispatch.com/story/news/ crime/2018/10/25/ex-york-city-cop-pay-fine-domestic-assault-case/1760474002/.

Dugan, Laura. 2002. "Domestic Violence Legislation: Exploring Its Impact on Domestic Violence and the Likelihood That Police Are Informed and Arrest, Final Report." National Institute of Justice. Document No.: 196853. https:// nij.ojp.gov/.

Dugan, Laura, Daniel S. Nagin and Richard Rosenfeld. 2003, November. "Do Domestic Violence Services Save Lives? *National Institute for Justice Journal*, 250: 20– 25.

Duster, Chandelis. 2021, March 8. "Congress Moves to Reauthorize Violence Against Women Act." CNN.com. www.cnn.com/2021/03/09/politics/vawa-reauthorization-house/index.html.

Ebbert, Stephanie. 2020, May 12. "When Is a Drop in Domestic Violence Bad News?" *Boston Globe*. www.bostonglobe.com/2020/05/12/metro/when-is-drop-domestic violence-bad-news.

Elazar, Daniel J. 1966. *American Federalism; A View from the States*. New York: Crowell.

Epstein, Deborah. 1999. "Effective Intervention in Domestic Violence Cases: Rethinking the Roles of Prosecutors, Judges, and the Court system." *Yale Journal of Law & Feminism*, 11 (1), 3–50. http://digitalcommons.law.yale.edu/yjlf/vol11/iss1/3.

Evans, Dabney P., Shila Rene Hawk, and Carrie E. Ripkey. 2021. "Domestic Violence in Atlanta, Georgia before and during COVID-19." *Violence and Gender*, 8(3): 140–147.

Evans, Megan L., Margo Lindauer, and Maureen E. Farrell. 2020, December 10. "A Pandemic within a Pandemic: Intimate Partner Violence during Covid-19." *New England Journal of Medicine*, 383: 2302–2304.

Everytown for Gun Safety. 2021, June 4. "Mass Shootings in America." https://everytownresearch.org/maps/mass-shootings-in-america-2009-2019/.

"Navigator: Domestic Violence, Minnesota." https://everytownresearch.org/navigator/states.html?dataset=domestic_violence&states=MN.

"Gun Law Navigator." https://maps.everytown.org/navigator/states.html?dataset=domestic_violence&states=.

Everytown for Gun Safety Support Fund. 2021. "Gun Law Navigator: Domestic Violence." https://everytownresearch.org/navigator/index.html.

Farole, Donald J. Jr. and Lynn Langton. 2007. "County-Based and Local Public Defender Offices, 2007." *Census of Public Defender Offices, 2007*. US Department of Justice, Bureau of Justice Statistics. https://bjs.ojp.gov/content/pub/pdf/clpdo07.pdfs.

Farris, Emily. 2022. "Address Confidentiality Programs." www.addressconfidentiality.com/.

Federal Bureau of Investigation. 2022. *Uniform Crime Reports*. Database.

Few, April L. 2005. "The Voices of Black and White Rural Battered Women in Domestic Violence Shelters." *Family Relations*, 54(4): 488–500.

Fording, Richard C. 2018. "Unpublished Supplement to 1998 AJPS Article." https://rcfording.com/state-ideology-data/.

Fuchs, Erin. 2013, September 26. "Why Rape Is Much More Common in Alaska." *Business Insider*. www.businessinsider.com/

Gendreau, LeAnne and Michael Fuller. 2020, December 2. "Domestic Violence Cases in Conn. Increasing Amid Pandemic, through Holiday Season." NBC Connecticut. www.nbcconnecticut.com/news/local/lt-gov-bysiewicz-to-bring-attention-to-rise-in-domestic-violence-cases-amid-pandemic-holiday-season/2374323/.

Georgia Commission on Family Violence. 2018. "Fatality Review Project." https://gcfv.georgia.gov/.

Gilardi, Fabrizio and Fabio Wasserfallen. 2019. "The Politics of Policy Diffusion." *European Journal of Political Research*, 58(4): 1245–1256.

Godwin, Marcia L. and Jean Reith Schroedel. 2000. "Policy Diffusion and Strategies for Promoting Policy Change: Evidence from California Local Gun Control Ordinances." *Policy Studies Journal*, 28(4): 760–776.

Goodman, Lisa A. and Deborah Epstein. 2008. "The Advocacy Response." In Lisa A. Goodman and Deborah Epstein, eds., *Psychology of Women. Listening to Battered Women: A Survivor-Centered Approach to Advocacy,*

Mental Health, and Justice. Washington, DC: American Psychological Association, pp. 29–47.

Goodmark, Leigh. 2018. *Decriminalizing Domestic Violence*. Oakland: University of California Press.

Gordon, Linda. 1988. *Heroes of Their Own Lives: The Politics and History of Family Violence: Boston, 1880–1960*. New York: Penguin Books.

Goss, Kristin A. 2015. "Defying the Odds on Gun Regulation: The Passage of Bipartisan Mental Health Laws across the States." *American Journal of Orthopsychiatry*, 85(3): 203–210.

2020. *The Paradox of Gender Equality*. Ann Arbor: University of Michigan Press.

Governor Tom Wolf. 2018, October 12. "Governor Wolf Signs Domestic Abuser Gun Ban, Urges Legislature to Close Gun Show Loophole." www.governor .pa.gov/governor-wolf-signs-domestic-abuser-gun-ban-urges-legislature-close-gun-show-loophole/.

Graham, Erin R., Charles R. Shipan, and Craig Volden. 2013. "The Diffusion of Policy Diffusion Research in Political Science." *British Journal of Political Science*, 43 (3): 673–701.

Granitz, Peter. 2013, March 22. "Murkowski Clarifies VAWA Dispute." Alaska Public Media. www.alaskapublic.org/2013/03/22/murkowski-clarifies-vawa-dispute/.

Gray, Virginia. 1973. "Innovation in the States: A Diffusion Study." *American Political Science Review*, 67(4): 1174–1185.

Grossback, Lawrence J., Sean Nicholson-Crotty, and David A. M. Peterson. 2004. "Ideology and Learning in Policy Diffusion." *American Politics Research*, 32 (5): 521–545.

Grumbach, Jake. M. 2018. "From Backwaters to Major Policymakers: Policy Polarization in the States, 1970–2014." *Perspectives on Politics*, 16(2): 416–435.

Gupta, Alisha Haridasani and Aviva Stahl. 2020, March 24. "For Abused Women, a Pandemic Lockdown Holds Dangers of Its Own." *New York Times*. www.nytimes.com/2020/03/24/us/coronavirus-lockdown-domestic-violence.

Halstead, T. J. 2001. "Firearms Prohibitions and Domestic Violence Convictions: The Lautenberg Amendment." Congressional Research Service. RL31143. congress.gov.

Hartman, Jennifer and Joanne Belknap. 2003. "Beyond the Gatekeepers: Court Professionals Self-Reported Attitudes about and Experiences with Misdemeanor Domestic Violence Cases." *Criminal Justice and Behavior*, 30 (3): 349–373.

Hays, Scott P. 1996. "Patterns of Reinvention: The Nature of Evolution during Policy Diffusion." *Policy Studies Journal*, 24(4): 551–566.

Healy, Melissa. 2020, August 18. "Domestic Violence Rose during Lockdown – And Injuries Are Dramatically More Severe, Study Finds." *Los Angeles Times*. www.latimes.com/science/story/2020-08-18/intimate-partner-violence-spiked-80-after-pandemic-lockdown-began.

Heim, Shannon M. 2011. "Revisions to Minnesota Domestic Law Affords Greater Protection to Vulnerable Victims." *William Mitchell Law Review*, 30(2): 950–970. https://open.mitchellhamline.edu/cgi/viewcontent.cgi?art icle=1399&context=wmlr.

Helgeson, Baird. 2014, April 27. "Gun Restrictions on Domestic Abusers, Stalkers Gain Bipartisan Support in Minnesota." *Star Tribune*. www .startribune.com/minnesota-is-close-to-new-gun-limits/256849681/.

Hess, Cynthia, Jessica Milli, Jeff Hayes, et al. 2015. *The Status of Women in the States: 2015*. Washington, DC: Institute of Women's Policy Research. http:// statusofwomendata.org/wp-content/uploads/2015/02/Status-of-Women-in-the-States-2015-Full-National-Report.pdf.

Hetherington, Marc. J. and Thomas J. Rudolph. 2015. *Why Washington Won't Work*. Chicago: University of Chicago Press.

"Hidden Problem." 1977, July 1. *St. Louis Post-Dispatch* (1923–2003). p. 32. http://login.library.coastal.edu:2048/login?url=https://www.proquest.com/ historical-newspapers/july-1-1977-page-32-60/docview/1901785023/se-2? accountid=26722.

Hlavaty, Kaylyn and Homa Bash. 2018, November 19. "Family Member: Aisha Fraser Was Attacked and Killed While Dropping Off Her Daughters." News 5 Cleveland. www.news5cleveland.com/news/local-news/oh-cuyahoga/aisha-fraser-killing-details.

Htun, Mala and S. Laurel Weldon. 2018. *The Logics of Gender Justice: State Action on Women's Rights around the World*. New York: Cambridge University Press.

Htun, Mala and Francesa R. Jensenius. 2020. "Comparative Perspectives on the Caregiving Crisis, Welfare States, and Men's Roles." *APSA Comparative Politics Newsletter*, XXX(2): 22–32.

Human Rights Watch. 2020, July 3. "Submission to the UN Special Rapporteur on Violence against Women, Its Causes and Consequences Regarding COVID-19 and the Increase of Domestic Violence against Women." www. hrw.org/news/2020/07/03/submission-un-special-rapporteur-violence-against-women-its-causes-and-consequences.

Hunter, Michelle. 2020, September 29. "Woman Killed by Boyfriend and Man Shot by Deputies in Avondale Have Been Identified." Nola.com. www.nola .com/news/crime_police/article_eeb0bc78-0282-11eb-a25e-63577a550f2a .html.

Institute for Women's Policy Research. 2015. "Status of Women in the States: 2015 Full National Report." http://statusofwomendata.org/wp-content/ uploads/2015/02/Status-of-Women-in-the-States-2015-Full-National-Report.pdf.

Jones, Loring. 2008. "The Distinctive Characteristics and Needs of Domestic Violence Victims in a Native American Community." *Journal of Family Violence*, 23(2): 113–118.

Joslyn, Mark R., Donald P. Haider-Markel, Michael Baggs, and Andrew Bilbo. 2017. "Emerging Political Identities? Gun Ownership and Voting in Presidential Elections." *Social Science Quarterly*, 98(2): 382–396.

Kansas City Star. 2018, February 19. "More Women Die When Domestic Abusers Own Guns. Do Kansas and Missouri Lawmakers Care?" www .kansascity.com/opinion/editorials/article200998154.html.

Karch, Andrew. 2012. "Vertical Diffusion and the Policy-Making Process: The Politics of Embryonic Stem Cell Research." *Political Science Research*, 65(1): 48–61.

Karni, Annie. 2021, April 9. "Ghost Guns: What They Are, and Why They Are an Issue Now." *New York Times.* www.nytimes.com/2021/04/09/us/politics/ ghost-guns-explainer.html.

Kelley, Lauren. 2020, July 14. "Who Bears Witness to a Hidden Epidemic?" *New York Times.* www.nytimes.com/2020/07/14/opinion/sunday/domestic-vio lence-coronavirus.

Kim, Junghack, Bruce D. McDonald III, and Jooho Lee. 2018. "The Nexus of State and Local Capacity in Vertical Policy Diffusion." *The American Review of Public Administration*, 48 (2): 188–200.

Kivisto Aaron J., Magee Lauren A., Phalen Peter L. and Ray Bradley R. 2019. "Firearm Ownership and Domestic versus Nondomestic Homicide in the U.S." *American Journal of Preventive Medicine*, 57(3): 311–320.

Kluger, Jeffrey. 2021, February 3. "Domestic Violence Is a Pandemic within the COVID-19 Pandemic." *Time Magazine.* https://time.com/5928539/domestic-violence-covid-19/.

Kolinovsky, Sarah. 2019. "House Republicans, at NRA's Urging, Vote against Violence Against Women Act." https://abcnews.go.com/Politics/house-repub licans-nras-urging-vote-violence-women-act/story?id=62198856.

Krutz, Glen S. 2001. *Hitching a Ride: Omnibus Legislating in the U.S. Congress.* Columbus: The Ohio State University Press.

Kueppers, Courtney. 2020, April 1. "Kemp Shares Number for State's Domestic Violence Hotline for Those in Need." *Atlanta Journal-Constitution.* www.ajc .com/news/kemp-shares-number-for-state-domestic-violence-hotline-for-those-need.

Lacombe, Matthew J. 2019. "Political Weaponization of Gun Owners." *Journal of Politics*, 81 (4):1342–1356.

LaCombe, Scott J. and Frederick J. Boehmke. 2020. "Learning and Diffusion Models." In Luigi Curini and Robert Franzese, eds. *The Sage Handbook of Research Methods in Political Science and International Relations.* Newbury Park, CA: Sage, pp. 311–328.

Lang, Marissa J. 2020, March 27. "Domestic Violence Will Increase during Coronavirus Quarantines and Stay-at-Home Orders, Experts Warn." *Washington Post.* www.washingtonpost.com/local/domestic-violence-will-increase-during-coronavirus-quarantines-and-stay-at-home-orders-experts-warn/.

Lasswell, Harold D. 2011 (1936). *Politics: Who Gets What, When, How.* Montreal, Canada: Literary Licensing.

Lauer, Hallie. 2020, June 16. "Abuse Hotlines Light up after Region's Move to Green Phase." *Pittsburgh Post-Gazette.* www.post-gazette.com/news/crime-courts/2020/06/16/.

Laws of Alaska. 1996. "Domestic Violence Prevention and Victim Protection Act of 1996." SLA 64. www.legis.state.ak.us/PDF/19/Bills/HB0314E.PDF, Section 12.

2006a. "Harassment/Assault/Stalking." SLA Chapter 87. www.legis.state.ak.us/PDF/24/Bills/HB0343Z.PDF.

2006b. "Protective Order for Sexual Assault/Abuse." SLA Chapter 36. www.legis.state.ak.us/PDF/24/Bills/SB0054Z.PDF.

Leckrone, J. Wesley. 2013. "State and Local Political Culture." *The American Partnership*. https://theamericanpartnership.com/2013/12/18/state-and-local-political-culture/.

Levendusky, Matthew. S. 2009. "The Microfoundations of Mass Polarization." *Political Analysis*, 17(2), 162–176.

Levy, Marc. 2018, March 21. "Senate OKs Bill to Toughen Gun Laws in Domestic Abuse Cases." https://www.wfmj.com/story/37777329/pennsylvania-senate-oks-bill-to-toughen-gun-laws-in-domestic-abuse-cases.

Lundy, Rose. 2021, March 7. "Calls to Domestic Violence Were More Frequent – and Dire – during Pandemic." *Maine Monitor*. www.themainemonitor.org/calls-to-domestic-violence-hotlines-were-more-frequent-and-dire-during-pandemic/.

MacDonald, Evan. 2018, December 7. "Aisha Fraser Mason's Uncle Wants '11 Questions' Law for Ohio to Help Protect Domestic Abuse Victims." Cleveland.com. www.cleveland.com/expo/news/erry-2018/12/b9c33054881924/aisha-fraser-masons-brother-wa.html.

Mahoney, Scott. 2018, May 12. "Alwin King, 29, Gets 3 Years Probation for Shooting Woman in the Leg." *Chronicle*. http://www.chroniclet.com/cops-and-courts/2018/05/12/Alwin-King-29-gets-3-years-probation-for-shooting-woman-in-the-leg.html.

Mallinson, Daniel J. 2019. "Who Are Your Neighbors? The Role of Ideology and Decline of Geographic Proximity in the Diffusion of Policy Innovations." *Policy Studies Journal*, 49(1): 67–88.

Martin, Luke X. 2021, June 28. "New 2nd Amendment Protections In Missouri Split Law Enforcement." NPR. www.npr.org/2021/06/28/1010320106/new-2nd-amendment-protections-in-missouri-split-law-enforcement.

Maryland Police Training and Standards Commission. 2016. "Lethality Assessment Program Report – In Response to House Bill 1371. https://mdle.net/pdf/HB1371-Report_regarding_Lethality_Assessment_Program_12-1-16.pdf.

Mason, Lilliana. 2015. "'I Disrespectfully Agree'": The Differential Effects of Partisan Sorting on Social and Issue Polarization." *American Journal of Political Science*, 59(1): 128–145.

2018. "Ideologues without Issues: The Polarizing Consequences of Ideological Identities." *Public Opinion Quarterly*, 82(1): 280–301.

Mauer, Marc. 2013, February 27. "The Changing Racial Dynamics of Women's Incarceration." Sentencing Project. www.sentencingproject.org/publications/the-changing-racial-dynamics-of-womens-incarceration/.

Messing, Jill T., David Becerra, Allison Ward-Lasher, and David K. Androff. 2015. "Latinas' Perceptions of Law Enforcement: Fear of Deportation, Crime Reporting, and Trust in the System." *Journal of Women and Social Work*, 30(3): 328–340.

Messing, Jill. T., Jacquelyn. C. Campbell, Janet. S. Wilson, et al. (2014). Police Departments' Use of the Lethality Assessment Program: A Quasi-Experimental Evaluation. U.S. Department of Justice, Award No. 2008-WG-BX-0002.

Mettler, Suzanne. 1998. *Dividing Citizens.* Ithaca, NY: Cornell University Press.

Mettler, Suzanne and Mallory SoRelle. 2014. "Policy Feedback Theory." In Paul A. Sabatier and Christopher M. Weible, eds. *Theories of the Policy Process,* 3rd ed. Boulder, CO: Westview.

Michener, Jamila. 2018. *Fragmented Democracy.* New York: Cambridge University Press.

Minard, Anna. 2013, June 12. "When Domestic Violence Becomes a Mass Shooting." The Stranger.com. www.thestranger.com/seattle/when-domestic-violence-becomes-a-mass-shooting/Content?oid=17004357.

Minnesota Code of Laws. 2018. "Domestic Assault." www.revisor.mn.gov/stat utes/cite/609.2242.

2022. Office of the Revisor of Statutes. revisor.mn.gov/laws.

Minnesota Statute 609.2242; Revised Code Washington 939.51. Revisor.mn.gov/laws.

Montana Domestic Violence Fatality Review Commission. 2020. https://leg.mt .gov/content/Committees/Interim/2019-2020/Law-and-Justice/Committee-Topics/Required-Reports/2019-domestic-violence-review-commission-report-doj.pdf.

Montana House Judiciary Committee. 2019. http://sg001-harmony.sliq.net/00309/Harmony/en/PowerBrowser/PowerBrowserV2/20170221/-1/34673?agendaId=143824#agenda.

Mooney, Christopher Z. 2001. "Modeling Regional Effects on State Policy Diffusion." *Political Research Quarterly,* 54(1): 103–124.

2020. *The Study of US State Policy Diffusion: What Hath Walker Wrought?"* New York: Cambridge University Press.

Moore, Katherine. 2015. "No More Simple Battery in West Virginia: The Newly Amended § 61-2-9 and § 61-2-28." *West Virginia Law Review,* 117 W. Va. L. Rev. Online 21. https://wvlawreview.wvu.edu/west-virginia-law-review-online/2015/02/16/no-more-simple-battery-in-west-virginia.

Mozes, Alan. 2020, August 18. "Study Finds Rise in Domestic Violence during COVID." WebMD. www.webmd.com/lung/news/20200818/radiology-study-suggests-horrifying-rise-in-domestic-violence-during-pandemic#1.

Murchison, Adrianne. 2020, June 25. "Police Work to Handle Rise in Domestic Violence Calls during Pandemic." *Atlanta Journal-Constitution,* www.ajc.com/news/local/police-work-handle-rise-domestic-violence-calls-during-pandeimc.

National Association of Confidential Address Programs. 2021. "Spring 2021 Newsletter." www.nacap.org/uploads/8/8/9/9/88992652/nacap_spring_2021_newsletter.pdf.

National Center on Domestic and Sexual Violence. 2008. "Timeline of the Battered Women's Movement." www.ncdsv.org/images/NYCHRADSS_TImelineBWM_2008.pdf.

National Coalition Against Domestic Violence. 2018, June 6. "Domestic Violence and the LGBTQ Community." https://ncadv.org/blog/posts/domestic-violence-and-the-lgbtq-community.

2021. "Statistics." www.ncadv.org/learn/statistics.

National Congress of American Indians. 2018, March 20. "VAWA 2013's Special Domestic Violence Criminal Jurisdiction (SDVCJ) Five-Year Report." www .ncai.org/resources/ncai-publications/SDVCJ_5_Year_Report.pdf.

2021. "Demographics." https://www.ncai.org/about-tribes/demographics.

National Council of State Legislatures. 2017. "Full-and Part-Time Legislatures." National Conference of State Legislatures. www.ncsl.org/research/about-state-legislatures/full-and-part-time-legislatures.aspx.

2019. "Domestic Violence/Domestic Abuse Definitions and Relationships." www.ncsl.org/research/human-services/domestic-violence-domestic-abuse-definitions-and-relationships.aspx.

2021. "State Partisan Composition." www.ncsl.org/research/about-state-legisla tures/partisan-composition.aspx#Timelines.

"Partisan Composition of State Legislatures 1990–2000." www.ncsl.org/docu ments/statevote/legiscontrol_1990_2000.pdf.

National Domestic Violence Hotline. 2021. "Types of Abuse." www.thehotline .org/is-this-abuse/abuse-defined/.

National LGBTQ Task Force. 2022, March 11. "President Biden Signs Violence Against Women Reauthorization." www.thetaskforce.org/president-biden-signs-violence-against-women-reauthorization/.

National Research Council. 1996. *Understanding Violence Against Women.* Washington, DC: National Academy Press. https://ncadv.org/signs-of-abuse.

Neumann, Janice. 2020, July 22. "Domestic Violence Advocates, Victims Face Special Challenges during Pandemic." *Chicago Tribune.* www.chicagotribune .com/suburbs/daily-southtown/ct-sta-crisis-center-court-advocates-st-0723-20200722-cltfsmbshvfizipbskjhuhc27e-story.html.

Obeidallah, Dean. 2021, March 21. "The Shameful Vote by 172 Republicans." CNN. www.cnn.com/2021/03/21/opinions/republicans-vote-against-vawa-women-obeidallah/index.html.

Office of Governor. 2021, October 8. "Governor Newsom Signs Legislation to Bolster California's Nation-Leading Gun Safety Laws, Support Survivors of Domestic Violence." www.gov.ca.gov/2021/10/08.

Office of Justice Programs. 2016. "National Institute of Justice Five Things about Violence against American Indian and Alaska Native Women and Men." https://www.ojp.gov/pdffiles1/nij/249815.pdf.

Office of the Chief Medical Examiner. 2016. "West Virginia Domestic Violence Fatality Review Panel Annual Report." www.wvlegislature.gov/legisdocs/reports/agency/H01_CY_2014_13578.pdf.

Office of Violence Against Women, 2019. "OVW Fiscal Year 2020 Improving Criminal Justice Responses to Domestic Violence, Dating Violence, Sexual Assault, and Stalking Grant Program." www.justice.gov/ovw/page/file/1252371/download.

2020a. "Awards by State and Program." www.justice.gov/ovw/awards.

2020b. "OVW Grants and Programs." www.justice.gov/ovw/grant-programs.

2021. "Solicitation Program Guide." www.justice.gov/ovw/page/file/1342606/download.

Orcutt, Ben. 2015, June 3. "Homicides Stun Cul-de-Sac: 'Why His Own Daughter?'" *Chesterfield Observer.* www.chesterfieldobserver.com/articles/homicides-stun-cul-de-sac-why-his-own-daughter/.

Orloff, Leslye E. and Paige Feldman. 2017. "Domestic Violence and Sexual Assault Public Policy Timeline." Washington, DC: American University College of Law.

Parker, Kim, Juliana Horowitz, Ruth Igielnik, Baxter Oliphant, and Anna Brown. 2017. "America's Complex Relationship with Guns." Pew Research Center. https://assets.pewresearch.org/wp-content/uploads/sites/3/2017/06/06151541/Guns-Report-FOR-WEBSITE-PDF-6-21.pdf.

Pennsylvania Coalition Against Domestic Violence (PCADV). 2005. "2004 Domestic Violence Fatality Report." Harrisburg, PA: PCADV, pp. 1–15.

Pennsylvania State Senate. 2016, December 21. "Memorandum: Tierne's Law – Enhanced Domestic Violence Protection." www.legis.state.pa.us/cfdocs/Legis/CSM/showMemoPublic.cfm?chamber=S&SPick=20170&cosponId=21562.

Petrocik, John R. 1996. "Issue Ownership in Presidential Elections, with a 1980 Case Study." *American Journal of Political Science*, 40(3): 825–850.

Petrosky, Emiko, Janet M. Blair, Carter J. Betz, et al. 2017. "Racial and Ethnic Differences in Homicides of Adult Women and the Role of Intimate Partner Violence – United States, 2003–2014." *MMWR Morbidity and Mortality Weekly Report*, 66: 741–746. DOI: http://dx.doi.org/10.15585/mmwr.mm6628a1.

Pinchevsky, Gillian M. 2017. "Understanding Decision-Making in Specialized Domestic Violence Courts: Can Contemporary Theoretical Frameworks Help Guide These Decisions?" *Violence Against Women*, 23 (6): 749–771.

Piore, Adam. 1996a, March 21. "Bill Seeks to Keep Guns from Spouse Abusers." Hackensack, NJ: *The Bergen Record*. www.loc.gov/item/sn84020452/.

1996b, September 6. "Democrats Urge Gun Ban for Domestic Violence Offenders, Gingrich Asked to Pass Bill." *The Record*.

Piquero, Alex R., Wesley G. Jennings, Erin Jemison, Catherine Kaukinen, and Felicia Marie Knaul. 2021, February. "Domestic Violence during COVID-19: Evidence from a Systematic Review and Meta-Analysis." https://cdn.ymaws.com/counciloncj.org/resource/resmgr/covid_commission/Domestic_Violence_During_COV.pdf.

Pleck, Elizabeth. 1989. "Criminal Approaches to Family Violence, 1640–1980." *Crime and Justice*, 11: 19–57.

The Progress-Index. 2015, June 18. "Police: Text Messages, Phone Calls, Reveal Stafford Shaw's Confession to Killing Estranged Girlfriend, Their Infant Child." www.progress-index.com/article/20150618/NEWS/150619663.

Primus, Eve Brensike. 2017. "Defense Counsel and Public Defense." In Erik Luna, ed. *Vol. 3 of* Reforming Criminal Justice: Pretrial and Trial Processes. Phoenix: Arizona State University, pp. 121–145.

Ptacek, James. 1999. *Battered Women in the Courtroom: The Power of Judicial Responses*. Boston: Northeastern University Press.

Queram, Kate Elizabeth. 2021, October 4. "Why States Are Expanding Domestic Violence Laws to Include Emotional Abuse." Route Fifty. www.route-fifty.com/health-human-services/2021/10/states-expanding-domestic-violence-coercive/185827/.

Quester, Nicole M. 2007. "Refusing to Remove an Obstacle to the Remedy: The Supreme Court's Decision in *Town of Castle Rock v. Gonzales* Continues to Deny Domestic Violence Victims Meaningful Recourse." *Akron Law Review* 40(2): 391–434.

Raissian, Kerri M. 2016. "Hold Your Fire: Did the 1996 Federal Gun Control Act Expansion Reduce Domestic Homicides?" *Journal of Policy Analysis and Management*, 35(1): 67–93.

Reaves, Brian A. 2017. "Police Response to Domestic Violence, 2006–2015." US Department of Justice Office of Justice Programs. https://bjs.ojp.gov/content/pub/pdf/prdv0615.pdf.

Resnik, Judith. 2002. "Reconstructing Equality: Of Justice, Justicia, and the Gender of Jurisdiction." *Yale Journal of Law and Feminism*, 14(393): 393–418.

Revised Code Washington State. 2019. "Domestic Violence Prevention: Definitions." https://app.leg.wa.gov/RCW/default.aspx?cite=26.50.

Root, Danielle. 2018, November 1. "Obstacles to Voting for Survivors of Intimate Partner Violence." Center for American Progress. www.americanprogress .org/issues/democracy/reports/2018/11/01/460377/obstacles-voting-sur vivors-intimate-partner-violence/.

Rosen, Andy. 2020, May 10. "Rollins Believes Many Domestic Violence, Child Abuse Cases Are Going Unreported." *Boston Globe*. www.bostonglobe.com/ 2020/05/10/nation/rollins-believes-many-domestic-violence-child-abuse-cases-are-going-unreported.

Rothman, Emily F., Jeanne Hathaway, Andrea Stidsen, and Heather. F. de Vries, 2007. "How Employment Helps Female Victims of Intimate Partner Violence: A Qualitative Study." *Journal of Occupational Health Psychology*, 12(2): 136–143. https://doi.org/10.1037/1076-8998.12.2.136.

Ryan, John B., Talbot M. Andrews, Tracy Goodwin and Yanna Krupnikov. 2020. "When Trust Matters: The Case of Gun Control." *Political Behavior*, pp.1–24.

Ryzik, Melena and Katie Benner. 2021, January 22. "What Defines Domestic Abuse? Survivors Say It's More Than Assault." *New York Times*. www .nytimes.com/2021/01/22/us/cori-bush-fka-twigs-coercive-control.html? smid=tw-share.

Sacco, Lisa N. 2019. "The Violence Against Women Act (VAWA): Historical Overview, Funding, and Reauthorization." *Congressional Research Service*. www.everycrsreport.com/files/20190423_R45410_ 672f9e33bc12ac7ff52d47a8e6bd974d96e92f02.pdf.

Sawer, Marion and Jill Vickers. 2016. "Introduction: Political Architecture and its Gender Impact." In Melissa Haussman, Marian Sawer, and Jill Vickers, eds. *Federalism, Feminism and Multilevel Governance*. New York: Routledge.

Schechter, Susan. 1982. *Women and Male Violence: The Visions and Struggles of the Battered Women's Movement*. Boston: South End Press.

Schiller, Wendy J. and Kaitlin N. Sidorsky. 2022. "Federalism, Policy Diffusion, and Gender Equality: Explaining Variation in State Domestic Violence Firearm Laws 1990–2017." *State Politics & Policy Quarterly*, pp. 1–23.

Schneider, Elizabeth M. 2000. *Battered Women & Feminist Lawmaking*. New Haven: Yale University Press.

Seib, Gerald F. 2020. *We Should Have Seen It Coming: From Reagan to Trump – A Front-Row Seat to a Political Revolution*. New York: Penguin Random House.

Selvaratnam, Tanya. 2020, March 23. "Where Can Domestic Violence Victims Turn during Covid-19?" *New York Times*. www.nytimes.com/2020/03/23/opinion/covid-domestic-violence.html?searchResultPosition=13.

Shipan, Charles R. and Craig Volden. 2008. "The Mechanisms of Policy Diffusion." *American Journal of Political Science*, 52(4): 840–857.

Shor, Boris and Nolan McCarty. 2011. "The Ideological Mapping of American Legislatures." *American Political Science Review*, 105: 530–551.

Sidorsky, Kaitlin. 2015. "Moving on Up? The Gendered Ambitions of State-Level Appointed Officials." *Political Research Quarterly*, 68(4): 802–815.

2019. *All Roads Lead to Power*. Lawrence: University of Kansas Press.

Sidorsky, Kaitlin and Wendy J. Schiller. 2020. "Litigating Lives and Gender Inequality: Public Defenders, Policy Implementation, and Domestic Violence Sentencing." *Journal of Women, Politics & Policy*, 41(3):320–333. www.tandfonline.com. DOI 10.1080-1554477X.2020.1800355.

Skocpol, Theda. 1995. *Protecting Mothers and Soldiers*. Cambridge, MA: Harvard University Press.

Skocpol, Theda and Vanessa Williamson. 2016. *The Tea Party and the Remaking of Republican Conservatism*. New York: Oxford University Press.

Smith, Kelly B. 2019. "Learning without Widespread Policy Adoption: Early Childhood Education in the American States." *Publius: The Journal of Federalism*, 50(1): 3–29.

Smucker, Sierra. 2019. "(Strategically) Absent Advocates: How Domestic Violence-Related Firearms Policies Passed in Pro-Gun States, 2013–2015." *Interest Groups & Advocacy*, 8: 121–164.

Sokoloff, Natalie J. 2008. "Expanding the Intersectional Paradigm to Better Understand Domestic Violence in Immigrant Communities." *Critical Criminology*, 16: 229–255.

Sokoloff, Natalie J. and Ida Dupont. 2005. "Domestic Violence at the Intersections of Race, Class, and Gender: Challenges and Contributions to Understanding Violence Against Marginalized Women in Diverse Communities." *Violence Against Women*, 11(1): 38–64.

Sokoloff, Natalie J. and Christina Pratt, eds. 2005. *Domestic Violence at the Margins: Readings on Race, Class, Gender, and Culture*. Piscataway, NJ: Rutgers University Press.

Soler, Esta. 1987. "Domestic Violence Is a Crime: A Case Study – San Francisco Family Violence Project." In Daniel J. Sonkin, *ed*. Domestic Violence on Trial: Psychological and Dimensions of Family Violence. New York: Springer, pp. 21–28.

Solnit, Rebecca. 2018, November 19. "How Many Husbands Control the Votes of Their Wives? We'll Never Know." *Guardian*. www.theguardian.com/commentisfree/2018/nov/19/voter-intimidation-republicans-democrats-midterm-elections.

Southall, Ashley. 2020, April 17. "Why a Drop in Domestic Violence Reports Might Not Be a Good Sign." *New York Times.* www.nytimes.com/2020/04/17/nyregion/new-york-city-domestic-violence-coronavirus.

Spangler, Todd. 2019, February 28. "Rep. Debbie Dingell: My Father Was 'Mentally Ill,' Shouldn't Have Had a Gun." *USA Today.* www.usatoday.com/story/news/local/michigan/2019/02/28/gun-debate-debbie-dingell-father/3019595002/.

Speth, Linda E. 1982. "The Married Women's Property Acts, 1839–1865: Reform, Reaction, or Revolution?" In D. Kelly Weisberg, ed. *Women and the Law: A Social Historical Perspective.* Cambridge, MA: Schenkman.

Spohn, Cassia and David Holleran. 2001. "Prosecuting Sexual Assault: A Comparison of Charging Decisions in Sexual Assault Cases Involving Strangers, Acquaintances, and Intimate Partners." *Justice Quarterly,* 18(3): 651–688.

Stevens, Holly R., Colleen E. Sheppard, Robert Spangenberg, Aimee Wickman, and Jon B. Gould. 2010. "State, County and Local Expenditures for Indigent Defense Services Fiscal Year 2008." www.americanbar.org/content/dam/aba/administrative/legal_aid_indigent_defendants/ls_sclaid_def_expenditures_fy08.authcheckdam.pdf.

St. Louis Post-Dispatch. 1977, July 1. "A Hidden Problem." stltoday.com

Staff. 2020. "Deanna Walters – Domestic Violence Survivor." Criminal Discourse Podcast. https://criminaldiscoursepodcast.com/deanna-walters/.

Stop Arming Felons Act. 1992. "Stop Arming Felons Act: Hearing on S.2304 before the U.S. Senate Subcommittee on the Constitution of the Committee on the Judiciary, May 5, 1992." www.ojp.gov/ncjrs/virtual-library/abstracts/stop-arming-felons-act-hearing-s2304-us-senate-subcommittee.

Thomas, Alex. 2018, September 11. "Manchin Arms Himself in Latest Ads; NRA Issues Election Call to Arms." WVMetroNews.com. wvmetronews.com/2018/09/11/manchin-arms-himself-in-latest-ads-nra-issues-election-call-to-arms/.

Tingley, Jane C. 2015. "Family and Intimate Partner Homicide." Virginia Department of Health. www.vdh.virginia.gov/content/uploads/sites/18/2018/02/2015-FIPS-Annual-Report.pdf.

Tjaden, Patricia G. and Nancy Thoennes. 2000a. *Extent, Nature, and Consequences of Intimate Partner Violence.* Washington, DC: U.S. Department of Justice, National Institute of Justice. https://www.ojp.gov/pdffiles1/nij/181867.pdf.

　　2000b. "Full Report of the Prevalence, Incidence, and Consequences of Violence Against Women." Center for Disease Control and Prevention. https:nij.ojp.gov/library/publications.

Treisman, Rachel. 2022, June 23. "The Senate Gun Bill Would Close the 'Boyfriend Loophole.' Here's What That Means." NPR.org. www.npr.org/2022/06/23/1106967037/boyfriend-loophole-senate-bipartisan-gun-safety-bill-domestic-abuse.

Uggen, Chris, Ryan Larson, Sarah Shannon, and Arleth Pulido-Nava. 2020, October 30. "Locked Out 2020: Estimates of People Denied Voting Rights

Due to a Felony Conviction." The Sentencing Project. www .sentencingproject.org/publications/locked-out-2020-estimates-of-people- denied-voting-rights-due-to-a-felony-conviction/.

United States Congress. "H.R. 3756: Treasury, Postal Service, and General Appropriations Act, 1997." https://www.congress.gov/amendment/104th- congress/senate-amendment/5241?s=1&r=40.

United States Senator for Alaska Lisa Murkowski. 2022. "Murkowski and Colleagues Introduce Bipartisan Bill to Reauthorize Violence Against Women Act." www.murkowski.senate.gov/press/release/murkowski-and-colleagues- introduce-bipartisan-bill-to-reauthorize-violence-against-women-act-.

US Census Bureau. 2018. "The American Community Survey." Various years (2001–2017) www.census.gov/programs-surveys/acs.html.

US Department of Health and Human Services (US DHHS), Centers for Disease Control and Prevention (CDC), and National Center for Health Statistics (NCHS). Bridged-Race Population Estimates, United States July 1st Resident Population by State, County, Age, Sex, Bridged-Race, and Hispanic Origin, 1990–1999, 2000–2009, 2010–2017. Available on CDC WONDER Online Database. http://wonder.cdc.gov/bridged-race-v2017.html.

US Department of Justice. 2018. "Easy Access to FBI's Supplementary Homicide Reports: 1980–2016." www.ojjdp.gov/ojstatbb/ezashr/asp/off_selection.asp.

US Department of Justice. 2021. "Rural Program." Office on Violence Against Women. www.justice.gov/ovw/page/file/1117481/download.

US Department of Justice. FY Budget 2022 Request; Addressing Gender-Based Violence. www.justice.gov/jmd/page/file/1398856/download.

US Department of Justice, Office of Justice Programs. 2014. "Restrictions on the Possession of Firearms by Individuals Convicted of a Misdemeanor Crime of Domestic Violence." www.justice.gov/jm/criminal-resource-manual-1117- restrictions-possession-firearms-individuals-convicted.

US House of Representatives. 2022. "From Title 34: Crime Control and Law Enforcement." https://uscode.house.gov/view.xhtml?req=(title:34% 20section:10461%20edition:prelim).

Vigna, Ariane. 2021, May 17. "Domestic Violence Survivors Face More Obstacles during Pandemic." *Amherst Bulletin*. www.amherstbulletin.com/ Domestic-violence-survivors-in-pandemic-40413217.

Walters, Mikel L., Jieru Chen and Matthew J. Breiding. 2013. "The National Intimate Partner and Sexual Violence Survey (NISVS): 2010 Findings on Victimization by Sexual Orientation." Atlanta, GA: National Center for Injury Prevention and Control, Centers for Disease Control and Prevention. cdc.gov.

Weisman, Jonathan. 2012, April 27. "Senate Votes to Reauthorize Domestic Violence Act." *New York Times*. www.nytimes.com/2012/04/27/us/politics/ senate-votes-to-renew-violence-against-women-act.html? searchResultPosition=20.

Weldon, S. Laurel. 2002. *Protest, Policy, and the Problem of Violence against Women: A Cross-National Comparison*. Pittsburgh: University of Pittsburgh Press.

2006. "Women's Movements, Identity Politics and Policy Impact: A Study of Policies on Violence against Women in the 50 United States." *Political Research Quarterly*, 59(1): 111–122.

Whitesell, Anne. 2019. "Who Represents the Needs of Domestic Violence Survivors in State Welfare Policy?" *Politics and Gender*, 15(3): 514–546.

Wildavsky, Aaron. 1984. "Federalism Means Inequality: Political Geometry, Political Sociology, and Political Culture." In Robert Golembiewski, ed. *The Costs of Federalism: In Honor of James W. Fesler*. New Brunswick, NJ: Transaction.

Wolf, Robert V. 2020. "In Practice: Courts Respond as COVID-19 Fuels Rise in Domestic Violence." Center for Court Innovation. www.courtinnovation .org/publications/courts-covid-dv.

Wooldredge, John and Amy Thistlethwaite. 2002. "Reconsidering Domestic Violence Recidivism: Conditioned Effects of Legal Controls by Individual and Aggregate Levels of Stake in Conformity." *Journal of Quantitative Criminology*, 18(1): 45–70.

Worden, Amy. 2005, November 30. "Unlikely Coalition behind Gun Law: The General Assembly Has Passed an Anti-Domestic Violence Bill to Give Judges the Power to Seize Firearms." *Philadelphia Inquirer*, A1.

WWBT NBC12 News 2015. "Search Warrant Offers Details of Grisly Chesterfield Murder Scene." www.nbc12.com/story/29229957/search-war rant-offers-details-of-grisly-chesterfield-murder-scene/.

Zeoli, April M., Alexander McCourt, Shani Buggs, et al. 2018. "Retracted: Analysis of the Strength of Legal Firearms Restrictions for Perpetrators of Domestic Violence and Their Associations with Intimate Partner Homicide." *American Journal of Epidemiology*, 187(7): 1449–1455.

Index

Page numbers for tables and figures are in italic.

Biden, Joseph, US Senator, 36, 105
Blymier, Brenda, 128
Boston Globe, 167
Boxer, Barbara, United States Senator, 37
boyfriend loophole. *See* domestic violence
  firearm laws (DFVLs)
Brown, Nadia, 115
Browne, Angela, 32
Bush, Cori, US Representative
  domestic violence victim advocate, 177

California
  coercive control, 182
  COVID-19 court restrictions, 169
  ghost guns, 181
  stalking, 65
Carlson, Jennifer, 20
Carrouzzo, Amber, 129
Case, Cale, 178
Center for American Progress, 151–152
Centers for Disease Control and Prevention
  (CDC)
  domestic violence homicides by race, data
    on, *156*
  intimate partner violence, definition of, 97
  National Violent Death Reporting
    System, 14
  women murdered due to domestic
    violence, number of, 14
Charleston Gazette, The, 85
Citizen ideology, 114
  Fording and Berry index (2018),
    114
Civil Rights Act of 1964 33
Clinton, Bill, 19–20, 36, 42
concealed carry permit, 23, 87, 104
Condon, Meghan
  dual arrests in communities of color, 156
  restorative justice, 158
Connecticut
  coercive control, 182
Cornish, Tony, 92
Costa, Jay, 83
COVID-19, 7, 27, 161–171
  court restrictions, 151
  court restrictions by state, *169*
  impact on incidence of domestic violence,
    150
  National Commission on COVID-19 and
    Criminal Justice, 163
  stay-at-home orders, 151, 168

stay-at-home orders and court restrictions
  by state, dates of, *169*
stay-at-home orders, timeline of, *163*
Crenshaw, Kimberlé
  racial stereotypes in domestic violence
    policing, 155

dating violence. *See* Violence Against
  Women Act (VAWA)
Democratic Party, 91, 111
  limiting access to firearms for domestic
    violence offenders, support for, 19
  VAWA reauthorization, support
    for, 111
Dichter, Melissa, 156
Diez, Carolina, 97
district attorney, *See* prosecutor
domestic violence
  dating partners, *See* domestic violence
    firearm laws (DVFLs) boyfriend
    loophole
domestic violence (DV), 1–2
  coercive control, 180–181
  deaths from, 96–97
  definitions of offenses, 25, 63–66
  disproportionate impact on women of
    color, immigrant women, and Native
    American women, 155–161
  domestic violence laws in the United
    States and selected states, scope of, *68*
  extension to dating/intimate partners,
    22–23, 65, 103
  factors in adopting related state policies,
    case studies of, 67
  false imprisonment, 22, 65
  federal action on domestic violence,
    timeline of, *34*
  federal domestic violence policy, 29
  federal laws and practices, proposed
    reforms to, 27
  impact on immigrant women, 159
  lethality assessments, 180, 182–186
  misdemeanants, 98
  offenses, 9, 64
  policy history of, 30–33
  policy reforms, recommendations for, 186
  political participation costs, 151–155
  Power and Control Wheel of domestic
    abuse, 9–10, 9, 137, 181
  public-private divide, 8
  same-sex partner domestic violence, 14, 48

Index

Made in the USA
Middletown, DE
23 July 2024

57909262R00135